AF519933

GEORGE ELIOT'S

ADAM BEDE

(A CRITICAL EVALUATION)

A Critical Study in Four Parts- Part I-Introduction to George Eliot, Part II-A Detailed Study of Adam Bede, Part III-Select University Questions and Answers, Part IV-Select Literary Criticism.

Latest Revised Edition

Authors

DR. S. SEN
M.A., Ph.D.

J.K. CHOPRA
M.A., M.Phil.

Thoroughly revised by

DR. G. S. MANSUKHANI
M.A., Ph.D.
Ex- Head of the Department of English
S.G.T.B. Khalsa College
University of Delhi
&
Retd. Deputy Secretary
University Grants Commission

UNIQUE PUBLISHERS
Education Redefined

Latest Edition, Unique Publishers (I) Pvt. Ltd. All rights reserved.

Price : ₹ 125.00
ISBN : 978-81-8357-153-1
Code : 3.9

***Published by*:**
Amarjeet S. Chopra
Unique Publishers (I) Pvt. Ltd.
Email : info@uniquepublishersindia.org
Website : www.uniquepublishersindia.org

***Regd. Office* :**
M-51, Lajpat Nagar-II, New Delhi - 110024
Fax: +91 11 46573070

***Delhi Office* :**
4574/15, Padam Chand Marg (Opp. Happy School)
Ansari Road, Daryaganj
New Delhi - 110002
Tel : +91 11 41564400/11/22
Fax : +91 11 43508440

***Corporate Office* :**
B-155, Sector-63
Noida - 201301 (U.P.)
Tel : +91 120 4575555
Fax : +91 120 4575563

***Printed at*:**
Sanjeev Offset Printers

NOTE :

1. No part of this book may be reproduced or transmitted by any means/form, electronic, mechanical, photocopy, recording or any other way, without prior written permission from the publishers.
2. Due care has been taken to ensure that the information provided in this book is correct. However, the publishers bear no responsibility for any damage resulting from any inadvertent omission or inaccuracy in the book.
3. All trade marks are the properties of their respective owners.
4. Any dispute arising due to any issue/issues related to the publication of this book shall be subject to the jurisdiction of Delhi Courts only.

PREFACE

George Eliot is the pen-name of Mary Ann Evans. The Victorian Era is crowded with female novelists and George Eliot is ranked first among them. George Eliot is a Victorian novelist and she is one of the 'founding fathers' of the modern psychological novel. *Adam Bede* is a full length novel and it gives an excellent picture of English country life among the humbler classes. *Adam Bede* was published in the beginning of 1858. In *Adam Bede,* the novelist takes the moral aspects painfully and brings us to notice the consequences of the deeds which are done ignoring the rules and regulations of nature and society as well.

The scope of this critical study is to discuss exhaustively those textual aspects of her novels that are indispensable for the students of English Honours and Post Graduate Classes of Indian Universities. Particularly beneficial from the examination point of view are the Select University Questions with Answers and the critical discussion of the various features of the novel. Suggestions for improvement are most welcome and will be favourably considered at the time of the publication of its next edition.

We also express our heart-felt thanks to the literary illuminaries whose names have been given in Select Bibliography.

New Delhi **The Editors**

PREFACE

[illegible]

The Editors

CONTENTS

PART - I
INTRODUCTION TO GEORGE ELIOT

PART - II
A DETAILED STUDY OF *ADAM BEDE*

PART - III

Or

Hetty's Narcissus Complex led to her tragedy. How far do you agree or disagree with this view?

Or

Write a note on the symbolic significance of Hetty Sorrel in the novel *Adam Bede*

Or

Comment on the "Change of Nature-background in keeping with the changes in the career and fortunes of Hetty" in *Adam Bede.*

Q. 2. Adam Bede had regenerated into more genuine human being through the power of love. Comment on the above statement. 195

Or

Give your own views about the "Gradual shedding of Adam's hardness, pride and sense of self-righteousness".

Or

Consider the role of Mr. Irwine and Bartle Massey in the process of Adam's regeneration.

Or

Adam gained enough education and had grown more mature through a process of suffering.

Q. 3. Write a note on the significance of the minor characters in *Adam Bede.* 200

Or

George Eliot has presented a cross section of the Midland society in *Adam Bede.* Write a note on the minor characters in the light of the above statement

Or

The minor characters of *Adam Bede* present a comprehensive picture of Midland life and society. The farmers, clergymen, gardeners, school-master, carpenters, milk-maids and inn-keepers all come out alive in the novel. Give your own views.

Q. 4. Write a note on the three suppers and their symbolic significance. 205

Or

"The first of these suppers is designed to remind Adam of his origin in Nature"—How far would you agree with this view ?

Or

Give in your own words an account of George Eliot's artistic and philosophic intentions in the portrayal of Adam's growth.

Or

Write a note on the restoration of Adam's humanity and his regeneration.

Or

The novel abounds with religious and symbolic elements. Comment.

Q. 7. Consider Arthur as a man of weak moral fibre who yields to temptation. 215

Or

Through Arthur-Hetty Sorrel love story, the novelist tries to impart a moral lesson depicting the ill consequences of surrendering to temptation. How far would you agree with this view ?

Or

The novel *Adam Bede* is a study in moral weakness and its consequences. How far would you agree or disagree with this view ? Give reasons for your answer.

Or

"If Arthur had been conventionally wicked Squire's son setting out to seduce the village maiden he could hardly have made a better start. Yet George Eliot enables us to look at this scene—with the additional knowledge that there is no prospect of Arthur's marrying Hetty—and still remains convinced that he means no ill."
Make an analysis of Arthur Donnithorne's character in the light of the above statement.

Or

"His (Arthur Donnithorne's) is the tragedy of a weak man who is unable to line up to his good intentions." Give in your own words an account of Arthur Donnithorne's moral conflict.

Or

How far is Arthur Donnithorne responsible for Hetty's tragedy ?

Or

The novel *Adam Bede* traces the movement from weakness to sin and from sin to Nemesis. Comment.

Q. 8. "*Adam Bede* is uneven in the precise sense of having its weight wrongly distributed." Write a note on the technical flaw of the novel in the light of the above statement. 221

Or

The Dinah-Adam marriage is forced, unnatural and lacks credibility. How far would you agree with this view?

Or

Is the ending of *Adam Bede* suitable? Give your own views.

Q. 9. "Eliot's stories grow like plants out of a theme or idea in a given social environment." Justify. 224

Or

Write a note on the plot structure of the novel *Adam Bede.*

Or

Comment on the organic wholeness of the novel *Adam Bede.*

Or

"The simple well-combined pattern conveys the sense of a social structure enclosing four human beings as completely as the soil enclose the roots of a growing plant and, in so doing, it illustrates one aspect of the author's vision of life." How far would you agree or disagree with this.

Q. 10. According to George Cgreeger, in Arthur, Hetty finds, "for a brief time at least, the objectification of her day-dreaming desires, but these in turn are a projection in fantasy of her own ego, sexually translated." Give your own comment. 229

Or

Hetty's love of Arthur is in reality the exterminations of her day dreams. How far would you agree or disagree with this view ?

Q. 11. Consider *Adam Bede* as a novel of rural life. 232

Or

George Eliot gives a picturesque and realistic presentation of country life in her novel *Adam Bede.* Comment.

Or

"Finally George Eliot uses landscape to define, reinforce and foreshadow the events of the plot and moral situation". Write a note on Eliot's presentation of the rural backdrop in *Adam Bede* in the light of the above statement.

PART - IV

PART - I
INTRODUCTION TO GEORGE ELIOT

CHAPTER - 1

SOCIAL AND HISTORICAL BACKGROUND TO THE VICTORIAN NOVEL (1830-90)

1. An Era of Peace

It would be fairly correct to describe the Victorian Age as an era of peace. By the middle of the century, the influence of the French Revolution had died down and peace, hopes and ideals were being entertained.

2. Material or Economic Developments

New activities, commercial enterprise and enlarged availability of markets led to increasing use of mechanical devices. The Industrial Revolution was at the centre of material prosperity. But it brought a number of social evils in its wake—squalid slums, exploitation of cheap labour (especially children), and increasing migration from the countryside to the cities. The Utilitarian Philosophy was used by corrupt manufacturers and businessmen to exploit workers. A few enlightened people tried to introduce social legislation to fight these evils. Writers of this era, such as Dickens, Thackeray, George Eliot, Carlyle, Ruskin and Arnold spoke against such materialistic values in their works.

3. Intellectual Development

Materialism did not completely deaden intellectual activity in this era. A spirit of questioning was dominant. There was a revolution in scientific thought, following upon the works of Darwin (*Origin of Species*, 1859) and his school. There was a great outburst of social political theorizing—such as that of Herbert Spencer and John Stuart Mill. In addition, popular education became a practical thing. This in its turn produced a new hunger for intellectual matter, leading to increased production of the Press and other forms of literature. But the scientific and philosophical developments also led to the rise of pessimism. Old customs and faiths had lost their hold, but a new order had not yet been established. A gloomy view of life, for instance is reflected in the work of George Eliot. It was, on the whole, a complex age, and this complexity is reflected in its literature.

CHAPTER - 2

LITERARY FEATURES OF THE VICTORIAN AGE

The sixty years (1830-90) generally included under the heading of the Victorian Age exhibit several dissimilar features; yet, we can detect certain common characteristics in the novels of the day about which we can generalize.

1. Morality of the Age

Morality occupied a dominant place among the writer's concern in its earlier years as people demanded it. George Eliot, however, breaks off a great deal from conventional morality, but even she cannot totally escape its influence. In most of the other novelists' works, however, there is a deliberate refusal to acknowledge the physical aspects of man's being. Prudishness about sex was prevalent.

2. Spirit of Revolt

Many writers of the time revolted against the deadening effects of certain conventions. Satirizing or denouncing the snobbishness, the hypocrisy and the dubious values of the society is quite common in the literature of the time, especially in the novels.

3. Influence of Intellectual Developments

New ideas in science, religion and politics influenced literary products. The scientific temper and philosophical mind is very much reflected in George Eliot's works. She, too, is not ready to accept conventional Christian practices without questioning their relevance and significance.

4. Conventional Plots

The Victorian novels are generally characterised by a loose plot with a touch of melodrama or sentimentality. However, George Eliot's plots are more coherent and realistic than those of the average Victorian novelists.

5. Varied Interests and Subject Matter

The Victorian novels usually have a very wide range of moods and subjects, crowding together a variety of interests.

(1953). Her novels are largely dependent on personal experiences. There is great truth and intensity in her novels, but the seriousness is unrelieved by humour. However, she brought energy and passion to the novel. Emily Bronte wrote less than her sister, but her single novel, *Wuthering Heights* (1847) is unique in English literature. It breathes the very spirit of the desolate wild moors, and the passions of its characters have an elemental force which is poetic. Unflinching realism marks the style. Anne Bronte's works, the chief of which is *Anne Grey* (1847), are not as good as her sisters' novels.

The importance of the Bronte sisters lies in their pioneering efforts in laying bare the human soul. Individual personality gains importance. Imagination and emotion combine with intellect in their work. In their concern with the human soul, they were to be followed by George Eliot and Meredith.

4. George Eliot (1819-80)

George Eliot was the pen-name of Mary Ann Evans. She started her career as writer only late in her life. Pre-occupation with the individual is carried further in her novels. Her style is lucid and her work lightened by her humour. (See the next section for a detailed discussion of her life and works).

5. George Meredith (1828-1909)

He was a poet as well as a novelist. His novels include : *The Ordeal of Richard Feveral* (1859), *Evan Harrington* (1861), *Emilia in England* (1964), *Rhoda Fleming* (1865), and *The Egoist* (1879). His style is precise of phrase and epithet, elaborate in detail and imaginatively powerful. His plots are weak, but the characters are subtly analysed.

There are several other novelists of this period who are, however, not of the first rank. They include Benjamin Disraeli, Charles Reade, Anthony Trollope, Wilkie Collins, Charles Kingsley, George Borrow, Elizabeth Gaskell and Robert Louis Stevenson among others.

CHAPTER - 4

LIFE AND WORKS OF GEORGE ELIOT

Life of George Eliot : Mary Ann Evans, later to be famous as George Eliot, was born on 22nd November, 1818, at Arbury Farm. The youngest daughter in the family, she was deeply influenced by her father. Her childhood impressions and experiences were never forgotten. She quite often felt insecure and unhappy, for her plain looks were constantly contrasted with her pretty sister, Christina. She showered her love and affection on her brother Isaac. Her early education was mainly obtained from observing nature and from extensive reading. She was deeply influenced by Walter Scott. She also relished Maria Edgeworth's stories. In 1836, her formal education at school came to an end when her mother died and she had to keep house for her father. She had a religious fervour right from an early age, and even when she discarded Christianity, she clung to the ethical conceptions of God, duty, responsibility and man's destiny.

In 1841, on moving to Coventry, Mary Ann Evans' mental horizons widened to a great deal. Here she met several intellectuals in various fields of knowledge. Slowly, she developed skepticism and discarded the old beliefs. This led to a great spiritual conflict as well as open conflict with her father who was a devout churchman.

In 1849, after her father's death, Mary Ann Evans went on a tour of Europe. Returning in 1850, she felt lonely and idle. She met John Chapman, a young publisher and was easily persuaded to become assistant editor of the *Westminister Review.* Her position brought her into contact with various distinguished men and women including Herbert Spencer, Carlyle, Emerson, and Mrs. Gaskell. She also met George Henry Lewes, one of the best drama critics of the age. He was married but separated from his wife whom he could not divorce under certain conditions of the existing Victorian laws. A mutual attraction developed between Mary Ann and George Lewes, for both had similar interests. After much serious thinking, Mary Ann began to live with Lewes as his mistress. As a result, she was ostracized by her family and society—for living in sin. But Lewes and Mary Ann found profound happiness in each other.

It was under Lewes' influence that Mary Ann became the novelist George Eliot. With the death of Lewes in 1878, the literary career of George Eliot came to an end. In 1880, she married J.W. Cross, twenty years her junior though a great friend for a long time. She died the same year at Chelsea.

Works of George Eliot

1. *Scenes of Clerical Life* (1858). It consists of three stories dealing with the tragedy of ordinary lives. *Amos Barton* teaches the significance of the anguish suffered by an ordinary man. *Mr. Gilfils's Love Story* is a vision of the past, and *Janet's Repentance* presents a conflict between religion and irreligion. Already George Eliot's humanity is apparent in these works, though her style and manner as a novelist are still in the making.

2. *Adam Bede* (1859). A full length novel, it gives an excellent picture of English country life among the humbler classes. The story involves Adam Bede, a village carpenter and Hetty Sorel, a pretty but vain girl whom he loves. Hetty, however, is seduced under the promise of marriage by Arthur Donnithrone, a young Squire. She becomes pregnant and later murders her illegitimate child. She is arrested, convicted of the murder of the child, and transported. After a time, Adam wins the heart of Dinah Morris, a young preacher. It is a movingly told story and is notable for its fine characters such as Mrs. Poyser, Hetty and Adam Bede himself. Besides being realistic and rich in humour, the novel expounds George Eliot's ethical philosophy.

3. *The Mill on the Floss* (1860) is a partly autobiographical story involving Maggie Tulliver and her brother Tom. A moving tragedy, set in an authentic rural background, it is probably George Eliot's most profound study of the inner recesses of human personality.

4. *Silas Marner : The Weaver of Raveloe* (1861) again gives excellent pictures of village life and has scenes of rich humour skilfully blended with the tragedy. Silas Marner is a handloom weaver. Basically good, he has become bitter and cynical because of a false accusation of theft brought against him. For years he endures a lonely life with the chief interest of saving money. But he is saved from his despair when he finds a little girl by chance. He lavishes all his love upon her and brings her up as a daughter. After sixteen years, the real father of the girl, a Squire, claims her but fails to win the girl from Silas.

5. *Romola* (1863) begins a new phase in George Eliot's writing. The ethical interests which was underlying all her previous works now become more and more the dominating factor in her novels. It is the story of Romola, a girl of high moral sense bred under the

influence of Savanarola, and Tito Melema, a handsome, clever but easy-going young man. The novel is set in medieval Florence, but the historical setting does not come alive. The note of spontaneity is lacking in spite of the memorable study of degeneracy in the character of Tito Melema that the novel presents.

6. *Felix Holt the Radical* (1866) is probably George Eliot's least important novel. It is set in the period of the Reform Bill. It gives a picture of the upper middle class and industrial life.

7. *Middlemarch, A Study of Provincial Life* (1871-72) has been regarded by most readers and critics to be George Eliot's greatest novel. The novel's name is that of the town in which the scene of the story is laid. In fact, there are two stories running parallel in the novel : in both cases there are complications arising from marriage. In one case, Dorothea Brooke finds her lofty ideas frustrated in her marriage with the Rev. Edward Casaubon. In the other case, Rosamand Vincy cannot find happiness with Dr. Lydgate, a man who struggles to meet his family's demands while being true to his professional ambitions. The novel is noteworthy for its deeply studied characters who suffer through their own blindness and folly, and the powerful and inexorable realism of the complex picture of life in a small town.

8. *Daniel Deronda* (1876) is coloured by George Eliot's pre-occupation with moral problems. Indeed, it is more of a dissertation than a novel. It is the story of marriage between two persons who are equally self-centred.

9. *Impressions of Theophrastus Such* (1879) is a collection of miscellaneous essays.

CHAPTER - 5

GEORGE ELIOT AS A PIONEER OF MODERN NOVEL *OR* GEORGE ELIOT'S REALISM AND PSYCHOLOGICAL ANALYSIS

Introduction

The Victorian Era is crowded with female novelists, among them, the prominent were Charlote Bronte, Emily Bronte and Mrs. Gaskell. Last, but not the least, George Eliot is ranked above all the other three, not for a variety of work she has given to the English novel, but for introducing a new form which is much deep and philosophised form of novel. Not only females but males also could not compete with her in her sharp understanding of the atmosphere and then portraying it into her novels, with much efficiency doing all the modifications that where required.

New Trends in the English Novel

The Victorian Age provided us with a great novelist, George Eliot. "She stands at the gateway between the old novel and the new, no unworthy heir of Thackeray and Dickens and no unworthy fore-runner of Hardy and Henry James." Her psychological insight into human motives was deep and sincere, which render profundity to her novels. Her contribution to the English novel cannot be written in a few lines but her novels like *Adam Bede, Silas Marner, Middle-march, Romola, Mill on the Floss,* themselves prove her greatness as a novelist.

Realistic Approach

Her early novels, *Adam Bede, Mill on the Floss and Silas Marner,* are the real descriptions of the life of the people staying in the English Midlands. The particular regions, Warwickshire, Derbyshire, were well known by the novelist and she started her career as a novelist, by giving a realistic picture of the natives, their beliefs, their cultures and habits. Even the dialects spoken by them is not ignored, and appreciated as well. She spent her childhood days wandering in the fields, eating the sweet fruits of the trees grown by her own relatives and neighbours experiencing the joys and sorrows of the tough village life and later every aspect could be seen in her novels. Says Hugh Walker, "It is notorious that in the earlier novels George Eliot drew very freely on the stories of her memory. Scene after scene, character after character in these novels has been identified with some place or person within the range of her early experience. Her mansions and cottages, her lanes and meadows, are those to which she had been accustomed to derive in childhood with her father, or over which she had rambled with her brother. Still more are the characters of her novels, the figures with whom she had been familiar, and almost in proportion to the familarity is the frequency of their appearance. No other group was so often laid under contribution as her own family. Her father, her mother, her brother, her sister, her aunt and herself, all appear in her pages."

Dissection of Human Mind

George Eliot is not much concerned with outward appearances but the inward looks could not escape from her sharp eyes and contemplated mind. This outlook was sufficient to produce a great change in the course of the novel. Although such a study of human relations as was made by George Eliot required her to employ a complex method, it did not require her to employ the artificial intricacy of the earlier novel of intrigue. Thus, developed psychological novel. In the words of E.A. Baker, "Her mind was always active; experience set it immediately and instinctively analysing and generalising, to discovering why and how things happened. And when she turned her attention to the world around her, it was this analysis that started her creative imagination working."

Philosophical Concepts

Another feature of George Eliot is that every sentence written by her has some deeper meaning which can be understood if is deeply studied. An average reader cannot find out the philosophical concepts rendered in much quantity, faith in the duty, emphasised the importance of morals and values in deciding one future and this is what her philosophy represents. "Again and again it has been pointed out that fiction in her hands is no longer a mere entertainment; it strikes a note of seriousness and even of sternment; it is turned into a searching review of the gravest as well as the pleasantest aspect of human existence, reassuming the reflective and discursive rights and duties pertaining to the novel at its beginnings without however sacrificing any of the creative and dramatic qualities that had developed in the intervening centuries." (E.A. Baker). She stresses again and again that the major flaw in character leads him towards the path of destruction.

As in *King Lear,* Lear suffers and finally meets a tragic death because of one mistake he had done by not understanding the silent love of his daughter Cordelia. In the same way, Hetty is destined to suffer, as she crosses the limit of her virginity, thus is given harsh punishment. Consequently, a number of miseries faced by her, ends with her own ending.

Conclusion

Nevertheless, although she had so much in common with other Victorian novelists, she was different from them in at least one important respect, and this difference caused her eventually to produce an essentially new type of novel.

CHAPTER - 6

PLOT CONSTRUCTION OF GEORGE ELIOT

Introduction

Every work of art has a technique. While spontaneity is the essence of charm, method has the strength of harmony and symmetry. Among Victorian novelists, Dickens, Thackeray, Trollope, Mrs. Gaskel, were the prominent. But George Eliot is considered the most prominent, for where others were writing in the tradition of Henry Fielding, George Eliot modifies that tradition. In some respects, she follows the tradition but in her art of plot-construction, the departure is felt. "The traditional English novel", says David Cecil, "consisted of a number of characters and incidents knit together by an intrigue centering round a young attractive hero and heroine and rounded off with their happy marriage. The plot did not, except in the single case of *Vanity Fair*, arise from the characters, it was imposed by the author on them".

Situation Determining Plot

"But George Eliot began with an idea of character or situation her plot was intended to follow, not a standardised formula, but what she conceived to be the logical development of that idea ! and this might entail something quite different from the accepted Victorian notion of a plot. It might entail no marriage, no happy ending, no character answering to the Victorian conception of hero or heroine. Often it did not. In *Silas Marner* the hero is an elderly bachelor; *The Mill on the Floss* ends very badly and has no hero at all. In *Middlemarch* there is no central figure of any kind; the main interest is divided between four separate groups of character; and none of these, except Dorothea Brooks, approaches the conventional heroic type. Finally, since the action of George Eliot's stories arises logically from the characters, those strokes of fortunes, coincidences, sudden inheritances, long lost wills which are the stock-in-trade of the ordinary Victorian plot, are inevitably omitted. They are the first novels which set out to give a picture of life wholly unmodified by those formulas of a good plot which the novel had taken over from comedy and romance. Her story is conditioned solely by the logical demands of situation or character; it ends sadly or happily, includes heroes or omits them, deals with the married or the unmarried, according to reason and observation lead her to think likely. In fact, the laws conditioning the form of George Eliot's novels are the same laws that condition those of Henry James and Wells and Conard and Arnold Bennett. Hers are the first examples in English of the novel in its mature form; in them it structurally comes of age."

Logical Arrangement of Incidents

The exposition of her novel comprises a particular idea or theme. Like all the Victorian novelists, she also portrayed life from the rural areas and the minutest description is not left out in her novels. But these scenes and characters remain in the background, because her major concern is the dissection of human mind. In the words of David Cecil, "Her mind was always active; experience set it immediately and instinctively analysing and generalising, to discover why and how things happened. And why she turned her attention to the world around her it was this analysis that started her creative imagination working. It is inspired, not by what she felt or fancied, but by what she thought; not by a wish to convey her impression of life but her judgements on it. And it embodied itself not in a picture but in a theme. She did not have a vision of Barchester or Cranford and then invent situations on which to hang her picture of this vision; she had a vision of human society as the expression of certain principles, and she embodied it in a picture of a specific place—Middlemarch. Her novels are built round an idea or theme, and everything not relevant to that idea is rigidly excluded. The end is implicit in the beginning, successive events are logically and causally connected with each other and as the action proceeds, it is seen to be the logical and natural outcome of the character or characters concerned and those characters themselves are the result of their social environment." Thus the catastrophe in *The Mill on the Floss* is worked out in the last chapter, entitled, "The Last Conflict". This ending follow logically from Maggie's love of her brother and her emotional nature. The death of Maggie is the only solution for the complicated problems of her life; and symmetry requires that Tom and Maggie who had walked hand in hand on the banks of the floss should finally go down into it hand in hand. So, the theme echoes that deviation from right path leads to destruction and the plot develops according to this theme.

Organic Whole

Character and action are well integrated with the social background and atmosphere of the novel. As Joan Bennet points out, "The outer circle within which the dramatic situation is contained is an organic human society." George Eliot's novels are well imbued with the spirit of a particular time and place. The outer circle in *The Mill on the Floss* is the society of St. Ogg's represented by the Dodsons and the Tullivers and a few others, "Narrow, rigid, tradition ridden and materialistic, it crushes and represses individual and uncommon aspirations."

George Eliot : An Innovator

This cannot be denied that in some respects George Eliot is a novelist in the Fielding tradition, as the stories written by her are complete in themselves. But if her novels are seen from different angles, we will find a revolutionary change in her style. Without a limited canvas, she could draw a variety of people with different thoughts and emotions. Her work can be equalled with Jane Austen in form and style. But where Jane Austen's philosophy for traditions and manners is a law of nature, George Eliot was aware of the ethical, religious and social conventions of the world. She paints and the effect of these surroundings can be seen in the evolution of her characters.

Conclusion

We conclude by the words of George Eliot. "It is the habit of my imagination to strive after as full a vision of the medium in which a character moves as of the character itself." Again, "My stories grow in me like plants" said George Eliot, beautifully describing the organic form which she conceived in her novels.

CHAPTER - 7

ART OF CHARACTERIZATION OF GEORGE ELIOT

Introduction : George Eliot's Command over Difficult Material

The work of any great novelist is assessed by his art of characterization and George Eliot proves herself in this respect. In *Adam Bede,* she had contrived to add the claim of a delightful philosophy to the pleasure of good story. The reader will at once remember that he could not help linking all the characters in that story. The general influence of the book was to reconcile us to human nature; to make us think better of our fellow men, to make us feel that in the weakest there is something to be admired, in the worst something to be loved; to give us not only the temporary delight of listening to a pleasant tale, but also the permanent good of an increased sympathy with our kind. In the words of David Cecil "It is in the treatment of character that George Eliot's more active intellect gives her the most conspicuous advantage over the typical Victoria".

Rural Characters

George Eliot picked her characters from the world with which she was well acquainted—her personal experience in the English Midlands. Later novels of George Eliot include some of the characters from the higher class which lack strength and vitality what was in abundance where characters were drawn from 'humble and rustic life.' Wordsworthian influence can be seen in her early novels.

Psychological Presentation of Character

This was the distinction of George Eliot to probe into the minds of the common people and make us aware of their innermost thoughts. This deep interest in motives partly flowed from her relative maturity—she was nearly forty when she wrote her first novel and was well versed in philosophy and science. Compton Rickett says, "The writer who could visualise for us the hedonistic Tito, the fine old puritan Dr. Lyons, the erratic Gowendolen, the steadfast Marry Garth; the commonplace Fred Vincy and the brilliant Lydgate; the rough uncultured Bob Jakin and the polished scholar Casuboum dealing justice to each, fairly appraising their merits and no less keenly exposing their weakness, was a writer with no ordinary power of psychological portrayal. Nor is she a whit inferior in the subtlety of her method, as is evidenced by the delicate nuances of the characterization of Mary Garth and Rosamund Vincy and Romola."

Realistic Portrayal of Characters

The realism in Eliot's novel can be guessed since the publication of her first novel, *Scenes of Clerical Life,* the readers were surprised to find the characters, who are known to us in one or another way. George Eliot has characterised them realistically and "they are seen clearly, objectively, humorously and inspite of their moral and intellectual deficiencies, with respect and sympathy." The small community of Shepperton is represented by these spokesmen having individual traits as well. Her memories of mother, can be visualised in the character of Mrs. Hackit, who is shrewd but kind woman. She manages the dairy like Mrs. Evans and Mr. Hackit is a hard working farmer like her own father, Robert Evans, he is "a shrewd, substantial man, whose advice about crops is always worth listening to and who is too well off to want to borrow money."

Development in Characters

Another feature of her characterization is that her characters are never flat. This is true at least of the characters that really matters. Her characters are always shown in a process of development. Indeed, the major aim of her is to show this very development in character. When the novel begins, a character is shaped already by the circumstances—heredity and environment—of the past. Then starts a process of change. It may be the impact of some incident or some other characters, of some book or philosophy but there is always something which gives the character a new dimension. For example, Tito Melema in *Romola,* is a scholar, with aim to overpower the world, falls in circumstances which cause his downfall, thus changing his existence on—this earth—such a grand change undergo Eliot's characters. In this connection Long remarks, "Her heroes and heroines differ radically from those of Dickens and Thackery in this respect. That when we meet the men and women of the later novelists, their characters are already formed, and we are reasonably sure what will they do under given circumstances. In George Eliot's novels the characters develop gradually as we come to know them. They go from weakness to strength, or from strength to weakness, according to the works that they do and the thoughts that they cherish. The novelist exhibits the mode by which step by step a character goes down, readjusting his principles to suit his practice till imperceptibly he is transformed, changed or ruined."

Female Characters

Some critics have pointed out that the major fault of George Eliot in her art of characterization is that most of her heroines are portraits of George Eliot herself. Romola, Dorothea, and Maggie are all self-portraits of George Eliot herself. Her delineation of women characters in general is more or less perfect, or rather comparatively, superior to her delineation of men characters. Virginia Woolf says in this connection : "The ancient consciousness of woman, charged with suffering and for so many ages dumb, seems in them to have brimmed and overflowed and uttered a demand for something—they scarcely know what—for something which is perhaps incompatible with the facts of human existence." George Eliot is exceptional in her portrayal of female characters and their tragedy of unfulfilled wills. Her major concern is to unfold their inner feelings with masterly strokes. Compton-Rickett points out : "Maggie's cry was for fuller life, Romola's for ampler knowledge, Dorothea's for larger opportunity for doing good." These themes were dealt with by George Eliot, which makes her to bring a revolutionary change in the history of English novel.

Conclusion

George Eliot invests her characters from the rural areas and these are the very spokesmen of the community to which they belong. Indeed, she studies her characters in relation to their environment. She explored and understood the human mind with an acumen much in advance of her contemporaries. Let us conclude with David Cecil's words : "She stands at the gateway between the old novel and the new a massive caryatid, heavy of countenance and uneasy of attitude, but noble, monumental, profoundly impressive."

CHAPTER - 8

INFLUENCE OF THE ENGLISH MIDLANDS

The Midland

The English Midland, more specially Warwickshire and Coventry about which George Eliot writes and renders her literary works. It is a calm and peaceful area with no forests at all. The beauty of the midland plains gave George Eliot an ecstasy and after watching the conflicts in religion, she turned towards these places in the last days of her life, for mental peace and order.

Attraction for Landscapes

George Eliot passed her childhood in the lap of nature and not a single scenary could have escaped from her sight-loving eyes. Parkinson says, "Quite a feature of the scenary—and indeed of Warwickshire generally—is that the hedges are everywhere closely planted with trees, whose height, as well as the riotous wastefulness of the hedge-rose give evidence of a kindly soil and climate." Her early home named as Griff House has stretched flat fields in its backward portion. Passing these fields, on the way, there are "round-pool" the "wokery elms" and probably to the "Red Deeps" where the secret meetings of Magie Tulliver and Philip Wakem occurred. *Brother and Sister,* her autobiographical poem, includes all about her early life and the environment around her. In her novels, we see a true copy of her own home, Griff House.

Recollections of Childhood

In her young age, George Eliot accompanying her father, used to go for a long walk through countryside. Both of them enjoyed the journey and during these trips she observed the nature with sharp eyes and later her novels described the scenery. Not a minutest detail of nature could escape from her novels. The knowledge of rural-dialect which helped her much to understand the country was not within the boundaries of an ancestral pack, but among the midland villages and markets by the tree-studded hedge-rows, and where the heavy berrges seen in the distance to float mysteriously among the rushes and the feathered grass. With her father, she visited Staffordshire and Derbyshire which were the scenes of activity of his early manhood. The background against which the drama of *Adam Bede* takes place is that of the borders of Straffordshire and

Derbyshire; that of *The Mill on the Floss* in Lincolnshire; whilst *Silas Marner, Felix Holt* and *Middlemarch* have Warwickshire landscape as their background.

George Eliot stepped in school in Coventry and the impression of the scenery stamped a mark on the mind. George Eliot's birth place was near Nuneaton where she could see the people working in fields and their life full of adventures and hard work for them, is the key to her success. Thus, all of her novels reveal the hard realities of this peasant class and their traditions, customs and ideas remaining in the background, are given much importance, which enables the reader to probe into their hearts. "Thus, looking upon the same environment, George Eliot has rendered the same service for rural England in the days of Queen Victoria that Shakespeare did for the time of Queen Elizabeth painting a never-to-be forgotten picture of life as it really was."

The Impact of Industrialisation

Warwickshire is a region of vast fields, the oak and the ash are planted closely on both sides, thus a beautiful and comfortable country. Agriculture being the main occupation of the people, there were smell of the smoke of industries here and there in the village. Finally, it was realized that the industries are being set up in this village, thus polluting it. Now in the village, industry and agriculture exist simultaneously. In her childhood, George Eliot became aware of the emergence of two contrasting factors, described it in her introduction to Felix Holt : "In these midland districts the travellers passed rapidly from one phase of English life to another; after looking down on a village dirty with coal-dust, noisy with the shaking of looms, he might skirt a parish all of fields, high hedges, after the coach had rattled over the pavement of a manufacturing town, the scenes of riots and trade-union meetings, it would take him in another ten minutes into a rural region, where the neighbourhood of the town was only felt in the advantage of a near market of corn, cheese and hay."

Place of Worship

On South Arbury farm George Eliot was born, which is near Arbury Park. In her first novel we find scenes of clerical life, in fact the real picture of all the natural scenery she has been encountered with in her early life. Walking on foot covers one mile from the grassy park, to the Arbury Hall, and the Chevered Manor or Mr. Gilfil's love story. On the left side of the hill, Astley Church is standing, which is described with changed name (Knebley Church in the story).

On South of Nuneaton, walk of one mile bringforth Chilver's Colton Church (Shepperton Church) whereas in Knebly Church, George Eliot talks about twelve apostles. In fact, there are eighteen saints in the church. So the modifications and alternations are done where they are needed. But the originality is never crushed under these slight modifications.

Description of the Inns

A few inns are also ignored while portraying other places. While portraying the inns, much attention is paid. Newdegate Arms' is the real name for the old Port Arms'. Near this is the Bull Hotel, whose role is significant in *Jonet's Repentance*. The traveller to Rosseter stops at 'Donnithorne Arms' in the second chapter of *Adam Bede*. At the entrance of the village of Hayslope, this inn stands. The original name for this inn is the 'Bromley Davenport Arms', at the entrance of the village of Ellastone in Staffordshire. Says Charles Olcott, "The green lay at the extremity of the village, and from it the road branched of in two directions, one leading further up the hill by the church, and the other winding gently towards the valley. This is an exact description of the fork in the road just beyond the Bromley-Davenport Arms."

Conclusion

We may sum up that she started her career as a novelist describing her own land, its culture, values and morals. The Midland setting, remaining at the background plays an important role in furthering the novel with full vitality. The very recognition of her own soil, enable her to probe into the minds and hearts of the people, which heighten her status in the history of English novel.

CHAPTER - 9

PHILOSOPHY AND IDEOLOGY OF GEORGE ELIOT

Faith in Evangelical Christianity

George Eliot came under the influence of her Evangelist aunt Mrs. Elizabeth Evans and a dint of Christianity remained with her, as she was brought up in the family, which was sticked with orthodox Christianity. In her youth, she used to visit the church regularly. Later, her relationship with Brays and other intellectuals, made her an irreligious and an agnostic. David Cecils says, "George Eliot was not religious".

Logical Bent of Mind

Intellect in her, infact, provokes her to question the doctrines prescribed by the orthodox-christianity. The progress of science and other new inventions brought about a revolutionary change in the thoughts of educated people and the same case was with George Eliot. In the words of Basil Willey, "Probably no English writer of the time, and certainly no novelist, more fully epitomizes the century; her development is a paradigm, her intellectual biography a graph, in its most decided trends. Starting from evangelical Christianity, the curve passes through doubt to a reinterpreted Christ and a religion of humanity : beginning with God, it ends in Duty."

Disbelief in Almighty Power

Calvacade of the English Novel by Wagenknecht, thus describes her loss of faith in the established concepts, "George Eliot's revolt against her inherited faith was based on intellectual ground alone; at no time was there a moral revolt. It was inevitable, therefore, that, being what she was, she should have spent the rest of her life trying to preserve the Christian morality without supernatural sanctions. The rationalist in her would not accept the Christian concept of God, and she regarded any faith in the supernatural as inconceivable. She represents the whole predicament of the religious temperament cut off by rationalism from the traditional objects of veneration, and the traditional intellectual formulations. She was not, of course, a practising Christian, but in her estrangement from the religion about Jesus she none the further from the religion of Jesus. She knew the hunger and thirst after righteousness, and the need for renunciation—the need to lose one's life in order to gain it. And though her religious consciousness was pre-eminently moral, it was not exclusively, so, she also had the faculty of reverence, the capacity of acknowledge the reality of the unseen."

Inward Enlightenment

Neither George Eliot was an athiest, nor agnostic. Her moralistic approach towards religion, can be visualized in all of her novels. Her philosophy celebrates duty, and the fortune is underestimated in all of her novels. David Cecil points out, "And this means that she conceives her vision of human existence only in those aspects that relate to her standard of criticism. Now this criticism was exclusively and consistently a moral criticism. George Eliot, though she was a thinker, was not a particularly original thinker. And her conception of life was that held by the dominant school of thought in advanced circles of her day. She was a thorough-going Victorian rationalist. The progress of thought and discovery to her made it impossible to believe in the supernatural; she had given up the Puritan theology that had soaked itself too deeply into the fibre of her thought and feeling for her to give it up as well. She might not believe in heaven and hell and miracles, but she believed in right and wrong and man's paramount obligation to follow right, as strictly as if she were Bunyan himself. And her standards of right and wrong were the Puritan standards. She admired truthfulness and chastity and industry and self-restraint; she disapproved loose living and recklessness and deceit and self-indulgence."

A Distinguished Philosophy

She believed that every man is the maker of one's own fate. Only the present actions decide what the man would be in the future. Nobody can escape from the punishment for one's earlier misdeeds neither a person is exempted from the rewards for one's honest and good deeds. We may sum up her philosophy in one line. "As you sow, so shall you reap."

Conclusion

To conclude with the words of A.E. Baker, "Emancipated herself from the Evangelical creed in which she had been brought up, but she was always religious-minded. The phase of rationalism through which she passed after abandoning the belief in heaven and hell of her Evangelical upbringing did not last long. Pantheism she found unsatisfying and she resigned herself to the conviction that there is no answer to our cravings for a definite faith. But hundreds of passages in her novels imply that she could never eradicate a profound sense, not merely of divine immanence, but of divine transcendence. Her puritanism, her worship of duty rested all her life upon the consciousness of an inner reality which adherents of the creeds readily identified with the Divinity. The monitor within represented something higher than ourselves, either of another order of being or simply the loftiest ideal conceivable to man. The latter question remains inscrutable; but the terms in which she constantly speaks of duty and conscience, and the Supreme Power, which fashioned us, are the terms of one who could hardly help believing."

CHAPTER - 10

HUMOUR OF GEORGE ELIOT

Humour in Her Novels

Philosophical mind of George Eliot could not render much humour in her novels. Still, her novels have some humour of every shape and variety. Her earlier novels—*Scenes of Clerical Life, The Mill on the Floss, Adam Bede* and *Silas Marner* contain very mild and refreshing humour whereas this kind of humour is absent in her later novels.

Her much concentration in her later novels, remain on psychological analysis of characters and other is her physiological concepts, which diverted her mind from other important factors. Humour is one of them.

Two Types of Humour

She is compared with Thomas Hardy, for her rustic humour which comes in the form of comments and action of these simple people. Hugh Walker says that in her novels, "we can distinguish two types of humour. One is that which Shakespeare has embodied in the person of Falstaff, in whom it is combined with extraordinary mental gifts. No character in imaginative literature is so fertile in expedients and so rich in suggestion as Falstaff : he is at once mirthful himself and a cause of mirth in others. So too is Sam Weller; his wit and humour are conscious, and he laughs with, and often at, his interlocutor. It is not so with the tribe of Dogberry and Sir Andrew Aguecheek. Though the cause of mirth in others, they are themselves far from mirthful. We read with delight their speeches, uttered with the most sober purpose. Such characters are unconsciously humorous. Now this is the sort of humour in which George Eliot excels. There is wit as well as wisdom in her works; there are plenty of bright and illuminating phrases whose effect depends, at least as much upon their lively expression as upon their truth. But there is no character of the Falstaff type, none even who shows the roguery of a Touchstone. The humour is mainly found in characters of humble rank, or of imperfect education and moderate intelligence; and greatly would they have been surprised at the idea that their talk was amusing." *Adam Bede*, *The Mill on the Floss* and *Silas Marner* are the novels in which humour found its important and magnificent place.

Mrs. Poyser in *Adam Bede*

Natural humour in Mrs. Poyser, has ranked her among some noteworthy humorists. Her amusing remarks attract everybody's attention no matters whether the person is very solemn or loves fun. How Mrs. Poyser makes Molly weep, when unfortunately, he breaks a jug : "It's all very fine to look on and grin, but there's times when the crockery seems alive, and flies out of your hand like a bird. What is to be broken will be broke, for I never dropped a thing; I kept the crockery all these years as I bought at my own wedding." Aphorists and proverbs of Mrs. Poyser creates real humour and comedy. Says A.E. Baker, "Very solemn and superior people would fain identify humour with folly and buffoonery, whereas on close examination it turns out to be near akin to, if not the same thing as, wisdom."

Witty Remarks in *Silas Marner*

In *Silas Marner,* the Rainbow is a full chapter attributed to the humour only. Leslie Stephen says "The condescending parish clerk and the judicious landlord and the contradictious farrier, with their discussions of village traditions, their attempts at humour, and the curious mental processes which take the place of reasoning are delicious and inimitable. One secret is that we can sympathise with their humble attempts at intellectual intercourse. The brutality which too often underlines a good deal of more refined satire comes out in the "unflinching frankness", which at the 'Rainbow' is taken for the 'most piquant form of joke.' The presumption of the assistant clerk, who hopes that he may have his own opinion of his vocal performances, is tempered by the remark that, "there'd be two opinions about a cracked bell, if the bell could hear itself," and finally crushed by the critic who tells him that his voice is "well enough when he keeps it up in his nose." It's your inside "as isn't right made for music; it's no better nor a hollow stalk"

Humour Aroused by the Dodsons in *Mill on the Floss*

In the *Mill on the Floss,* the Dodsons come as the rustic chorus. Their character and habits, their occupation, their culture and traditions are themselves bringforth through the speeches made by them. The Dodson sisters are never satirised but the way they live is a source of amusement, as they are the typical of that society.

Their religion was a simple, semi-pagan kind, but there was no heresy in it—if heresy properly means choice—for they didn't know there was any other religion, except that of chapel-goers which appeared to run in families, like asthma. How should they know?

The vicar of their pleasant rural parish was not a controversialist, but a good hand at whist, and one who had a joke always ready for a blooming female parishioner. The religion of the Dodsons consisted in revering whatever was customary and respectable : it was necessary to be baptised, else one could not be buried in the churchyard, and to take the sacrament before death, as a security against more dimly understood perils but it was of equal necessity to have the proper pall bearers and well cured hams at one's funeral, and to leave an unimpeachable will. A Dodson would not be taxed with the omission of anything that was becoming, or that belonged to that eternal fitness of things which was plainly indicated in the practice of the most substantial parishioners, and in the family traditions—such as obedience to parents, faithfulness to kindred, industry, rigid honesty, thrift, the thorough scouring of wooden and copper utensils, the hoarding of coins likely to disappear from the currency, the production of first rate commodities of the market, and the general preference for whatever was home-made.

This Dodson Code, whereas, represents the complexity of whole class, there the individuality of the sisters also contributed much to the humour.

Satire on the Victorian Age

George Eliot, being a Victorian novelist, saw much of the life which could be satirised and mended, so she used this method in many of her novels where the eccentricities and hyprocricy of people of that very age, was represented and laughed at by the readers. She was not a harsh satirist, who took stick in her hand to mend people or has used harsh and vulgar language, instead her superior brain possessing philosophical ideas renders a very mild kind of satire. In the words of David Cecil, "Her fools are ridiculous because they act in a way inconsistent with the absolute standards of right living she conceives them. She does not say, for this reason George Eliot's satire is at once milder and more serious than that of her predecessors; she shows us human beings as smaller and as more pathetic."

CHAPTER - 11

GEORGE ELIOT'S CONTRIBUTION TO THE ENGLISH NOVEL

Philosophy in Literature

In both male and female Victorian novelists, George Eliot is the most philosophical, which is her strength and weakness as well. Whereas it hinders her practical approach there her literature is imbued with seriousness and depth. As Samuel C. Chew observes "In George Eliot's hands the novel was not primarily for entertainment but for the serious discussion of moral issues." This moralistic approach, infact required deeper study and sharp thinking, which naturally intellectualised the English novel. Even her contemporaries like Dickens and Thackeray could not uplift the standard of novel to the extent where it required profound understanding. Her greatest novels include *Adam Bede, Silas Marner, Middlemarch, Romola and The Mill on the Floss.*

Plot-Construction

David Cecil points out, "George Eliot did not care much for plo-construction, as least of the traditional kind; she was governed not by the story but by her idea. She worked out her plots in conformity with that idea, giving all kinds of jolts and jerks to the expectations of the reader. Her plots were intended to follow not a standardised formula but what she conceived to be the logical development of that idea." Literature consisting the factors like fortune, coincidences, shattered wills were in vogue, in Victorian Age, which were invariably committed by her from her novels. Hers are the, "first novel which set out to give a picture of life wholly unmodified by those formulate of a good plot which the novel had taken over from comedy and romance. Her story is conditioned solely by the logical demands of situation or character; it ends sadly or happily, includes heroes or omits them, deals with the married or the unmarried, according to as reason and observation lead her think likely. In fact, the laws conditioning the form of George Eliot's novels are the same laws that condition those of Henry James and Wells and Conard and Arnold Bennet. Hers are the first examples in English of the novel in its mature form; in them it structurally comes of age."

Realism : Memories of the Past

George Eliot rightly says that though, "life did change for Tom and Maggie, they were not wrong in believing that the thoughts and loves of their first years would always make part of their lives." In the early novels; *Adam Bede, Mill on the Floss* and *Silas Marner,* took the material from the memories of her own experience of childhood lived happily and she could make us see what she transformed by her loving memories of the past. Says Hugh Walker, "It is notorious that in the early novels George Eliot drew very freely on the stories of her memory. Scene after scene, character after character in these novels has been identified with sense place or person within the range of her early experience."

Pioneer of Psychological Fiction

George Eliot is recognized as one of the pioneers of psychological fiction. Like Browning, she deliberately sets out to explore and lay bare the springs of human motives and human mistakes and analyse the inviolability continuity of the cause and effect in human action. Lettice Cooper aptly observes : "Her analysis of motives is penetrating and she has more understanding than any English novelist before Freud of the undercurrents of mind and heart. Because her human beings are more complicated, and more mixed than those of the novelist who receded her, they are much near to the truth of human nature."

Characterization in Her Novels

According to David Cecil, "It is in the treatment of characters that George Eliot's more active intellect gives her the most conspicuous advantage over the typical Victorian." She did not put much efforts in the ornamentation of her characters but was much concerned with their inner reality. As Jesome Thale says, "She directed her whole attention to the portrayal of the inner man." She was, in fact, one of the first major novelists in English literature to probe and analyse the innermost thoughts of her characters.

George Eliot's art of characterization lies in the fact that her characters evolve or grow just as the story proceeds or just as the characters and the situations or incidents act upon each other. Observed by Long rightly : "Her heroes and heroines differ radically from those of Dickens and Thackeray in this respect that when we meet the man and woman of the later novelists, their characters develop gradually as we come to know them. They go from weakness to strength, or from strength to weakness, according to the works that they do and the thoughts that they cherish. The novelist exhibits the mode by which step by step a character goes down, re-adjusting his principles to suit his practice, till imperceptibly he is transformed, changed or ruined," The result is that Maggie Tulliver at twenty-two is not the Maggie Tulliver that we would have expected to be from what we know her to be when she was twelve.

George Eliot : A Sociological Novelist

Fielding and Thakerary had practised the panoramic narrative method, loaded with realistic detail, but no one before George Eliot had established the close, organic relationship between the nature of the individual and the nature of the society in which the individual has developed and in which he has to function. She is the first sociological novelist. Long before the subject was studied as it is today, she observed that someone should investigate :

> ....the natural history of our social classes, especially of the small shopkeepers, artisans and peasantry and the degree in which they are influenced by local conditions, their maxims and habits, the point of view from which they regard their religious teachers, (and the interaction of the various classes on each other).

Style

"George Eliot's style is lucid, and to begin with simple, but later, in reflective passages, it is often overweighed with abstractions. Her dialogue is excellent for the revelation of character, and her command of the idioms of ordinary speech enables her to achieve a fine naturalness. Only rarely does she rise to the impassioned poetical heights of the Brontes, but her earlier novels, particularly *The Mill on the Floss.* are full of fine descriptions of the English countryside, and her faculty for natural description she never lost entirely." E. Albert and Cazamian writes, "Her style, through many a page, through whole chapters and episodes, has the indefinable quality that suggests a lesson in psychology, ethics or history."

George Eliot's Place in the History of the English Novel

George Eliot occupies an important position in the history of English fiction. She elevated the art of novel writing to a level of seriousness so that it was no longer considered to be mere entertainment. She was a pioneer in psychological analysis in fiction—something which has become the mainstay of the English novel. Her serious concern with the problems of the human personality and its relationship with forces outside itself did much to determine the future course of the English novel. "In her best work, there is a depth and reality that no English novelist has surpassed; nor can any of them surpass her in her power of taking the reader into her created world"—we can add little to that comment by Lettice Cooper on the art of George Eliot.

Conclusion

George Eliot is of great importance in the history of fiction. Her serious concern with the problems of the human personality and its relationships with forces outside, itself did much to determine the future course of the English novel. (E.Albert)

PART - II
A DETAILED STUDY OF *ADAM BEDE*

CHAPTER - 12

INTRODUCTION AND A CRITICAL APPROACH OF *ADAM BEDE*

The Origin of *Adam Bede*

"*Adam Bede* on 22nd October, completed the first volume by the following March: wrote the second during her tour to Germany and completed the third on November 16th. The novel was published in the beginning of 1858. Eliot claims that the story of the novel was inspired by the true story of a girl who was condemned for murdering her own child. An anecdote by her aunt, the Methodist preacher, Mrs. Samuel Evans led George Eliot to conceive the idea of *Adam Bede*. Her aunt, Mrs. Evans once narrated the real story of a girl whom she had visited. The girl was a condemned criminal—a very ignorant girl, who had murdered her child and refused to confer. Her aunt being a Methodist preacher stayed with her praying through the night and at last the poor girl broke out into tears and confessed her crime. Mrs. Evans even accompanied her to the place of execution.

George Eliot claims that the character of Dinah grew out of her recollection of her Methodist aunt, yet very much different. The character of Adam and one or two incidents connected with him were suggested by her father's early life. She says : "When I began to write it, the only elements I had determined on, besides the character of Dinah, were the character of Adam, his relation to Arthur Dommithorne, and their mutual relations to Hetty i.e. the girl who commits child murder—the scene in the prison being of course, the climax towards which I worked. Everything else grew out of the characters and their mutual relations."

Time of Action

Adam Bede was published in 1859 but its action took place in 1799. Those were stirring times when momentous events were taking place both at home and abroad. *Adam Bede* cannot be considered to be a historical novel in view of the fact that no such events are mentioned in the novel. Apart of Methodism no historical events has any significance in the novel. Methodism has been presented through the character of Dinah. Apart from highlighting methodism, the novel is concerned with universal human beings and their activities that take place in the solitudes of the countryside.

The Setting and Atmosphere of the Novel

The setting of the novel is in the village of Hayslope in the country of Loamshire and Snowfield and Stoniton in the country of Stonyshire, in the English Midlands where the novelists had been bred and brought up. The characters, scenes and sights with which she had been familiar since her childhood boosted her imagination enabling her thus to portray real characters in real setting that comes alive out of the pages of the novel as we read it. The presentation of the of the countryside is so faithful and marked with the Midland flavour with such fidelty that when the novel was first published under anonimity people came to the assumption that the novelist must be resident of those parts. Many conjectures regarding the authorship of the novel was made but least suspicion arose that the authoress could have been the inexperienced and unknown Mary Evans.

The Characters

The novel abounds with characters major and minor. The novelist has crowded the canvas of the novel with characters. She has represented a cross section of the whole Midland society starting from the carpenters' family to the Squires' family. George Eliot presents a whole village with all the people in it thus enlarging the scope of its canvas : First, there is the Bede family, the village carpenters that consists of Adam Bede, the central figure, his brother Seth, mother Lisbeth and father Thias. Then, there are the Poysers, tenants of the Hall Farm. This family consists of Mr. Martin Poyser, his old father, his wife Mrs. Poyser—their two nieces. Dinah and Hetty, and their children and others. Yet another groups consists of the old Squire or landlord of the village and his grandson, Arthur, the heir to the state. They all live at the Chase with a number of attendants. Rev. Mr. Irwine, the Rector of Hayslope and bioxton, his mother Mrs. Irwine, a majestic lady, and his two unmarried sisters who also form a part and parcel of the Loamshire world.

Bentle Marsey, the school teacher, Jonathen Burgess, the carpenter, Wiry Ben, a romping girl called Bess, Molly, the maid servant

of Leslie Stephen, "*Adam Bede* for most of us mean pre-eminently Mrs. Poyser and owes its popularity to her presence. Her dairy is nearly the centre of the whole microcosm. We are first introduced to it as the background which Mrs. Poyser displays her conversational powers. The little rustic world is painted in colours, heightened by affection. There is, it may be, a little more of Goldsmith's beautifying touch than of Crabbe's uncompromising realism. But it is marvellously life-like, and Mrs. Poyser's delightful shrewdness seems to guarantee the fidelity of the portraits. She has no humbug about her, and one naturally takes it for granted that they must be as she sees them. Which makes the kitten-like beauty of Hetty Sorrel irresistible to young Captain Donnitherne. But Mrs. Poyser is the presiding genius. She represents the very spirit of the place, and her influence is the secret of the harmony of the little world of Squire and Parson and parish clerk and schoolmaster and blacksmith and carpenter and shepherd and carter. Each of these type is admirably sketched in turn, but the pivot of the whole is the farm. It is, indeed needless to insist upon her excellence for Mrs. Poyser became at once one of the immortals." In her later novels, Mrs. Poyser was expected with same temper and moods, but again she could not enthrone the readers' hearts as it could in *Adam Bede.*

CHAPTER - 13

HISTORICAL BACKGROUND OF *ADAM BEDE* *OR* RELIGIOUS BACKDROP OF THE NOVEL AND ITS SIGNIFICANCE

Aloofness of Hayslope

Published in 1859, the novel *Adam Bede,* had its origin in Europe and England and the time then chaotic, affected the novel to some extent but not too much, for Hayslope, an untouched community which is the very background of the novel, remained unaffected area by these stirring events. It seems as if nothing mishappened there at all, because this rural community did not bother for the far-off towns inherited by persons with strange and complex ideas. So, they totally remained separate from their complexity in any way.

Examples of a Few Historical Occurrences

It is wrong to consider *Adam Bede* a historical novel, for not a single political issue entered the play or tried to disturb its coherence in any way. It did not concern with the political ups and downs. The Civil War was fought in the United States, the custom of making slaves, was diminished, the West was overpowered, and the Americans faced a tremendous change in their lives due to the Industrial Revolution. Garibaldi emerged in Italy and rising of new star of independence could be expected. Japan was fully prepared for entering into a new world. The serfs were freed by Russia, who were continued to be slaves for hundred of years. Prussia came into being as a big European power, first getting victory over Austria, then over France and then the German Empire was provided with sufficient military and political force. There were mutual misunderstanding within defeated France paving a way for the establishment of the Third Republic. Now, it can be realized that how *Adam Bede* turned its back from all these historical events, as George Eliot says, in 1799. As a matter of fact, none of the great happenings in the world that were contemporary or prior to the action of the novel seem to have had any effect on Hayslope. The American colonies had fought Great Britain for their independence and won, establishing themselves as the United States. Liberation movements were beginning to flare all over Latin America, and France had executed her King and Queen in the ten bloody years of her revolution. Napoleon Bonaparte had begun his far-flung conquests and was on the verge of proclaiming himself Emperor of France. By 1799, England had been at war with France for six years, her great leaders, Wellington and Nelson, battled to contain Napoleon. To these French wars, the only reference in the novel is that Arthur Donnithorne goes out to France with his regiment, falls ill, is advised rest at home and so comes back to Hayslope. Otherwise, all these great happenings sound as remote to the people of Hayslope as if they happened on the other side of the moon. They have no impact at all on Hayslope life or on Adam, Seth, Hetty, Arthur and Dinah, the principal figures in the novel. The only historical event that makes its impact on the novel is the movement for religious dissent from, or non-conformity with, the established church, known as Methodism.

Brief Description of Religious Tolerances

It is not to be forgotten that the church of England was established due to the settlement between the Catholicism and Protestantism and there have been continuous movements ever since the days of Chaucer. The dispute hanged on till Ninteenth century, with not any sound solution. Methodism or 'Evengelical Methodism' was the most important form religious dissent of the 18th century. In the novel Mr. Irwin stood as representing the established church, whereas Dinnah Morris, the heroine of the novel, echoes the Methodism, thus the novelist compares both of the religion, impartially. Methodism may be defined as, "a movement a reaction against the apathy of the church of England that prevailed in the early part of the eighteenth century". The name 'Methodist' was originally applied to the members of a religious society established at Oxford in 1729 by the Wesleys and other members of the University, "having for its object the promotion of piety and morality. It was subsequently extended to those who took part in or sympathised with this movement." The Eighteenth century developed the term 'Evengelical' which lays more stress on faith and tries to sustain the concepts of *Bible*.

Innovator of Methodism

The 'Methodist' Movement was started by John Wesley who was born in 1703 in Lincolnshire. He got his education at Oxford and took holy orders in 1725. England of Eighteenth century declared him the greatest religious figure. In 1729, group of young men followed his doctrine and collectively formed a society named 'The Methodist Society', which gave importance to fasts and festivals of the Church. They took oath to keep their religion sacred and the corruption of the world should not enter their pious home any way.

1739 was the year of great importance for Wesley because he developed spirituality which added his knowledge of religion. Now, it was realized by him that he had a new way to cover and let others do above, which will give a unique shape to the religion. Considering whole of the England as his Parish, he made several journey to preach them and to make them able to see that holylight which would clear all the religious doubts. Coming in contact with his humble preach, thousands of English people converted and became the part of 'the new birth' of religion. The lower classes were numerous in number, who followed his principles and were benefited with the sayings of the established church.

Wide-spread Methodism

Now, the necessity of some institution was felt to provide a religious uniformity for the thousands of converts and the Methodist society was getting popularity which led to the increase in number of organisations to serve the people. Lady preachers were appointed; band meetings were held : there were class meetings and meetings in houses. Some women were much confident to preach, what they did successfully. They worked under the same organisation, in the very beginning, but with the growth of society, it started working independently, and in 1744, witnessed the First Wesleyan Conference. It did not separate itself from the basic organisation i.e. the established church till after Wesley's death in 1791.

Dinah Representing Methodism

Dinah is an example of orthodox Methodist, who perched to follow God's will. They believed in miracles, in instantaneous conversion, in revelations by dreams and visions; they drew lots; and sought for Divine Guidance by opening the *Bible* at hazard. Dinah is a staunch Methodist, who believes in all this and whenever she has to take some crucial decision, *Bible* is the only source, which provides her not only the solution but relief also. To whom should she give her hand, to Adam or to Seth, was decided by Dinah, with the help of *Bible*.

Impact of Her Impreachment

Methodist preachings come on the scene when Dinah dictates the religious principles on the village Green. The very glance of the sermon, makes the readers conscious about its characteristics and features, which lays stress on God's sympathy and love for the poor and miserable. Dinah presented in front of the people, the example of Jesus Christ, so that God's agony garden became very true to the listeners. Then she opposed the vanity and arrogance, which is a very part of the world. How she preaches for a simple living and high thinking, is evident from one of her speeches : "Wear no gold, no pearls or precious stones, use no curling of hair, buy no velvet, no silks, no fine linen, no superfluities, no mean ornaments, however much in fashion. I do not advise women to wear rings, ear-rings, necklaces, laces etc." Another thing which was given importance, were the poor and how they can be saved and helped. The sermons were much powerful to convert Chad Bers who had worn earring, tries to hide them, though, the natives of Hayslope did not pay much attention to it. On the other hand, the people of lower class of Snowfield accepted it with open heart.

It is *Epiligue,* which make us to learn that women preachers, "did more harm than good with their preaching". Dinah also says bye to this profession and develops interest in domestic works. This brings loss for the movement, for she unlike others, was a devout and honest preachers who did only good and did not cause disreputation for the church in any way. It is obvious how she consoles Lisbeth in her solemn and sad state and visits prison to give strength to poor Hetty and inspires her to defend herself from the guilt which she has not done. All these examples lift her image in the eyes of readers and it cannot be denied that she imparts a strong impact on the listeners

Everlasting Effect

There is no doubt that Hayslope became a major centre of tremendous change in religion, which affected the people's attitude towards life and the themes, "of God and godlessness, love and jealousy, life and death, sin and repentance, are universal and come about regardless of the Nepoleons and the Hitlers, or perhaps inspite of them. What happens in Hayslope in *Adam Bede* can well happen in almost any agricultural community on earth and in almost any period of recorded history." The fertility of soil and the friendliness of nature cannot be questioned but the man working on the land, which was of some other's, would not live life to its brim. However there was a rapid growth of industries in England, though the country was dominated by agriculture. Except for the universal emotions, the only significant aspect of the background of *Adam Bede* is the village of Hayslope were the need to work hard and skilfully in order to survive, and the fermentation caused by Evangelical Methodism. These people of rural background are not of extinct case rather we can find them here and there in every human being in the countryside.

India is best evidence of this kind, where people are enjoying the pure nature of countryside who are unspoiled by the hyprocrisy of the town people. They still apply orthodox implements while cultivating their lands. Fact remains, that tragedies of Sophocles had their origin in these rural areas and the Hetty-Adam-Arthur Donnithorne story looks towards to the countryside for its source.

CHAPTER - 14

CHARACTERIZATION IN *ADAM BEDE*

Character and Characterization

Characterization is a literary genre : a short and usually witty sketch in prose of a distinctive type of person. Characters are the persons, in a dramatic or narrative work, endowed with moral and dispositional qualities that one expressed in what they say—the dialogue—and what they do—the action. E.M. Forster in *Aspects of the Novel* (1927), introduced popular new terms for an old distinction in discriminating between flat and round characters. A flat character (also called a "type", or "two dimensional"), Forster says, is built around "a single idea or quality" and is presented in outline and without much individualizing detail, and so can be fairly adequately described in a single phrase or sentence. A round character is complex in temperament and motivation and is represented with subtle particularity, thus he is as difficult to describe with any adequacy as a person in real life, and like most people, he is capable of surprising us.

Characterization : Its Eminence

We can estimate the novelist's writings better by his art of characterization and in this respect George Eliot wins our hearts. George Eliot is eminent writer among her contemporaries because of her psycho-analytic approach and power of characterization as well. She not only presents the characters which make us able to see the real people of Hayslope and Stonyshire, but not losing their individual importance. David Cecil says, "It is in the treatment of characters that George Eliot's more active intellect gives her the most conspicuous advantage over the typical Victorian".

Portrayal of Rural People

Most of the women writers look into their inner self, whenever some creative writing is to be done. Same case is with George Eliot. She never forgot her childhood experiences which gave a realistic touch to her work. It was English Midland, for which she looked for the inspiration, for here she could have got the raw material. In her later works she took the characters from the higher society which lacked the subtlety and strength what was much while portraying the characters from "humble and rustic life". Wordsworthian influence can be felt almost in all of her famous novels.

Eliot's interest in rustic life can be seen in her work and to give it a realistic touch she uses the dialect spoken by the humble and simple rustics.

Subjective Approach

Most of the characters, if we analyse them deeply, will come out as one of her friends or relatives or any other from her acquaintances. Her early novels reveal this very fact. In her first novel, *Scenes of Clerical Life,* the characters portrayed are the real people with whom she had some recognition. The thoughts of the ordinary, humble men and women is celebrated in her novels and all of these characters remain in the background, here her art of characterisation is praised. They never goes to the extreme in their habits and nature. Neither they are extra-ordinary excellent, nor over-foolish; instead they are just like real men, mixture of virtues and vices possessing natural instincts and emotions. Violent passions and supernatural elements in the character never can be seen in the novels of George Eliot. This would not be exaggeration that her novels are the "real drama of life on this universe".

Psychological Analysis of Characters

George Eliot was chiefly concerned with exploring and trying to understand human motives. She was, in fact, one of the first major novelists in English literature to probe and analyse the innermost thoughts of her characters. Compton Rickett observes her work and writes, "The writer who could visualise for us the hedonistic Tito; the fine old puritan Dr. Hyons; the erratic Gowendolen; the steadfast Mary Garth; the commonplace Fred Vincy and the brilliant Lydgate; the rough uncultured Bob Jakin and the polished scholar Casaubom dealing justice to each, fairly appraising their merits and no less keenly exposing their weakness, was a writer with no ordinary power of psychological portrayal. Nor is she a whit inferior in the subtlety of her method, as is evidenced by the delicate nuances in the characterization of Mary Garth and Rosamund Vincy and Romola."

The Poysers : Realistic Portrayal of a Rural Family

The realism in Eliot's novel can be guessed, as after the publication of her first novel, *Scenes of Clerical Life,* the readers were surprised to find the characters, who were known to them in one or another way. George Eliot has characterised them realistically and "they are seen clearly, objectively, humorously and inspite of their moral and intellectual deficiencies, with respect and sympathy."

The influence of her father can be seen in her portrayal of character like Adam Bede. Her father Robert Evans, like Adam Bede, was popular among his countrymen for his honesty, high character and praiseworthy skill. Plantations, timbers and mines, were the fields which he had mastery. Sir Francis Newdigate getting impressed by Robert's extraordinary capability, bringforth his hand of friendship towards him. Thus, both of them come closer and the source was taken while describing the friendship between Adam Bede and Arthur Donnithorne. Whereas the character of Dinah Morris is concerned, George Eliot said, "The character of Dinah grew out of my recollections of my aunt who is a very small, black-eyed woman, and (as I was told, for I never heard her preach) very vehement in her style of preaching." Mrs. Elizabeth Evans, her aunt, who was represented by the character of Dinah Morris, was a preacher of Methodism. She was famous for her philanthropic heart, in Derbyshire. In the words of Gey Roslyn, "In the novel the descriptions of Dinah are descriptive also of Elizabeth, the heroine of fact, and the heroine of fiction are alike in walking, talking, dress, occupation and the fortunes of life."

Ordinary Aspects of Life

Midlands remained her home for around thirty years of the beginning of her life and in that kind of atmosphere, she was brought up and studied the manners and life of the lower classes. In her own words, she described that she lived among craftsmen, farmers, tradesmen, mechanics, gardeners and inn keepers and these kinds of people were celebrated in all of her novels. The people of Midlands, remained in her memories and later came on the pages of her novels. Even the occupations and professions were followed and described in a fair way, with which George Eliot had been familiar. Adam Bede is a carpenter. Dinah Morris is worker in a factory and a preacher as well. No doubt Hetty Sorrel is beautiful and childlike but having uncommon fancies. According to Henry James, "She is unmistakably a painter of bourgeois life as Thackeray was a painter of life of drawing rooms."

Portrayal of Female Characters

Another important feature of her novels is their very deep concern with human psychology. In her characterization she displays both subtlety and variety. Her studies of the inner man, more particularly the inner woman, are marvellous. Nobody can compete with her in her protrayal of tragedy of unfulfilled female aspirations. She probes deeply into the hearts of frustrated women and their emotions found outlet in her works. Compton Rickett points out,

"Maggie's cry was for fuller life, Ramola's for ampler knowledge, Darothea's for larger opportunity for doing good." The characterization of Hetty Sorrel in *Adam Bede,* was a victory in itself. It is her extreme beauty which added vanity in her, thus led her toward the path of destruction. Inspite of a very wealthy life, she faced cruelties, sorrows, sufferings and intolerable pains in her life. Joan Bennett writes, "George Eliot portrays with insight and convincing truth Hetty's physical charms and her shallow, pleasure-loving, heartless nature, without ill-will but without any strength of purpose to withstand temptation."

Nobody could find out the weaknesses in Hetty Sorrel, which made her to suffer, but it was Dinah Morris, who can foresee the drawbacks in her and realises that she lacks some of the essential qualities with which a woman should be endowed, and Dinah takes the advantage of these defects in her. Walter Allen remarks, "It is almost as though Hetty's very prettiness is scored up as a bad mark against her." Biographies reveal that George Eliot was taking revenge on herself through the beautiful Hetty's sins. There are many beautiful women who not only bring ill-luck for themselves but destroy the lives of men also. In the words of V.S. Pritchett, "George Eliot was punishing herself and Hetty has to suffer for the sins George Eliot had committed, and for which to her perhaps contentious dismay, she herself was never punished". Like Hetty, Maggie Tulliver, Gwendolen Harleth and Mrs. Tranoome also suffered, for all of them diverted from the right path and laid the examples that sinners are given severe punishment for their misdeeds.

Minor Female Characters

From the Mildlands, she introduced her minor female characters. Mrs. Poyser in *Adam Bede,* proves her artistic hand in portraying minor female characters as major ones. If we probe into the life of George Eliot, we see a deep similarity between her mother and Mrs. Poyser. What is emphasized by J.W. Cross, "His (Robert Evans) second wife was a woman with an unusual amount of natural force; a shrewd practical person, with a dash of the Mrs. Poyser vein in her."

Development in Characters

The characters of George Eliot are not flat rather they are round character who develop as the story proceeds. How the circumstances and situations bring a grand change, is noteworthy in *Adam Bede.* Hetty, earlier a pretty, childlike girl with uncommon fancies, in the end is a sincere, honest and a complete woman who has attained a pre-mature wisdom. Arthur Donnithorne sheds his pride and ego, gives 'way to a new humanitarian approach towards life'. Again, Dinah Morris is completely changed girl in the end.

Religious Class

Religious class is never ignored by George Eliot while drawing other characters. Methodist movement started at that period gave her the stuff to introduce the eclasisastic issues in her novels and she portrayed the clergymen in positive way. Dinah Morris in *Adam Bede,* is an example of preaching under the leaders. The defects in clergy class is also shown through Mr. Irwine yet he is treated with understanding and sympathy.

Conclusion

Lifelike characters are drawn by George Eliot in her novels, yet the modification is not ignored, where it needed. They are real people with normal emotions and natural instincts. Nothing is exaggerated while protraying them. Reader while reading and analysing them feels, as if he himself knows the character as one knows his near friend. She herself probes into their hearts and enables the reader to make a personal assessment of them. This kind of task is done by rare novelists and George Eliot has not only tried but she has succeeded while doing so and her contribution in the field of characterisation is noteworthy.

CHAPTER - 15

PLOT OR STRUCTURE OF *ADAM BEDE*

Introduction

The plot in a dramatic or narrative work is the structure of its actions, as these are ordered and rendered towards achieving particular emotional and artistic effects. There is a great variety of plot forms, depending on what the author writes—a tragedy or a comedy or something else. The character who remains the centre of attraction is the hero or the protagonist, whereas the character for whom we are contemptuous, is called antagonist. A plan made by a character to degrade other one, is termed as intrigue. A plot has unity of action if it has a single, complete, and ordered structure and all actions are directed towards the intended effect, in which none of the component parts, or incidents, is not necessary, and as Aristotle said, all the parts should be "so closely connected that the transposal and withdrawal of any one of them will disjoint or dislocate the whole."

An Organic Plot

Adam Bede is famous for its psychological-novel hitherto ignored thing, and its well-knit plot is much popular among his contemporaries as well as for the newcomers. The novel was not divided in parts while publishing it. Not in a single magazine, it was given into various episodes, rather it came as a book on the very first publication. While revising the book, some loose odds and ends were arranged and some irrelevant matter was excluded. Every action and each character is necessary to advance the action. The novel is a compact whole, and a single action excluded from the novel would destroy the organic unity and beauty of the novel, as well.

Construction of Four Stories

She was quite aware of the construction problem while writing the novel, is apparent to us what George Eliot described in her own genesis of the novel. Four different stories are integrated in the novel (a) Adam-Hetty love story (b) Arthur-Hetty love story (c) Adam-Dinah love story (d) Relationship between Arthur and Adam. The main problem for George Eliot is to integrate these four stories into a single plot. The main story concerns with Hetty Sorrel, how she is tempted towards sexual relationship with Arthur, the Squire's son and is compelled to murder her own child. "The inter-linking of the various stories is made possible by the relations of Adam and Arthur to each other and to Hetty and the marriage of Adam and Dinah rounds up the whole, and satisfies contemporary conversion by linking the lives of the hero and heroine at the close."

Thematic Unity

Presence of thematic unity is also realised as we go through the story. It is based on a single theme, later split into a various themes such as moral weakness, childhood experiences, self-righteousness and many others. All these themes cover the stage by character like Arthur, Hetty and Adam. These themes are interlinked and are taken step by step.

A Compact Whole

George Eliot's novels have "organic wholeness" where the story, the characters and the social environment are well-integrated. George Eliot keeps the social environment in the background and the characters are celebrated, depicted thoroughly. For example, in *Adam Bede* the life of Hayslope envelops the tragedy. We are acquainted with its inhabitants, mostly the people from every class of the society; farmers, labourers, schoolmaster, artists, innkeeper and Squire. The whole community is full of zeal and remain working for their livelihood. What kind of a work, a person does also modifies man's personality to some extent. There is no doubt that Hayslope kept itself aloof from the struggling and conflicting life of cities, yet a dirt of Methodism and religious conflicts, could be seen here and there in the Hayslope, which affected young minds also. The third book describes how the people gathered at Donnithorne Chase to celebrate the young Squire's anniversary. Thus, the life lived by the people at that time is well studied by Eliot, who described them through the central characters who are shown with all of their virtues as well as vices. After the climax, when Hetty Sorrel is subjected to death, taking a feeling of guilt in her consciousness, and it would have been felt by another author that the work is complete, to balance the third, the sixth book is added. This book is actually meant for the re-establishment of order which had been lost earlier. Thus, a kind of poetic justice is also given in this text.

Social Environment at the Background

The social environment remains at the background yet its effect is noteworthy. Hetty, an innocent girl is happy in her dreamworld, suddenly faces the reality, which has worn the mask of happiness, later shows the bitter truth, when Hetty is destroyed by Arthur, the son of the Squire. Consequently, not only Hetty, but Arthur also suffers and illusion shatters, comes out the reality from it. The Poysers who have attained reputation in the society is obvious, by the opinion of neighbours and the surroundings where they reside, work they do, give a way for the tragedy which comes to Hetty just before her marriage with Adam. She realises her pregnancy, which is illegal in the eyes of society and can bring miseries for the family, intentionally leaves the place, and murders her own child. All this happens, because the atmosphere she had been provided with from the very childhood, shakes her existence and finally the terrible death comes to her. The same situation is encountered by Arthur also, who is brought up in a joint family under the guidance of his grandfather who is the Squire with high conception of love and esteem. He also inherits the land and ideas as well from his relations, which compels him to pay the high price for one mistake, which is a sin in the eyes of society and religious authorities as well.

No doubt, the outer circle affects our inner-sense to much extent. Rector's benignity, the zeal among Methodists, the simplicity of country people, all have collective impression on the minds of central characters, and the situations in which they fall off. The fact can not be questioned that the outer circle contains naturalistic scenes of comedy or of pathos and practical minded characters, yet one or in other way, are concerned with the main story, which requires full-attention. Thus we see, that character and action are well integrated with the social background and atmosphere of the novel. As Joan Bennett points out the, "outer circle within which the dramatic situation is contained is an organic human society." George Eliot's novels are well imbued with the spirit of a particular time and place. The outer circle in *Adam Bede* is the society of the Poysers, Squires and a few others. "Narrow, rigid, tradition-ridden and materialistic, it crushes and represses individual and uncommon aspirations." And Hetty is a victim of this repressive environment.

Impact of Physical Environment

Social environment remaining at the background, affects the story and is well-integrated with time and action. In the way, physical environment is also very important in context of its impact on the lives of central characters. People living in Hayslope have the fertility and tenderness of Loamshire, but they have also its turbulances and hardness. Dinah tries her best to convey the religious message to people, who are unresponsive and unreceptive for they are living a simple life and with the over-confidence, that the way they are living, is the best and nobody has any right to alter their ideas, thinkings and traditions as well. Their hardness of attitude is, symbolised, by Hetty's stubbornness during her trial, not a single word comes out of her mouth in order to defend herself resulting the death sentence for her.

Dinah Works as Bridge

Dinah works as a bridge between Loamshire and Stonyshire. Stonyshire, the land of rocks, hard and barren is the place from where she comes, but the people here are not like that of Loamshire. There is a kind of zeal in people, and the response here is much positive. They are infact, spiritually alive and conscious about the outer world. So, whenever a feeling of emptiness foreshadows Dinah's optimistic view, she returns in this very place, in order to revitalise her vocation. That is why, without celebrating harvest festival, she leaves Hayslope in order to escape from the proposed hand of Adam. Another elements which is to be noticed is the very changing nature of physical environment with the moods and situations of the characters, mainly of Hetty. She spends her childhood days in the charming atmosphere of Hayslope; from here she shifts to Stonyshire, a lifeless rocky place where she is convicted and sentenced to death. Seasonal changes are never ignored, when the fortunes of the characters are changing. For example, the marriage of Adam and Dinah takes place on "a rimy morning in departing November," a season when trees shed their leaves and the actual appearance of atmosphere is seen which was earlier in disguise and an illusion. Thus the atmospheric sadness is balanced with the ecstasy of Adam-Dinah wedding. The painful memories of Hetty, somehow is kept alive and fresh in the hearts of both of them.

Parallelisms and Contrasts

The structure of the novel is symmetrical. The six books of the novel have three parts, each with a definite theme. Book I describes the gathering of whole community to hear the sermons of Dinah Morris. In Book III, the birthday feast of Arthur is enjoyed by the villagers. Athur-Hetty love started at this very situation, is significant from the point of development of action. In Book VI, the description of Harvest Supper is to balance the order and a kind of satisfaction is rendered to the reader and a self-satisfaction for the author.

Realistic Picture of Rural Life

It is injustice to ignore the efficiency of novelist, while handling the rural life capturing all of its features and not a single aspect is left undiscussed. Dorothy V. Ghent says, "The pace of *Adam Bede*, is set to Mrs. Poyser's clock, to all that slow toil and activity that have made daylight and living valuable. Slower, organically, invisibly slow at the months of Hetty's pregnancy; the Poyser's clock, the clock at the Chase, do not keep this time with their eights and nines and half past nines. This other deep, hidden animal time drags the whole pace down to that of poor Hetty's journey in despair, a blind automatism of animal night where the ticking of the human clock cannot be heard."

Some Defects

Eminent critics have all noted that *Adam Bede* is a great novel but it has its defects and weaknesses. Mostly the criticism find its way in its abrubt ending. The marriage of Dinah and Adam is criticised, for it is not properly motivated or it was a thoughtless decision. It only follows the convention that hero and heroine of the novel must be united at the end. The comments of Lettic Copper verify it : "The weakness of the book, besides the oppressive virtue of Adam and Dinah is, as with many Victorian novels, the sacrifice of probability to plot, and the tidiness of the ending. George Eliot was moving towards a new kind of novel in which representation of life was to be more important than the resolution of a plot, but she was still partly bound by the old convention : Hetty's pardon, so dramatically and improbably brought to the place of execution by Arthur Donnithorne, is an artificial device to spare the reader. In the relationship between Hetty and Arthur and in all that grows out of it, there is a sense of destiny which is falsified by this resolution. Again while Adam's love for Hetty is utterly convincing and the thing that brings him most to life as a human being, his final marriage to Dinah has none of that inevitability, but seems like a mechanical device to round off the story."

Conclusion

Adam Bede is, on the whole, absorbing and it grips our attention. Notwithstanding some flaws, it remains a great novel. These are flaws in a rich tapestry of rural life of the time and the novel keeps our interest alive up to the last page. The novel can be appreciated wholeheartedly, if it is judged keeping in mind the age in which it is written and how it captured the ancient aspects of period in a single novel.

CHAPTER - 16

PYSCHOLOGICAL REALISM IN *ADAM BEDE*

Introduction

George Eliot is a Victorian novelist, but she is one of the 'founding-fathers' of the modern psychological novel. In fact the modern psychological novel was born between 1913 and 1915 with the publication of Marcel Proust's *Remembrance of Things Past* in 1913 and Miss Dorothy Richardson's first volume of *Pilgrimage* in 1915. But the seeds of this kind of novel, were sown much before in the Victorian age, by George Eliot. W.J. Long thus praises her, of all the women writers who have helped and are still helping to place our English novels at the head of the world's fiction and she holds at present unquestionably the highest rank. A psychological novelist is required to have a deep understanding of the characters. Not only the inner struggles of his characters are depicted but the very souls of them is disclosed to the readers. There were many novelists in the modern age, who followed the technique and added many psychological novels in the English literature. Prominent among them were Dorothy Richardson, James Joyce, Virginia Woolf.

Pioneer in This Field

The Victorian age is flooded with female novelists, among them George Eliot is ranked first, because of her capability to depict real passion and her skill in presenting various moods of the characters. As W.J. Long points out, "George Eliot sought to do in her novels what Browning attempted in his poetry, that is, to represent the inner struggle of a soul and to reveal the motives, impulses and hereditary influences which govern human action. Browning generally stops when he tells his story and either lets you draw your own conclusion or else gives you his in a few striking lines. But George Eliot is not content until she has minutely explained the motives of her characters and the moral lesson to be learned from them. Moreover, it is the development of a soul, the slow growth or decline of moral power, which chiefly interests her. Her heroes and heroines differ radically from those of Dickens and Thackeray in this respect that when we meet the men and women of the latter novelists, their characters are already formed, and we are reasonably sure what they will do under given circumstances. In George Eliot's novels the characters develop gradually as we come to know them. They go from weakness to strength or from strength to weakness, according to the works they do and the thoughts that they cherish."

Deep Concern with Human Psyche

Most of her novels reveal the human-psyche to some extent and *Adam Bede* is the prominent among them. Her novels are all novels of character. "She", says Compton Ricket, "was the first novelist to lay the stress wholly upon character rather than incident; to make her stories spiritual rather than physical dramas." Her studies of the inner man, but more particularly the inner woman, are marvelous. As A.E. Baker rightly points out, "George Eliot's sphere was the inner man; she exposed the internal clockwork. Her characters are not simply passive, and they do not stand still; they are shown making their own history, continually changing and developing as their motive issue into acts, and the acts become part of the circumstances that condition, modify, and purify or demoralise the will." David Cecil remarks, "We get behind the clock face and see the works, locate the mainspring, discover how it makes the wheel turn. We know just how a character will behave and why; we know exactly what special mixture of common human ingredients make him act differently from other people."

George Eliot : A Psycho-Analyst

George Eliot puts all the emphasis on the inside, very little on the outside. David Cecil observes in this connection, "We do not remember her serious characters by their appearance or the way they talk, indeed we do not remember these things, clearly at all. Her portraits are primarily portraits of the inner man."

Adam Bede is the best example of Eliot's efficiency in handling pyschological novels. The novel is admired for those parts which describe the minds of characters, dissecting their souls. This is the reason why critics ranked *Adam Bede* as, "the first psychological novel." This is the psychological treatment of Adam, Seth, Hetty, Dinah, Arthur and the Poysers, which laid examples for the psychological novelists of the future. In fact, Eliot is the first novelist who tried her hand to introduce a new kind of novel i.e. a psychological novel, which gave her much popularity. In the words of David Cecil, "She stands at the gateway between the old novel and the new, a massive caryatid, heavy of countenance and uneasy of attitude, but noble, monumental, profoundly impressive."

Brilliant Psychological Insight

A Journey in Hope, one of the chapter in *Adam Bede* is a deep study of Hetty's brain and heart which widens the reader's scope to analyse the situation fully. Adam's character is also revealed through Hetty's inner turbulence. The story continues when there is much more inner activity than outer. Only one single episode is treated mainly but sometime various minor actions are also interwoven. Throughout the novel, she continues with her psychological analysis.

The psychological approach of Eliot is excellent. This is proved in her work *Adam Bede* where she not only enables the reader to probe into the hearts of the characters, but also to let the reader see what the character himself does not see. Lisbeth, the widow of Thias Bede, shorty after the death of her husband, was in the Bede home where the body was kept. Where Thias was laid, the place was cleansed and purified, after this ritual she contemplated the big loss, sitting on chair in the kitchen : At another time Lisbeth's first thought would have been, "Where is Adam?" But the long period of twenty-six years of married life shattered at once, with the sudden death of her partner, but the memories are restored, "She had forgotten his faults as we forget the sorrows of our departed childhood, and thought of nothing but the young husband's kindness and the old man's patience." This sentence of a few words, not only depicts the mind of a just-widowed lady, who pardons every fault of her husband and only the happy moment passed together are overlapping her brain, but there is also an insight in Eliot's own unloved childhood.

Study of Arthur Donnithorne's Mind

Psycho-analytic approach of George Eliot ranked her above her contemporaries as well as her predecessors. In this connection David Cecil writes, "Drawing from the inside out, starting with the central principle of the character, she is able to show how it reveals itself in the most apparently inconsistent manifestations, can give to the most varied coloured surface of character that prevalent tone which marks it as the expression of one personality. Her characters always hang together, are of a piece, their defects are the defects of their virtues. We are not surprised that a man, so anxious for the good opinion of others as Arthur Donithorne, should selfishly seduce Hetty, because we realise that the controlling force in his character is the desire for immediate enjoyment; so that his wish to sun himself in the pleasant warmth of other people's liking goes along with his inability not to yield to the immediate pleasure of Hetty's embraces. George Eliot can follow the windings of motive through the most tortuous labyrinths, for firmly grasped in her hand is always the central clue."

Conflict in Mind

Complex characters created by George Eliot must possess mixed states of mind which is not left to the reader to study them. But the work is done brilliantly by her, is realised by the reader while turning the pages. Behind all her writings there lies a sense of tragedy of life, in which sin or folly brings its own retribution. Her preoccupation with this theme gives *Adam Bede* some of the features of moral treatise. As Samuel C. Chew observes, "In George Eliot's hands the novel was not primarily for entertainment but for the serious discussion of moral issues". *Adam Bede* reveals that she believed in the dominance of circumstances over the human beings, not completely, yet a single temptation how changes Hetty's life fully. How temptation leads a person on the path of destruction, is shown in the novel with which we are concerned, "No other English novelist has given us so vivid a picture of the process of moral defeat, as Donnithorne's gradual yielding to his passion for Hetty. With an inexorable clearness she reveals how temptation insinuates itself into the mind, how it retreats at the first suspicious movement of conscience how it comes back disguised, and how, if once more vanquished, it will sham death only to arise suddenly and sweep its victim away on a single irresistible gust of desire when he is off his guard."

Purification Through Remorse

How the characters in *Adam Bede,* Hetty, Adam, Arthur and Dinah as well repent whatever mistakes they had done, which not only purifies their hearts, but the moral chaos is also portrayed. "She exposes all the complex writings of a spirit striving to make itself at ease on the bed of a disturbed conscience, the desperate casuistry by which it attempts to justify itself, its inexhaustible ingenuity in blinding itself to unpleasant facts, the baseless hopes it conjures up for its comfort; she can distinguish precisely how different an act looks before it is done, shrouded in the softening darkness of the secret heart, and after, exposed in all its naked ugliness to the harsh daylight of other people's judgement." Thus, we are able to see Arthur's heart which is filled with feeling of guilt and not able to have a wink of sleep, "With rare penetration and insight George Eliot isolates and detects the various warning elements in Arthur's mind, his genuine compunction, his horror of being disapproved, of is instinctive resentment at disapproval, however justifiable, his inextinguishable hope that things will come right in the end, his irrational conviction that with him, at least, things always must come right. One grows quite uncomfortable as one watches so merciless, so delicate an exposure of human weakness. The truth it embodies is universal. In exposing Arthur Donnithorne, she also exposes her reader." (Davil Cecil)

Depiction of Arthur's Semi-Conscious Motives

Arthur's motives and ideas are opened to readers which provide them with the much information what is going on within his head. Sleep did not come to his anxious mind. Arthur wanted to go home without saying anything he was too painfully embarrassed in mind, as well as too weak in body, to wish for any further explanation to night. And yet it was a relief for him that Adam reopened the subject in a way the least difficult for him to answer. Arthur was in a wretched position of an open, generous man, who has committed an error which makes deception seem a necessity.

Conclusion

George Eliot possess great repulation in the history of fiction. She is much concerned with the human-psyche and its relationship with forces outside which determine the fate. She is more a preacher and a moralizer than any of the great contemporary. Besides this she had quality to reflect the country life in England in the period she lived and felt the necessity of preaching and moralizing.

CHAPTER - 17

THEMES OF *ADAM BEDE*

Adam Bede : Thematic Significance

It cannot be questioned that George Eliot was a popular author, for her novels concern with not a single theme rather various themes if the novel is seen through different angles. She is never stamped as a "difficult novelist" if her novels are read carefully. It depends upon the reader's intellect, whether he or she is able to grasp the very deep aspect of the novel. Actually *Adam Bede* is a novel which dissects human mind and then analysis is done, which discloses a lot of themes underlying it. *The Times* pronounced : "There can be no mistake about *Adam Bede.* It is a first-rate novel, and its author takes rank at once among the masters of the art."

Flaw in Adam

Critics gave their views that Adam is shown as over-virtuous. What George Eliot had considered an ideal person should be, she rendered all those aspects to Adam. But, a deep analysis of his mind make us aware of the flaws in his character. He is hard, arrogant with little sympathy for ordinary sinners. In this world, nobody is perfect and imperfection should be pardoned, but Adam Bede lacked this integrity. Gradually, he comes out of all these faults and converts into a complete and real human being. Dinah's affection for him and later, their marriage, brings about this grand change in him. The process of his education occupies the centre of the novel. If the process is taken carefully the point would become clear.

Stone-hearted Person

In fact, Adam is a stone-hearted person at the very beginning. The very fault in him lies in his over-confidence which makes him to think that he is righteous and it is not wrong in any way. This is told to us by the hymns he sings and the ending with the same hymn is not only appropriate but it also gives him the impression how much significant the hymn is?

Confidence on His Vision

He does not harm anybody, knowingly. Not for a single moment he thinks when he hurts anybody. He is much confident about his doings, "I've seen pretty clear, ever since I could cast up a sum, as you can never do what's wrong without breeding sin and trouble more than you can ever seen." His confidence is shaken when he catches his friend red handed while making love with his beloved Hetty, in the woods. He realises his mistakes, "how incomplete his mental seeing has been! He understood it all now—the locket, and everything else that had been doubtful to him a terrible scorching light showed him the hidden letters that changed the meaning of the past." Here starts the process of his education and self-realisation.

Conflict in Head and Heart

In the very beginning of the novel, we realise that Adam may be intelligent and honest, yet, not a sincere man because the head dominates the heart in him. He is stern, cruel, harsh and hasty with unforgiving aspect in him which stamped him as a stone-hearted man. Whenever such kind of conflict rises between head and heart, intellectual curiosity turns into hardness and pride. Adam's pride gave rise to various disputes on all sides. His hardness also faced the same responses. Adam's hardness consists in his having "too little feeling with the weakness that errs inspite of foreseen consequences' George Eliot says that if this fellow feeling is absent, "how are we to get enough patience and charity towards our stumbling, falling companions in the long and changeful journey?" The first part of *Adam Bede* provides us with the answer to the question which had been haunting us again and again. The early chapters of the book show Adam controlling his own life. He has not any sympathy for those who stumble and fall—like his own father, for example. "The function of old Thias Bede as a character is, indeed, precisely that of revealing the extent of his son's hardness. The same is true of Arthur. Toward both men Adam is unforgiving, and even when he repents of his severity, the repentance is futile because it reflects no genuine increase in his capacity for sympathy."

Passionate Love for Hetty

Neither for Arthur, nor for his father, Adam has any kind of deep feeling. Instead, all his love is meant for Hetty and this extreme love, causes much of his sufferings. When, he himself, undergoes all these hardships, then he realises to share other's problems. The possibility of regeneration is felt through a human agent exercising the power of love. There are two agents—one is Mr. Irwine and other Bartle Massey. Both of them contributed their best, to raise Adam from these undesirable circumstances. Too much despair fills Adam's heart with violence and revenge on Arthur. Both of them prevent him to do so. Irwine convinces him that another crime will not foreshadow Hetty's crime rather it would add more difficulties and tensions in her life. Adam is somewhat convinced but the tempest in his mind was controlled by Bartle Massey.

Attainment of Knowledge

Bartle puts much efforts to melt Adam's hardness which makes him to decide that he would stand by Hetty. It suggests the gradual change in him to forgive Arthur and to develop a new love. He realises the truth that "love does not exist without sympathy, sympathy does not exist without suffering in common."

Influence of Feuerbach

Written by Feuerbach, *The Essence of Christianity* was translated into English by George Eliot. The influence of Feuerbach can be seen in George Eliot, in her works. In the above mentioned book, Feuerbach talks about the religious significance of water, wine and bread. All of three are sacred for him. The reason for the sacredness of water lies in the fact that it is a force of nature and it keeps us reminding that we have our origins in nature, the same origin of other lower creatures. Thus necessity of water symbolises our oneness with nature and Baptism as well. Wine and bread are man made things which look towards nature for the raw-material, thus symbolises that man is much superior to other lower creatures who are not so efficient to modify natural things. In the Christian ritual of Baptism, only water is used, for innocent and pure-hearted children. Whereas for the mature man, the Lord's supper which includes wine and bread, is served. It suggests that man is much above animals. If the man is hungry and thirsty, he will no more remain a human being and taking of bread and wine restores him to his humanity. This truth is revealed to us through three suppers which is taken by Adam and his humanity kept ever-present in him."

Importance of Three Suppers

U.C. Knoepf Lamacher says, "the first of these suppers is designed to remind Adam of his origin in nature." i.e. in water. Adam's unawareness of the fact that a mature person should be varied from nature, is stressed by the second scene "a need soon to be accentuated by Hetty's unnatural murder of her natural child." In the third scene, Adam realises the importance of this distinction which has religious concern.

Dinah Lacks Maturity

Already mentioned that Adam is not a complete, well integrated man, in the very beginning of the novel. His heart is dominated by the head i.e. he is a fully practical, hard and self-righteous person. In case of Dinah, it is not realised at very beginning. She also can not attain the balance between the head and heart. It is after she was accepted by Adam, as his beloved, attains the knowledge and steps towards maturity and sincerity as well.

Over Emotionality

Neither she takes life practically nor she gets involve within it. Says Creeger, "implicit in her fear is also, I believe, a kind of unwillingness to become fully involved in life. In this respect she is like her creater who once said that it was pity her life could not be managed for her, while she stood by, the passive but interested spectator." It cannot be denied that she was not mild, compassionate and sympathetic but never tried her hand to involve in somebody's problems.

Withdrawal from Reality

"Such a psychological state represents a complete withdrawal from life, and withdrawal (or retreat) is characteristic of Dinah. Whenever the going gets rough, that is, whenever life begins, paradoxically, to seem too pleasant and reductive, Dinah flees back to Stonyshire, barren and sterile under the "overarching sky". The most notable of these strategic retreats occurs after Adam has told her of his love. Following his declaration, Dinah replies that she could return his love save for the fear that she would 'forget to rejoice and weep with others' even forget the divine presence. Her peace and joy come from having no life of her own. Adam's love only raises the fear that she will forget Jesus, the man of sorrows, and become hard: 'And think how it is with me, Adam : that life I have led is like a land I have trodden in blessedness since my childhood; and if I long for a moment to follow the voice which calls me to another land that I know not I cannot but fear that my soul might hereafter yearn for that early blessedness which I had forsaken, and where doubt enters there is not perfect love. I must wait for clearer guidance: I must go from you'. Here is clear expression of Dinah's fear of accepting full maturity, for the land which faces her (i.e. Loamshire and, of course, Adam) is a strange one; and who knows what life there may hold for her ? Better, then to the other land (Stonyshire and the self-contained world of childhood). There is at least no risk is run. If Hetty was incapable of growing up, Dinah is afraid too" (Creeger).

Love Brings Maturity

She overcomes her fear after she was told by Adam that he was in love with her. Dinah also responses positively and starts participating in her life symbolised by her returning to Stonyshire. Adam also leaves Loamshire and enters Stonyshire where he is able to find Dinah again and feels a great change in her. She is now a complete woman with intense love for him and with a strong desire to become his wife. Finally, in departing November, the wedding of Adam and Dinah is done. The ending is proper as both of them had painful experiences concerning with Hetty, which render them a sympathetic heart and thus love based on sympathy wins.

Message in George Eliot's Novels

All of George Eliot's novels have some didactic purpose as she believes that in every writing there must be something to teach. She gives more stress on morals and values. According to Leslie Stephen, "George Eliot believed that a look of art not only may, but must, exercise also an ethical influence". She thought that, "our deeds determine us, as much as we determine our deeds." We would surely suffer if we follow temptation and sin. Nobody can escape from the results of the past's deeds. She believes in the policy, "What will you sow, so shall you reap." The characters in *Adam Bede,* suffer due to what they had done in the past. Hetty and Arthur suffer because they were tempted by sex and breaks all the shackles of moral values and social customs.

Hetty with Ordinary Features

Hetty Sorrel, the heroine of the novel is neither an innocent nor a cunning girl. She is painted as a simple village girl with dreams of a handsome youngman, which is not an extraordinary feature for a girl of that tender age. Only once she is tempted by Arthur and she sways with her passions due to which she has to suffer a long and finally meets a tragic death. In the words of Henry James, "The central figure of the book by virtue of her great misfortune is Hetty Sorrel. Her suffering gives her special eminence. In the presence of that misfortune no one else assuredly, has a right to claim dramatic pre-eminence."

Contended Life of Hetty

A few pages of the first book reveal that Hetty was a pretty girl with normal passions, quite happy living with her aunt spending most of her time in a dairy. Mrs. Poyser is in habit of talking senselessly, which is known to her and she ignoring her rebukes, keeps on enjoying life to its brim. But as not a single person can be found without flaws, she has one i.e. her useless fancy to become a country lady.

Yielding to Temptation

Adam Bede, a handy carpenter loves her honestly and it is not a secret for Hetty also, but he is poor and so cannot match with her dream-lover. So, she rejects him as soon as her eyes catch the attention of Arthur, a real prince. She starts dreaming of him and is sure about her coming future, which would be bright and colourful. The words of novelist makes us aware of her dreamworld thus, "A new influence had come over Hetty—gay atmospheric, shaping itself into no self-confessed hopes or prospects, but producing a pleasant narcotic effect, making her tread the ground and go about her work in a sort of dream, unconscious of weight or effort, and showing her all things through a soft, liquid veil, as if she were living not in this world of brick and stone, but in a beautified world, such as the sun tights up for us in the waters. The poor child no more conceived at present the idea that the young squire could ever be her lover, than a baker's pretty daughter in the crowd, whom a young emperor distinguishes by an imperial but admiring smile conceives that she shall be made empress. But the baker's daughter goes home and dreams of the handsome young emperor, and perhaps weighs the flour amiss while she is thinking what a heavenly lot it must be to presence haunting her waking and sleeping dreams; bright soft glances had penetrated her, and suffered her life with a strange happy languor. Since then her inward life had consisted of little else than living through in memory the looks and words Arthur had directed towards her—of little else than recalling the sensations with which she heard his voice outside the house, and saw his enter, and became conscious that his eyes were fixed on her, and then became conscious that a tall figure, looking down on her with eyes that seemed to touch her, was nearer in clothes of beautiful texture with an odour like that of a flower garden born one the evening breeze".

Terrible Results

How all of her dreams shattered with only one mistake she was to make by Arthur's persuasion and the suffering is doubled when she is said good bye by her lover Arthur, when she is pregnant and has lost her virginity with nobody to help her. In this way, George Eliot brings out a moral aspect how a person is tempted and is made to sin. If sin is done then punishment must be given. Thus Hetty gets the punishment, when she is left alone to face all the hardships and then her futile attempt to search her lover, Arthur. Her premature delivery and the murder of her own son, is crime over crime.

Arthur's Hand in Hetty's Destruction

Not only Hetty is responsible for her suffering but Arthur is much involved in doing so. R.T. Jones writes in this connection, "the innocence that · Arthur represents consists in cultivating friendly relations with everybody, never willingly doing harm to anybody; and being willing to make amends for any harm he may accidentally do. This innocence is a master of intentions, of meaning well and meaning no ill, and is necessarily presented in descriptions of his thoughts rather than in actions, objectively regarded would be almost indistinguishable from those of calculated villainy."

Arthur Completes Circle

If Arthur, in vanity, persuades innocent Hetty, he is not escaped from the sufferings and punishment as well. His life is also destroyed. He is in a bad condition and tries to mend his fault by helping Hetty anyway. But not a single chance he gets from the fate, and suffers most. In these words he repents, "I was all wrong from the very first and horrible wrong has come of it. God knows. I'd give my life if I could undo it."

Conclusion

We may sum-up with the words of A.E. Baker, "She emancipated herself from the Evangelical creed in which she had been brought up, but she was always religious minded. The phase of rationalism through which she passed after abandoning the belief in heaven and hell of her Evangelical upbringing did not last long. Pantheism she found unsatisfying and she resigned herself to the conviction that there is no answer to our cravings for a definite faith. But hundreds of passages in her novels imply that she could never eradicate a profound sense, not merely of divine immanence, but of divine transcendence. Her puritanism, her worship of duty rested all her life upon the consciousness of an inner reality, which adherents of the creeds readily identified with the Divine. The monitor within represented something higher than ourselves, whether of another order of being or simply the loftiest ideal conceivable to man. The latter question remains inscrutable, but terms in which she constantly speaks of duty and conscience, and the Supreme Power, which fashioned us, are the terms of one who could hardly help believing." In short, the novelist takes the moral aspects painfully and brings us to notice the consequences of the deeds which are done ignoring the rules and regulations of nature and society as well.

CHAPTER - 18

ADAM BEDE : A REGIONAL NOVEL

Definition of the Regional Novel

A novel which deals with a particular place or region is called a regional novel. The novelist while writing the novel takes the aspects of the place with which she is concerned and the characters are attributed with all the features of that particular place. George Eliot experienced her life in English Midlands and wrote about its nature and characteristics.

Popularity of Regional Novels

The countries with a variety of speech, customs, habits, climate and character are rich in regional novels. Phyllis Bentley believes that "regional novels are in fashion, where within the limits of a national culture there is a considerable diversity, a considerable variety corresponding to geographical divisions, of patterns of life; in such a nation there exists considerable material for regional novels, and at one period or another of the national history writers will be stimulated by the presence of that material, to handle it."

The English Midlands

George Eliot's novels reveal the very aspects of the English Midlands, more specially Warwickshire and Coventry. The beauty of these Midlands plains caught the attraction of her eyes and these plains found their setting in her novels. Parkinson says, "Quite a feature of the scenery—and indeed of Warwickshire generally—is that the hedges are everywhere closely painted with trees, whose height, as well as the riotous wastefulness of the hedge—rose, give evidence of a kindly soil and climate."

Regional Characters in *Adam Bede*

In her second novel *Adam Bede,* George Eliot draws the characters from every walk of life of England's country-side. Says Phyllis Bentley, "Turning to George Eliot's characters we find that many of her important characters are truly regional. They are drawn from humble walks of life and are shown carrying on their day to day activity." Adam Bede is a carpenter, Hetty is a dairy worker and Dinah is a Methodist preacher. Not only major, but minor characters are also people of same land with similar notions.

The Setting in *Adam Bede*

The descriptions are so strong in this novel that are never questioned for their realistic features. The characters are lively and breathing with their customs, traditions and values. Finally, George Eliot uses landscape to define, reinforce and foreshadow the events of the plot and moral situation. *Adam Bede* is, in the very beginning of the novel, introduced in Jonathan Burge's workshop. Several scenes in the novel take the setting in the English Midland. The action of the novel takes place in Staffordshire and Derbyshire while called as Loamshire and Stonyshire. The scenes in the background, should not be considered insignificant. The fragrance of the pine-wood and bushes, the warmth of the sun render a sense of natural order and peace in the lap of countryside. Henry Auster says, "The atmosphere of sunny, harmonious, energetic rusticity is complicated, but not shattered, by the diversity of personalities and underlying tensions."

Interest in Humble Characters

Her deep concern in rustics is noteworthy in *Adam Bede* in which she accepts the very truth in it, "I turn, without shrinking, from cloud-borne angles. From prophets, skills, and heroic warriors, to an old woman bending over her plow pot, or eating her solitary dinner, while the noonday light softened perhaps by a screen of leaves, falls on her." She is parallelled with Thomas Hardy, in her capacity to draw rustic characters.

Mrs. Poyser : A True Copy

Not any character in this novel is provided with features and characteristics of the very rustics as Mrs. Poyser. Infact, she represents the whole community and its tradition. She stays in Hall Farm, which provides a background that bringsforth her character in wide range. This is the place where peace, love, energy and comfort resides and this feeling is shared by almost all of the characters, only Hetty is leftout. The remarks of Arthur Donnithorne catches the attentions, "I think yours is the prettiest farm on the estate......I know this his (Mr. Poyser) farm is in better order than any other within ten miles of us; and as for the kitchen. I don't believe there's one in the kingdom to beat it."

The Mansions

In *Adam Bede*, the Donnithorne Chase is the same estate of Wootton Hall quite near the Ellaston. Much earlier, the owner of it Sir Francis Newdegate had a son who introduced Robert Evans to the old squire and Robert Evans was appointed a beliff there. The story is reflected in *Adam Bede,* where with the efforts of Arthur Donnithorne, the management of the whole land comes in the hands of Adam Bede. In the novel, there are description of Wootton Hall; "The house would have been nothing but a plain squire mansion of Queen Anne's time but for the remnant of an old Abbey to which it was united at one end in much the same way as one may sometimes see a new farmhouse high and prime at the end of the older and lower farm offices. The fine old remnant stood a little backward and under the shadow of tall beeches, the sun was now on the taller and more advanced front, the blinds were all down, and the house seemed asleep in the hot midday."

A little cottage was inhabited by Robert Evans and between this cottage and the village of Norbury there was a little brick cottage where Bartle Massey, a school master used to live in. In *Adam Bede,* the same character is introduced with the same name. In the same school George Eliot used to go, which must be told by her father and incidents vividly described in her *Adam Bede.* One thing is to be noted here that the pictorial quality of *Adam Bede* is much better than her first novel *Scenes of Clerical Life.* Henry Auster thus, compares both of them, "What distinguishes the landscapes and interiors in *Scenes of Clerical Life* from those in *Adam Bede* is a matter of quality, not quantity : it is narrator's obtrusive, openly autobiographical feeling of personal acquaintance with the region."

Conclusion

Thus *Adam Bede* gives an excellent picture of English country life among the humble class. Her command on the idioms of ordinary speech enables her to achieve a fine naturalness. *Adam Bede* is full of fine descriptions of the English countryside and her faculty for natural description she never lost entirely. Her own words reveal the fact, "As to my indebtness to facts of locale, and personal history of a small kind, connected with Staffordshire and Derbyshire—you may imagine of what kind that is, when if tell you that I never remained in either of those countries more than a shadowy interrupted recollection. The details which I knew as facts and have made use of for my picture were gathered from such imperfect allusion and narrative or I heard from my father in his occasional talk about old times."

CHAPTER - 19

AN OUTLINE SUMMARY OF *ADAM BEDE*

The Bedes

Adam Bede, from the village of Hayslope in the country of Loamshire is an energetic deligent carpenter. He is till single, who along with his brother Seth, live with their parents Lizbeth and Thias Bede. After his rigorous manual labour are day long, he attends night school. Both the brothers are in love, Adam with Hetty Sorrel, who is the niece of Mr. Martin Poyser and Seth with Dinah Morris, a beautiful Methodist preacher.

Adam at Work

We are introduced to *Adam Bede*, as a young man who does not shy away from any tedious manual labour. He works with Seth and four other companions. Even when the others have called it a day, he continues to toil through the night, when he finds out that an order for a coffin from the neighbouring town of Broxton, which his father had taken, is yet to be completed. Immersed in his work, he hears a tap at the door late into the night. As believed by the locals, this was on omen indicating death in the family. Sure enough, the next morning they get to hear the news that his father had died as he was returning home in an intoxicated state.

Death of Adam's Father : Dinah's Visit

The death of Thias Bede makes Lizbeth inconsolable, but she draws strength from her two sons. Dinah Morris who has arrested the attention of Seth comes over to the Bede household. She tries to console Lizbeth in whatever manner that she can and does spent the night over to ensure the running machinery of the house is not affected. Dinah's kindness and considerations, coupled with her compassion and charm, makes her an ideal preacher. Twice had Seth proposed to her, and twice was his proposal turned down with the conviction that her call was towards the poor and the needy.

Hetty Sorrel and the Young Squire

While Dinah did all she could do to ease the pain, Hetty Sorrel showed scant respect to the feelings of the Bede household, by not even paying a courtesy visit. Because at this time her thoughts were occupied by Arthur Donnithorne, the grandson of the Squire. Incidentally the two were introduced to each other when Arthur Donnithorne had along with his friend Mr. Irwine, the Rector had visited Hall Farm, the very day that Thias Bede died, to pass the sad tidings. For all her vanity and conceit, Hetty Sorrel was indeed a beautiful woman, so Arthur Donnithorne found himself being attacted by her, and had invited her to the celebrations of his twenty first birthday when he would be coming of age.

Hetty's Daydream

Thias Bede was given a solemn funeral and though Hetty attended the funeral service she was too lost in her fantasy to be of the slightest comfort to Adam.

Birthday Celebrations

The birthday of Arthur was celebrated by the whole of Hayslope with much gaiety and in the thick of the merriment, Arthur had an announcement to make. He elevated Adam Bede to the post of the manager of the woods, and this went down well with the whole of Hayslope for Adam was known for his sincerity and admired for his diligence.

The Fight

As Adam Bede was immersed in his duty of manning the woods, unknown to him Arthur and Hetty had their scheduled meetings in the very woods itself. Like most youngmen who come from privileged backgrounds. Arthur was not essentially a bad person, but he did not have much resoluteness nor resistance. On one occasion when Hetty and Arthur were lost in their own world. Adam happened to be passing through. This evoked a deep rage in Adam and like all youngmen in love, he wanted to establish his manhood and his greater right to the affections of Hetty on physical strength. It was but expected that Adam would emerge the winner. When Arthur went into a state of unconsciousness, Adam took him to the Hermitage, a retreat in the woods. Arthur responded to Adam's messages and came around.

Hetty's Frustration

After that Adam asked Arthur not to fool around with Hetty, who in her state of excitement at the thought of being able to attract the attention of the future Squire, failed to see the chasm between their social standing. When convinced by Adam, Arthur wrote a letter to Hetty, explaining to her why their affair should end. As expected the letter totally devastated Hetty. Thereby Arthur also went to Windsor to join his regiment. Adam was still in love with Hetty and so he offered to marry her. Though broken hearted Hetty was sensible enough to realise that Adam was not a bad substitute, for he was quite prosperous by now.

Hetty Leaves Hayslope

But before the nuptials can take place there is already a twist in the tale. Hetty finds out that she will be having a child, and there is little that she can do to conceal her condition. With a myriad of thoughts running in her minds, suicide being one of them, she feels that Arthur might take her as his wife, out of pity atleast. On the pretext going to Snowfield to invite Dinah for the wedding, she sets off for Windsor.

The Journey in Hope

With just three guineas in her pocket she starts her mission of tracing Arthur. Travelling to Stoniton by coach, she realises that this entire exercise will cost her a lot more than what she has in her pocket. So she cuts down further on her cost by having skimpy meals hitching a ride and by now she looks so impoverished that even the coachman does not have the heart to take the tip which she was offering. The coach in which she was travelling stopped at the Green Man Inn, whose proprietor and wife were gentle and kind. Taking note of her condition they gave her food and free lodging. Adding more troubles to her already miserable condition, she got to know that Arthur had already left for Ireland. Just when she thought that her problems were coming to an end, unknown to her, this was an indication of the beginning of her nightmares. The knowledge of Arthur in Ireland shatters all her hopes and she was more convinced than ever that suicide was the only way out.

The Journey in Despair

The continuation of a cozy bed and a warm meal can be very healing at times, and the next morning she got up with a greater resolve and more in control of the situation. She gave a story of a long lost brother to the landlord and his wife whose only contact was Arthur. Now that Arthur had left for Ireland, she decided to go back and felt the necessity to raise some money by pawning off some of her jewellery. This the landlord agreed upon by advancing her three guineas, but refused any payment towards the bed and the meal. She came across the address of Dinah while rummaging through her purse, and for a fleeting moment she felt some sense of solace, in the thought of Dinah, but reality came counting down on her to make her feel more desperate than ever.

Hetty's homeword journey differed little in pattern with her onward journey. In her darkest moment she could not find solace even in her religious faith. After arriving at Stratford-on-Avon, she was on the lookout for a deep pool to drown herself. Surrounded by such grim thoughts she dogs off only to be horrified by the darkness enveloping her.

The Child Murder

She is woken from her slumber by an old man. She kept moving from one place to another till she gave birth to her child in the inn of a kind and compassionate woman. After quietly leaving the inn she was seen in a dishevelled condition by passers-by near a haystack. A labourer had espied the hand of an infant coming out from a heap of grass. The infant was dead, but Hetty could not bring herself to move away from the place where her child was lying still, and hence she was arrested for the murder of her child.

The Search

By this time the family of Hetty was worried, so Adam also took some initiative to trace her whereabouts, which led him to Dinah's cottage. There he learned that Hetty had gone to Leeds, so Adam came to the conclusion that she has left for Ireland and resolves to venture to Ireland.

The Arrest and the Trial

Adam returns to Hayslope to prepare for this mission to Ireland, but before leaving he takes the counsel of Mr Irwine. Adam tells the Rector all his possible suspicion between the affair of Hetty and Arthur. In return the Rector has the terrible news of Hetty's arrest for the murder of her child. The devasted Adam further gets to know that Arthur is on his way home as desired by the old Squire. Adam was torn between meeting Hetty and avoiding her. Bantle Massey, the man whose night school Adam had attended proved to be a real source of support in his darkest moments.

Hetty's Obstinate Silence : The Verdict

Though Mr. Irwine had arranged the best legal support for Hetty, she was of no help to herself, by her silence. Her resolute silence found her guilty and was sentenced to be hanged till death. The only sound which she emitted was during the reading of her sentence. At this moment when everyone had deserted her. Adam gave her unsolicitated support.

Dinah : The Confession

Dinah reached the prison prior to Hetty's hanging and was determined to spent every possible moment with her. Her gentle counselling touched Hetty and she finally came out with her side of the story. Then she knelt down with Dinah to pray for forgiveness.

The Last Moments, the Reprieve

With just a day left for Hetty, Adam came over to see her for the very last time. It was an extremely difficult and heavy moment as they were both aware that by tomorrow she would be hanged. Hetty informed Adam that she was trying to be charitable towards Arthur. Dinah, true to her word was with Hetty even as she walked towards the place of execution. The larger crowd gave a shout, when they saw a horseman waring a pardon in his hand, galloping towards the place of execution. It was Arthur, who did everything possible to defer the death sentence to life imprisonment.

The Reconciliation

With this grim tragedy put behind them the people of Hayslope quickly returned to their normal life, with the exception of Poysers, then of course Adam and Arthur. With the Poysers and Adam, nursing similar thoughts of leaving the neighbourhood, fate played a different plan on Adam. Adam and Arthur chanced to meet once again in the woods. But this time the wood was more sober and mellow in tone. Adam could also read remorse of Arthur's face. Arthur convinced Adam to stay on as the manager of his estate under the guidance of Mrs. Irwine. Arthur also urges Adam to do one more favour that to persuade the Poysers to stay on. Thus no one dislocated themselves from Haylope and the penitent Arthur took part in the war with the French.

Dinah and Adam's Marriage & Epilogue

In keeping with the convention George Eliot has to terminate the novel with the marriage of Adam and Dinah. This is possible by their being in close proximity during the final days of Hetty. To bring a sense of completeness to the novel Eliot informs us that Lizbeth is no longer around, and that Seth is a very happy uncle. Dinah is also not spared either. She is presented in a more domesticated form. After paying her price, Hetty also taste freedom before dying on her way to England. Arthur has not been keeping well so he is advised rest by the doctors, and the novel ends with a sense of normalcy finally returning to Hayslope.

CHAPTER - 20

DETAILED CHAPTER-WISE SUMMARY

BOOK 1

CHAPTER - 1

The Workshop

The story opens with the roomy workshop of Mr. Jonaathan Burge, carpenter and builder in the village of Hayslope. The hero of the novel Adam Bede works in this workshop as a carpenter.

Five more carpenters are at work with him. On a heap of soft shavings lies a rough grey shepherd-dog, admiring his master, Adam. Adam Bede is tall, dark-eyed youngman with jet black hair. He is large boned muscular man nearly six feet high and while working, he sings a hymn in a strong sonorous voice. The next workman is Adam's brother, Seth. They both are of equal height resembles each other except that Seth's eyes are grey and his look is more confiding and benignant.

The concert of the tools and Adam's voice is at last broken by Seth declaring finishing of his work. It produces a roar of laughter from the three workmen and smile from Adam, who politely says "Why thee'st forgot the panels". Seth gets confused and "wiry" Ben Cranage takes the red paint, saying he is going to write on't "Seth Bede, the Methody, his work". Thus humour is produced and the attention of the readers is at once caught.

Adam shook Ben and pinned him against the wall but Seth tries to compromise and normalcy of the work is observed. Ben again teases Seth, asking whether he has been thinking about the pretty person or her sermon. Seth good-humouredly replies "She's going to preach on the Green tonight". So he can go and hear her. Adam again warns him, on this Ben enquires if Adam is going to turn Methodist and disturb Parson Irwine. Here one is introduced indirectly to Dinah Morris, the Heroine.

The discussion on religion provokes and Adam states that he believes in freedom of conscience and worship. He stresses that people should stay quietly in the old church which has a lot to be learned. Seth comments upon the Methodist preachers's work. Adam clears his true intentions and on this Seth replies, "I know that well enough.

Thee't like thy dog Gyp-thee bark'st at me sometimes, but thee always like'st my hand after".

Just at six the work comes to an end. The men stopped working, but being indignant Adam asks them if they take no pleasure in their work. They apart with a poor response but Seth stays. This shows Adam's unique behaviour.

On being enquired by Adam, Seth replies that he intends to see Dinah Morris safely home to Poyser's farm after the preaching. Adam informs him about his night-school in order to improve his mind.

The dog Gyp runs forward to carry the basket for his loving master, just when Adam finished his work. After locking the workshop, Adam goes to Burge's house to deliver the keys. While walking along with Gyp, an elderly horseman stops and looks at him admiringly.

CHAPTER - 2

The Preaching

In the same evening excitement is seen in the village of Hayslope. Mr Casson, the landlord with red-face stands at door looking towards the village green, where certain grave-looking men and women are gathering. Mr Casson is in folly mode and is dignified in his bearing, for has been butler to the Donnithorne family for fifteen years.

The horse rider rode up to the inn to enquire about the cause of the gathering on the field. Mr Casson explained him about the preaching by a young Methodist woman going to be held there. He also confirmed that village Parson Irwine had no objections as he preaches only on Sunday afternoon. Moreover he lived at Bronton, over the hill. There were only two Methodists in Haylsope—Will Maskery and Seth Bede, whereas Treddleston had many who had come from there to attend it. The preacher came from Stonyshire but at present is staying with her aunt, Mrs Poyser, at the Hall Farm. The stranger also learned from Mr Casson that Squire Donnithorne is the owner of the whole land. They lived at the Donnithorne Chase in the valley.

The traveller waited to enjoy the young preacher and the beautiful landscape around. The whole crowd right from the old "Feyther Taft" to the babies was least serious about the preaching. They had only came to see "what war a - going- on like".

We are introduced to Chad Cranage, the blacksmith cracking jokes with "wiry" Ben Cranage nearby. Mr Joshua Rann, the village shoemaker and parish clerk, criticised the rise of Methodism which actually disturbed the dignity of the church. The stronger curiosity of the woman made them assemble there, where they could examine the quaker like costume of the female Methodists. Finally, the novelist has hinted at the religious disputes frame works the social background to the novel.

A small cart was placed under a tree which was actually the pulpit for the preacher to preach. There was mixed reactions among the Methodists. Like some were relaxing with their eyes closed, as if in prayer, while others looked with misery at the onlookers—specially at Bess, the daughter of Chad Cranage, who was standing with her large ear-rings.

Lastly the preachers, Dinah Morris arrived along with Seth Bede and Will Maskery. Dinah in her simple black stuff dress and delicate and feminine in appearance mounted the cart without any self-consciousness. She had a small oval face with smooth locks of pale reddish hair. The hair was drawn back and covered by a net quaker cap. Her eyes were frank and grey with a strong expression which could melt a light sneer. The stranger remarked her "A sweet woman" and said to himself, "but surely nature never meant her for a preacher".

First, Dinah prayed for God's blessing and then began to preach on. "The spirit of the Lord is upon me, because He hath anointed me to preach the gospel to the poor". She shared her past experiences with the viewers. She said that during her childhood she had heard John Wesley and how he had explained that the Gospel meant good news. It was noted by the traveller that Dinah had completely captured the attention of the viewers. Moreover, he himself could not resist the charm of her voice. All this still raised a doubt in his mind whether she could rouse the religious feelings in her listeners and could convert them into Methodism.

At the end of the sermon—the calling of sinners to repentance-brought a change in her manner. Under the inspiration of her simple faith the words were coming out from her mouth with deeper emotions. This transformation made her paler and eyes shining with mercy. She prayed earnestly to her audience to turn to God as still sometime is there.

There was many a responsive sigh and groan from her fellow Methodists, but the village could not easily moved Bessy Cranage, a naughty girl, started feeling frightened, as Dinah spoke of sin and repentance. Dinah directly pointed out Bessy and exhorted her to cast off the follies that were toxicating her soul and dragging her to Hell, where she may get lost far away from light and God. Frustrated Bessy pulled off her big ear-rings and threw it on the ground. Something miracle was suspected by the girl's father and was afraid that he too should be "laid hold on", return back to his work gave him self-control.

She (Dinah) changed her tone and started talking about the joys of Divine Peace and boundless love which would give comfort to the sinners. After one hour preaching the Methodists sang their closing hymn.

The eloquence and the sincerity of the heroine of the novel gives a dramatic texture to the novel.

CHAPTER - 3

After the Preaching.

Seth Bede was walking by Dinah's side along the path which lay between the village and the Hall Farm for an hour. Seth felt that "She's too good and holy for any man, let alone me", thus was unable to express his feelings of love for her. He asked her whether she would certainly return back to Snowfield on the following Saturday. She quietly responsed yes and said 'I'm called there to serve a suffering sister by her visions." The separation from her Aunt and the children and "that poor wandering lamb, Hetty Sorrel" made her disappointed.

This lead Seth to inform Dinah about the love of Adam for Hetty. This interaction lead Seth to turn the topic to marriage, which actually gave some support to him about his personnel love for her. Dinah regretted the proposal and thanked him for his love. The *Bible* was her guide and thus marriage was not approved by God. Seth accepted the concept of Methodisim, but was greatly disappointed. Dinah answered "It isn't for you and me to lay plans ; we've nothing to do but to obey and trust". She consoled him by pressing his hand with a look of despair in her eyes and he turned dejectedly away. He had just reached twenty three "and had only just learned what it is to love" without any ray of hope.

In this chapter we learn about Methodists and their mental images. It lays stress on miracles in instantaneous conversion and in revealing divine will in dreams and vision.

CHAPTER - 4

Home and It's Sorrows

In this chapter we are introduced to the Bede family, especially

Lisbeth Bede, the mother. Lisbeth was weak and thin but still an energetic aged lady. Her strong desire for the return of her beloved eldest son, Adam always inspired her to wait for him by looking from the doorway of her thatched cottage. She was tall like Adam and resembled him in many ways. But Adam did not inherit his broad brew and the look of hardness and intelligence from her.

On the arrival of Adam, Lisbeth greeted him very affectionately. On seeing the planks standing in the workshop in the same condition as they were in the morning, he asked about his father. Adam with frustation threw off his jacket and began to make the coffin. He had actually promised to deliver that the following morning. His father being irresponsible, had gone to Tredleston and probably got drunk. Lisbeth being an affectionate mother took hold of his arm and asked him to have food. Due to her repeated request for food, Adam got angry and told her to leave him as he had to do work.

Adam's mood had changed by the late evening and he asked for a light and a draught of water. He spoke politely to his mother. Meanwhile Seth had returned and observed that Adam was still working. He wanted to help Adam but Adam refused. Adam could observe his depressed looks and red eyes and asked whether he were in trouble. Seth responded , " It's what must be borne and can't be helped." Dinah's refusal to marry had made him sad.

Lisbeth being more attached to Adam, had no fear of Seth and spoke out her complaints and worries about Adam to him. She was afraid that Adam would either marry Hetty Sorrel instead of marrying Marry Burge and having a partnership in her father's business or leave home. She did not like the idea of Methodism and asked Seth to leave it. Anyhow, he made her mother to kneel down with him and prayed for his father and for Adam. Adam again refused Seth's help. Lisbeth placed some food for him on the bench and said, "Thee canst pick a bit while thee't workin."

There is comparison between the two brothers where both are innocent and hard working: Adam is energetic and dynamic but Seth is innocent and passive.

While sitting alone Adam recalled his happy old days. He was disappointed for his future life but was proud for his past days that he was Thias Bede's son. When he was eighteen he ran away due to sorrows and suffering. Later he decided to return as he had reached Stoniton. Adam being a responsible boy did not leave his mother and his brother. This scene shows Adams active and innocent nature.

Adam was still busy in making the coffin when it was almost past midnight. There was a loud knock on the door and Gyp gave a loud bark. Adam suddenly trembled when he recalled that his mother had told him such a sound meant that some one is dying. He set back to his work but after a while the sound was repeated again and Gyp again howled. Adam stood at door to look but he could see nothing. Adam went upstairs quietly and found that his mother and Seth soundly sleeping. The author being the historian of the Midlands, shows, her believes in superstitions that prevailed in that part of the country.

Adam and Seth carried the coffin to Broxton to deliver to the customs at early morning. They took a short cut across the fields and reached home by six o'clock. While crossing the field they happened to see the tall and heavy body of their father in the brook that ran through the field. He drowned into the river as he was drunk.

Adam hurriedly ran home to inform his mother and then ran back to help Seth with the body. The grief of the family was really unexplainable.

CHAPTER - 5

The Rector

Now we are introduced to two important characters—Mr. Irwine and Mr. Arthur Donnithorne in the novel. The Rector of Bronton, Reverend Adelphus Irwine, and Vicar of Hayslope was in the lofty dining room of personage due to rain in the morning. He was playing chess with his mother, she was, "a stately, beautiful old lady, with an aquilline nose, firm, proud mouth and small, intense black eyes. She was carefully dressed and her small brown hand was laden with pearls, diamonds and turquoises." His mother insisted for one more game as she had won the first, but her son "Dauphin" as she called her son with love, refused because weather had cleared and he wanted to go out.

Mr. Joshua Rann, the parish clerk, came in to inform him (Mr. Irwine) about the increasing influence of the Methodists in the parish. He was violent against the preaching on the village ground and told how Dinah "laid hold O'chad's Bess as the girl's been i' fits welly ever since." Will Maskery as tying to defame the rector by calling him "a dumb dog" and "an idle shepherd". This was disturbing for Joshua and he wanted some action to be taken against him. This episode shows the conflict between the established church and the Methodists.

But Mr. Irwine had different view about Maskery. He found a better transformation in him after following Methodism. Thus, he did not bother about him and thought it was unwise to create fuss: "We must live and let live in religion as well as in other things"; we must not mind what others say behind our backs.

Just then Arthur Donnithorne "a tawny whiskend, brown-locked, clear-complexioned young man", and a captain in the Loamshire Militia asked for the permission to see the Rector. The Rector greeted him warmly and asked Joshua to carry on with his informations. He gave the sad news of Thias Bede's death and said that his family wanted his body to be buried next to the white Thorn on account of a dream that Lisbeth Bede had.

When Joshua departed, Arthur and Mr. Irwine started a discussion on Adam's qualities. Arthur informed that very soon he would try Adam's promotion as a manager of his woods. They decided to go to offer condolence to Adam that very afternoon. They were going to call at Hall Farm on the way, as Arthur would see some whelps there, while Mr. Irwine wanted to talk to Dinah.

After having their lunch their warm conversation continued. Arthur discussed about his forthcoming twenty-first birthday which he would celebrate lavishly as his grand father had given him complete freedom. At present Arthur was bored by the dull shut up life at the Chase. Mrs. Irwine informed Arthur that she will wear her best brocade dress that she had worn at his christening. She praised Arthur for looking after his family well, even after the death of his mother i.e. just after three months of his christening. She inspired him "If I don't like a man's looks, depend up it I shall never like him." Arthur was also interested in literature and thus informed her about the poem *The Ancient Mariner* which he had recently read. It was published in a volume of poems entitled *Lyrical Ballads.* This shows the literary progress taking place when the novel was being written.

After lunch Mr. Irwine went upstairs to see his weak and diseased sister, Anne. She was looked after by her sister Kate. This shows the caring and humble personality of Mr. Irwine.

The Miss Irwines were quite superfluous existences; inartistic figures crowding the canvas of life without any effect. They were middle-aged ladies very different from their handsome mother. Mr. Irwine being large-hearted ignored his mother's rudeness towards his sister. Unlike his mother he did not consider his sisters uninteresting or superfluous. He was criticised by the Methodists for faults and not considered as an "earnest man" by them. He was neither laborious nor obviously self-denying, nor very copious in alms-giving. But he was not vindictive and intolerant. He was tender to other men's failing, thus sympathetic which is required by religious people like him.

CHAPTER - 6

The Hall Farm

Now in this chapter we are introduced to Mrs. Poyser and Hetty Sorrel, her husband's niece. They lived in the Hall Farm which was under repair as it was ruining. The history of house was plain now "It was once the Hall; it is now the Hall Farm. It is an old red brick house. The kitchen and the farm-yard being the centres of its activity.

Everything was looking at its brightest at this moment. There is always a stronger sense of life when the sun is brilliant after rain. At about half past three, in the afternoon the activities at the farm speeded up. There is quite a concert of noises. The farm doors were wide open and they were busy mending the harness. Mrs. Poyser could not resist the amount of dirt the workmen had brought into the house at dinner time, but by this time everything was well clean. Dinah was mending household linen and Mrs. Poyser was ironing. Hetty Sorrel was making up the butter in the dairy. Mrs. Poyser was shrewish in her appearance but was a good looking woman not more than thirty eight. Her tongue was not less keen than her eyes. There were some resemblance and certain contrast between her and her niece. She was keen and Dinah was gentle in expression.

It was churning day which made it inconvenient to have the "whittaws' and resulted in Mr. Poyser angry against her maid Molly than usual. A three or four years girl interrupted her mother to say that her toy iron was cold. Totty, had sunny hair and was dear to her mother. This changed her tone. Totty asked for cake and in her impatience knocked down the bowl of starch before moving off to the dairy.

Mrs. Poyser took up her knitting after an exchange of sharp words which actually is a source of humour. She started speaking to Dinah about her mother who had died young. Dinah was brought up by her aunt Judith, the Methodist. Mrs. Poyser was not happy with Dinah's preaching. She thus enforced her to stop preaching and live with peace at Hall Farm. Dinah refused and explained, "I can no more help spending my life in trying to do what I can for the souls of others than you could help running if you heard little Totty crying at the other end of the house." Both of them at the end were still unconvinced with each other.

Mr. Irwine, the Rector and Captain Donnithorne arrived. Mrs. Poyser was excited, "If there isn't captain Donnithorne and Mr. Irwine a' coming into the yard ! I'll lay my life they're coming to speak about your preaching on the Green, Dinah; it's you must answer 'em, for I'm dumb." But Dinah assured her about her ideas. She didn't preach without direction. She follows the supreme power of the world of God.

The stately cordiality of Mr. Irwine and Captain gave comfort to Mrs. Poyser. She was relieved by their compliments and good-humour. The Captain seated comfortably to watch the dairy and discussed the farm and its life. He talked about its attractions, but Mrs. Poyser, as a tenant, pointed out all its bad points and requested him to arrange some new gates for the Five closes. She became frank and continued her complaints.

The captain was inspired to see the dairy. Mrs. Poyser said, "Indeed Sir it's not fit for you to go in.......for Hetty's in the middle o'making the butter........ She thought that the Captain was really interested in her milk pans. At last the captain was taken by Mrs. Poyser to the dairy.

CHAPTER - 7

The Dairy

The dairy was certainly worth looking as it was a model of cleanliness, with a fresh fragrance of cheese and butter. Hetty blushed a deep rose-colour when Captain entered and spoke to her. Hetty was a beauty "like that Kittens or very small downy ducks making gentle rippling noises.... a beauty with which you can never be angry". Hetty's cheek was like a rose-petal, that dimples played about her pouting lips, her curly hair fell in dark, delicate rings on her forehead and about her shell-like ears. Hetty's moments during the butter making showed up her curved arms and rounded neck to advantage. She was particularly clever at making and handled the churn with grace and mastery.

The Captain after admiring the dairy expressed the hope that Mrs. Poyser would be ready for the great celebration on the thirtieth of July, his 21st birthday. He asked Hetty "Will you promise me your hand for to dance?" Mrs. Poyser answered for her, but Arthur was determined to make Hetty look at him and speak to him. She smiled and blushed and thanked him shyly and showed her willingness to dance with him.

Arthur asked Mrs. Poyser to bring her children and Hetty also to his birthday party. The proud mother hurried off to bring her daughter and in the meantime Hetty and Arthur were left alone. The Captain asked Hetty to come and have a walk at the Chase. Hetty informed him that the following afternoon she is going to Mrs. Pomfret, the lady's maid to learn lace-mending. This shows interest of Arthur in Hetty and their future love-affair proceeds.

Mrs. Poyser and Totty interrupts their conversations. In order to win the confidence of Mrs. Poyser and visit the farm-house, he gave the child Totty five six-pences and she ran away gleefully. After biding "Good-bye" to Hetty and receiving bow from her, Arthur left the dairy to rejoin Mr. Irwine. Mr. Irwine was busy with Dinah in an interesting conversation.

CHAPTER - 8

A Vocation

Just when the gentlemen arrived Dinah stood up but still continued her mending of the sheet. Mr. Irwine was impressed by her and his first thoughts were "what a well-favoured countenance!" Dinah replied that she came from Snowfield, in Stonyshire. But her kind aunt made her to rest as she was ill. Thus, she had come here. Dinah informs about her relations with her aunt, the Methodist, but now it is only Mrs. Poyser whom she know as a relative. She very unexpectedly took preaching as she used to teach children, speak in the class and pray with the sick.

Mr. Irwine wanted to know the circumstances which led her to take up the preacher's profession. She also told him how on one Sunday she met Brother Marlowe, an aged preacher, and went with him to Hetton Deeps, a lead-mining village twelve miles from Snowfield. The old preacher became ill and Dinah had to inform the people waiting for his preaching. Suddenly she shuddered and felt a urge in her soul "I trembled as if I was shaken by a strong spirit entering my weak body......and I spoke the words that were given to me abundantly. People gathered around me and many wept for their sins. That was the beginning of my preaching, Sir and I've preached ever since."

Dinah replied that when God makes His presence felt in our hearts we are like the Burning Bush, and only the brightness of the Lord is seen, when Mr. Irwine asked her if she felt embarrassed in preaching. She had never received any hard treatment from any one at Snowfield. Mr. Irwine later enquired whether she had found her audience quiet and attentive in the previous evening. She responded in the pleasant, quiet villages, she found a strong deadness to the word, while in the towns there was a rich harvest of souls. "I think may be it is so because the promise is sweeter when this life is so dark and weary, and the soul gets more hungry when the body is ill at ease."

Dinah was informed about Thias Bede's death by Mr. Irwine before departing. This news touched her heart and she decided to go to Mrs. Bede to help her. Mr. Poyser and Captain now returned from the dairy and the gentleman took leave of them. When Hetty came to bring some leaves for packing butter, she came to know about death of Adam's father. This news hardly brought any change in her. This shows the frivolous, inconsiderate nature of Hetty.

CHAPTER - 9

Hetty's World

Hetty was obsessed by Arthur's image and had no feelings for Adam Bede's troubles. She knew about her beauty which could fetch her several lovers. One of the example was young Luke Britton of Broxton, a shabby, silent youngman of whom her uncle disapproved. The gardener of the Chase, Mr. Craig too was her ardent admirer. He was sensible enough, he was knock-kneed, had a queer sing-song in his talk and was almost forty. Adam Bede too was her admirer and she also knew that her uncle wants her to marry him as he thought he had excellent prospects. Hetty at the same time never gave Adam any serious attention though she knew that he is better among all her lovers. Neither she wanted to marry Mary Burge nor she completely neglected him.

Adam was unable to arouse her love. As he was poor, Hetty knew she could never enjoy the luxuries which she always dreamed about. Hetty was clever and she could understand Arthur's advances and thought that he can fare any amount of trouble for her. Hetty was a simple farmer girl uneducated and high class gentleman's superiority attracted her.

She thought of her walk to the Chase the next afternoon and wandered whether the Captain would try to meet her.

Arthur too was lost in her thoughts and while riding by Mr Irwine's side on the way to Adam's house remained absent-minded The Rector asked him what attracted him in the dairy. Arthur thought it would be waste to tell a lie so told the truth that he had gone to dairy to have a look at Hetty Sorrel. He was interested in her. But Mr. Irwine advised him not to pay much attention to her because she is a poor girl who will be fascinated by his richness and thus would prove an unfit wife for a poor man. Arthur did not show much attention and plainly promised to follow his advice.

CHAPTER - 10

Dinah Visits Lisbeth

It was five when Lisbeth came down with the key of the chamber in which her husband's body lay dead. It was a house of mourning. Lisbeth was busy in cleaning every object in the room. She wanted to perform all rites connected with the funeral perfectly as mark of respect for her dead husband. She once dreamed that he lay in the coffin in white Thorn, thus wanted to bury his body here. Later she locked the room where her husband's body was lying and came downstairs.

Lisbeth was busy the whole day, the kitchen had none of her attention that day and was soiled and untidy. Lisbeth felt it was right that the things look strange and disordered. Seth came to her and offered to make tea and to make the house comfortable. She was agitated and scolded him for imagining that she could ever be comfortable again, since her husband was dead. They broke down and moaned. She asked about Adam and Seth requested her not to wake him as he was much tired and asleep in the workshop. Adam was awakened by Gyp's bark, though Lisbeth went in quietly.

Lisbeth burst out immediately with her tale of grief into his ears and said that "thee'st got nobody now but thy old mother to torment thee and be a burthen to thee". In spite of all his sympathy Adam was irritated by Lisbeth's constant expression of grief and by her fears regarding his future wife. Adam could no more hear his mother and went out, but she too followed him and asked him to go up to his father along with her. Seth too joined them as Adam had asked him. Lastly Adam left his brother and mother as he could no more tolerate his mother's tale of suffering.

Lisbeth was rocking and giving a low moan, when suddenly she felt a hand placed, gently on her. It was Dinah who tried to console her "Dear sister, the Lord has sent me to see if I can be a comfort to you." Dinah introduced herself and after her tenderness Lisbeth improved. She was influenced by Dinah's face and voice. Lisbeth could regain some measure of self-control and asked. Seth to make tea. Dinah told her early life's tale and some how made her to clean the kitchen. Lisbeth was attracted by Dinah's cool and friendly nature, wanted her to stay with her for that night. This shows that Dinah's healing spirit made Lisbeth comfortable and Dinah had some true qualities of a preacher.

Lisbeth washed and put on a clean cap as Dinah agreed to stay and gave her examples from the *Bible* about David's behaviour after the death of his child. Lisbeth gained comfort and asked her to read her from the *Bible*. "And so there was earnest prayer, there was faith, love and hope-pouring itself forth that evening in the little kitchen."

CHAPTER - 11

In the Cottage

It was half past four the next morning when Dinah rose and began to dress quietly. Adam after having a long rest had already gone down before her. He washed his head and face with cold water. He went into the workshop to look out the wood for his father's coffin, intending that he and Seth should carry and make it at Burge's workshop, so that his mother might not see and hear the sad task going forward at home.

Adam's quick ear heard Dinah's light step but he foolishly thought that it might be Hetty. For he had been asleep when Dinah had arrived the previous evening and he did not know of her presence. He went into the kitchen and was greeted by her "It was like dreaming of the sunshine and awakening in the moon-light." Adam glanced at her pale serene face and this interaction made Dinah for the first time in her life, feel a painful self-consciousness.

Adam thanked her for comforting his mother and asked him "who was it took the news to the Hall Farm?" Dinah reported it was Mr. Irwine who told her and her aunt. She knew his interest in Hetty well, thus told him that everyone at the farm would be pleased to see him as soon as he could go there. She informed that she could spend the day with Lisbeth, but refused to stay with her for another night. It was her last evening there so she had to return to the farm in the evening. She said that she will leave the Hall Farm the next morning.

All of them were at breakfast at 6 o' clock and kitchen too was clean according to Lisbeth's desire. Dinah moved about, serving breakfast to others. Lisbeth enjoyed the porridge and admitted that it was tasty as she was well-pleased. She also admired the cleanliness of the house as it was "well enough for a make shift".

After finishing breakfast Adam went to the workshop to take the wood, for his father's coffin to Burgess. As soon as Lisbeth came to know this, she wailed that no one but Adam alone should make the coffin of his father. Adam agreed to make it at home but wanted Seth's help. Lisbeth moaned and refused to let Seth offer Adam any help. Seth somehow persuaded Adam to agree to make it alone. All of them went to the workshop, Dinah too followed them. She said to Seth that she would see him again that evening. She put out her hand and said, "You'll have sweet peace in your mind today, Seth for your tenderness and long-suffering towards your aged mother."

When Dinah had left, Adam remarked that he was not surprised that Seth loved her, for she had a face like a lily. Here Adam had expressed his feeling for a woman who is going to be his future life partner.

CHAPTER - 12

In the Wood

Hetty used to visit the Chase on every Thursday, and as it was a Thursday morning she was supposed to visit again. While dressing Arthur Donnithorne made up his mind not to visit Hetty, thus told his valet to be prepared to set off with him at eleven-thirty, as he wished to go out to Eagledale to fish, and stay there for a week or so.

Arthur felt himself very heroic though he was yet an inexperienced youngman. He confessed his faults more candidly, but he felt that these faults were all of a generous kind. He was a good fellow and his picture of the future, when he would come into the estate, were made up of contented, prosperous tenants adoring their land lord, who would be the model of an English gentleman. One of first good actions he would perform in that future should be to increase Irwine's income for the vicarage of Hayslope. He disapproved of the way in which his grandfather's stables were managed. There was a foolish head groom, John and his assistant of Loamshire, totally raw lads. When Arthur told John to have Meg and Rattler saddled, he learned to his annoyance that Meg was lame. As there was no other suitable horse, his plans had to be changed.

Arthur made a decision to go to Norburne instead of Eagledale on Rattler. He also demanded to have lunch with his friend Gwaine who lived there. He wanted to avoid Hetty and thus decided to stay there till 5 P.M. He thought it would be wiser for him not to take any notice of her, and follow Mr. Irwine's advice accordingly.

His plan did not work out accordingly. His first part of plan could be followed only upto 3 o'clock. While returning and avoiding to meet Hetty on way, he again came back in time. The novelist says, "It is the favourite stratagem of our passions to sham a retreat, and to-turn sharp round upon us at the moment we have made up our minds that the day is our own."

He was amazed at the force of his desire to see Hetty and decided that he desired to meet her so very much only because a serious affair had been made of an idle matter. Irwine had taken his interest in Hetty too seriously, and he would meet Hetty only to show him that he was wrong. It was really all Mr. Irwine's fault. He set off for the Hermitage, which stood in Fitree Grove, the way Hetty was sure to come. It was serene, beautiful afternoon and presently Hetty appeared walking down as Arthur went up to her. He too seemed agitated and foolish as he turned and walked by Hetty's side. They were alone together, and Hetty felt as if she was riding a cloud.

Arthur turned round and walked by Hetty's side. He started talking to her and very skilfully took her in his confidence and drilled the whole information from Hetty about her coming to the Chase every Thursday afternoon to have lessons in lace and stocking mending. And asked her, 'What, are you going to be—a lady's maid? She respond positively. Hetty always returned home at about eight in the evening that day Arthur offered to show her the Hermitage some other time. He asked whether Craig, the gardener sees her home everyday. A deep blush overspread Hetty's face and tears began to roll down her cheeks on being suspected by Arthur of being in love with Craig. Arthur slowly puts his arm around her and spoke tenderly. As he gazed into her dark, beseeching eyes, he was carried off his feet, and it no longer made any difference to him what sort of English she spoke or what was her status in life. Hetty's basket fell to the ground with a rattling noise. Finally they separated with beating hearts. Arthur helped her to pick up the material of basket and departed from her in a chilling tone. He went away hurriedly towards the Hermitage and left Hetty back in a confused situation.

When he reached the Hermitage, Arthur opened the door and walked uneasily up and down the little room. He became quite sure that he was in love with Hetty. He knew he was wrong on his part and decided he must not see her alone again. But his mind kept thinking of her.

Though he had made up his mind not to meet her again, still he allowed himself to think that it would be very nice if he could meet her that evening and could remove doubts from her mind. He would behave in a quite, kind way to prevent her from going home with her mind full of false thoughts regarding his love for her.

This chapter contains a piece of psycho-analysis. We can clearly see the analysis of thoughts going inside Arthur's mind.

CHAPTER - 13

Evening in the Wood

Mrs. Pomfret, the gardener's mother had quarrelled with the housekeeper that morning. As Hetty's mind had been disturbed by Arthur's cold behaviour she could not concentrate on her needle work. It was about quarter to eight when she prepared to leave though, still she was deeply excited. Her teacher, Mrs. Pomfret noticed the new flush of beauty on her face and thought that such loveliness was a bad omen for a girl in her position of life.

Hetty wanted to avoid Mr. Craig, thus she walked towards the Fitree Grove very fast. She hoped to meet Arthur and waled with frivolous dreams. "It was as if she had been wooed by a river god, who might any time take her to his wondrous halls below a watery heaven. She had never read a novel and her expectations were as formless as sweet, languid odours."

Hetty began to weep as she was disappointed because she couldn't meet Arthur on the way. Anyhow when he saw Hetty crying, he spoke softly and kindly to her. Actually he was walking along side path and happened to meet her. When she told him that she had been sobbing as she thought that he will not come to meet her. On hearing this he put his arm around her waist and kissed her. Both of them walked with excitement in their hearts till they reached the gate at the end of the wood.

Arthur patted Hetty's cheek and bade good-bye to her as he was feeling uncomfortable. He hurriedly walked back to the Chase, and was glad that he got out of the Grove which seemed to be haunted by his evil genius. He was disturbed because he was dissatisfied with himself, irritated and mortified. This was so, as he knew he could not marry a farmer's daughter. His mind disapproved his thought of flirting with Hetty. In order to protect himself any more from this stupid temptation, he decided to go to Bront on Rectory early morning next day. He went to Mr. Irwine for better advice.

This chapter shows the powers of self-consciousness of ones mind like that in Arthur.

CHAPTER - 14

Return Home

Arthur and Hetty separated form each other at the same

afternoon and practically at the same time when Dinah bade farewell to Lisbeth and left for home with Seth. Dinah and Seth who were walking towards the Hall Farm was, being warmly observed by Adam and his mother. She praised Dinah and said she wish Dinah to be her daughter-in-law but said that Dinah, certainly, did not care sufficiently for Seth to marry him.

Dinah and Seth reached the Hall Farm, just when Hetty had reached there. They were saying good-bye. Hetty liked Dinah, for she always put in a kind word for her when her aunt found fault with her, and often helped her with the tiresome Totty. Hetty could not understand Dinah's serious talks. Dinah spoke of the Bedes and praised Adam, but Hetty answered absent-mindedly, for her thoughts were full of Arthur. Dinah was greeted by Mr. Poyser in fatherly way. Mrs. Poyser was trying to soothe feverish Totty, so she remained seated in her rocking chair.

Hetty was late before she was scolded by her aunt. Hetty tried to excuse herself by saying that the clocks at the Farm seemed to go faster than those at the Chase. Hetty then went to have her food. Dinah remained seated with her Aunt and talked about the Bede family as she had already had her food with the Bedes.

Soon Hetty returned and tried to take Totty from her aunt but Totty leaned forward and slapped her. Dinah came forward and spoke soothingly to Totty, who came to her arms willingly. This shows difference in the nature of two nieces.

All of them prepared to go to bed. Mr. Martin Poyser spoke friendly to Hetty as he said good-night, "You did not mean to be late, I'll be bound, but your aunt's been worried today". His soothing words were for Hetty in order to comfort her.

CHAPTER - 15

The Two Bed-Chambers

In this chapter we can compare Dinah and Hetty for various characters. They slept on the second story in adjoining rooms. There was little light, so Hetty decided, to move about and undress with comfort. She could see herself reflected clearly in her old mirror which had dim blotches on its surface. It was difficult to get a good view of her head and neck unless she sat down, and when she sat down the brass handles of the drawers hurt her knees and she could not get near the glass comfortably. "But devout worshippers never allow inconveniences to prevent them from performing their religious rites, and Hetty this evening was more bent on her peculiar form of worship than usual," says the novelist ironically.

Hetty opened the drawers and brought out two wax candles and lighted them. Then she set up on the table a small, but clear, looking glass. She felt proud of her beauty when she let down her dark silken ringlets. She was lost in Arthur's dream. She felt herself prettier than any other woman. She imagined she heard Arthur's soft voice repeating the things he had said to her in the wood. Then she took out an old black scarf and a pair of large ear rings from her drawer. They looked bright and beautiful like those, gold ones worn by ladies though they were artificial. She admired her own beauty and thought how much Captain Arthur loved her. She supposed he would marry her secretly first, and then everything would settle down well. She started dreaming about the riches of the Captain. Hetty thought that she would be a grand lady, ride in her coach, and dress for dinner in a brocade gown, with feathers in her hair. At the thought of all this splendour, Hetty rose and little mirror fell with a bang on the floor. She gave a start, and then began to pace backwards and forwards with the old black scarf round her shoulders and the glass earings in her ears. "How pretty and sweet is a prize for any man." It was in this way that Adam often thought of her, "people who love dowy peaches are apt not to think of the stone and sometimes jar their teeth terribly against it." Here we observe ironic comment on her beauty and frivolity.

Hetty and Arthur had different views about each other. Arthur, thought of her a dear affectionate little thing, but Hetty's mind always pictured herself as a main figure in fine clothes, admired by all. She liked to be with Arthur near her so that she would forget her past life. Mr. Poyser always defend her niece. But Mrs. Poyser often commented on Hetty's vanity and frivolity. She said that she was no better "than a peacock."

Hetty was dressed in scarf and earrings when suddenly she started to hear a tap on her bolted door. She hurriedly blew out the candles and put them in the drawer. There was a second tap but she had in time to remove the earings and her scarf fell to the ground. Hetty vexed and confused, went to open the door and found Dinah there. She had come to bid her good-bye as she was going to leave early in the next morning.

Dinah was sensible and serious than Hetty. She sat for sometime at her window looking out over the peaceful fields and meadows, when she went inside her bedroom. She closed her eyes and prayed for the dear friends she would so soon be leaving. She was disturbed by the sound in Hetty's room, but then it was all calm. So she decided to undress. She knew that Hetty is unprepared for serious matters of life and thus she was worried about Hetty. In this confused state of mind, she opened her *Bible* to follow the right way and read the words, "And they all wept sore, and fell on Paul's neck and kissed him." These lines were enough for Dinah to understand the situation and without any second thought she went to Hetty's room.

Both of them were different. As Dinah wore a long, white night dress while Hetty was different. Dinah's sweet and soft voice irritated Hetty, but she was glad that Dinah did not seem to notice her ear-rings. Dinah offered her help if she needed and said that she can depend on her for any help. She took Hetty's hand as she told her, that problems do come to everyone and she is quite young. If she needs strength she should pray to God for it.

Hetty remained untouched with her affectionate words. She began to cry as fear possessed her soul. Dinah did not realise that a pleasure seeking nature always shrinks from the possibility of pain. Hetty pushed her away when Dinah tried to kiss her as a stirring of a Divine impulse.

Dinah went quietly to her room and prayed for Hetty. Hetty in her dreams, was soon in the woods again. She dreamed of Arthur and his love of her.

This chapter gives a clearcut contrast of Dinah's and Hetty's nature.

CHAPTER 16

Links

Arthur Donnithorne wanted to talk to Mr. Irwine alone therefore he rose early next morning as Mr. Irwine would be at breakfast at 9:30. When he reached Brontes, he saw Adam at some distance and thus hurried to reach him. Arthur and Adam, both had mutual respect and admiration for each other, he had taken some lessons in carpentry from Adam when he was a young boy of eleven. Arthur warmly greeted Adam and chatted in a friendly way about Adam's future. Arthur admired the strength of Adam and thought that in a fight Adam would knock him down completely. But Adam being a learned person replied that he would never fight any man unless he behaved like a scoundrel. This is actually an irony of Sophocles because Arthur is to behave in times to come like a scoundrel and Adam would fight with him.

Arthur reached in time to have breakfast with Mr. Irwine. This made Mr. Irwine quite happy. Arthur's resolution to confess to the

Rector about his flirtation with Hetty weakened as soon as he found himself with him, and he decided to wait and talk about it later.

During their conversation, Mr. Irwine repeated a remark his mother had made : 'I'll never risk a single prophecy on Arthur until I see the woman he falls in love with". Arthur cared for other people's opinions very much so he decided to avoid Hetty. He thought he would solve his problems himself, but discussed with the Rector the possibility of a man, who is firm. And such a strongman is still carried away by the woman and betray into folly by a combination of circumstances. Mr. Irwine replied, "Why yes, a man can't very well steal a bank note unless the bank note lies within convenient reach; but he won't make us think him an honest man because he begins to howl at the bank note for falling in his way."

The Rector felt from this indirect discussion that Arthur wanted to tell him something and asked him if it was some temptation which faced him that he wanted to talk of, Arthur refused for such temptation, but he soon dismissed the idea and changed the topic.

Arthur's approach towards sin increases as his one opportunity of being saved had missed because of his own intention.

BOOK II

CHAPTER - 17

In Which the Story Pauses a Little

In this chapter Mr. Irwine's character is well discussed. It opens with recollection of Mrs. Poyser and Adam discussing the qualities of Mr. Irwine. He is contrasted with the new Rector Mr. Ryde who had succeeded him twenty years later. Mr. Irwine had good influence on the people. He may not have been a perfect clergyman, but he was loved and respected by the people of Broxton and Hayslope. Mr. Irwine's influence in his parish was a more wholesome one than that of the zealous Mr. Ryde. Adam had once remarked, "It isn't notions set people doing the right thing-its feelings..."

Mr. Ryde was away at a distance and he wrote books, but in mathematics and nature he was just ignorant. He meant well, but was short-tempered and often scolded the people for trifling faults. He lived above his income and was much more against the Dissenters than Mr. Irwine had been.

Mr. Irwine was greatly admired by Adam and others. He was a thorough gentleman and kind to all. He was not a great preacher. He didn't go into deep spiritual experience. His sermons were short moral homilies, but he lived upto his teachings and made people love him. He had the love and respect of the people which Mr. Ryde could not get. This chapter indicates Mr. Irwin's better position than Mr. Ryde.

CHAPTER - 18

Church

The chapter opens with the preparations for Mr. Thias Bede's funeral. Mrs. Poyser got herself ready and was waiting for other to leave for funeral service which was to take place in the village church at 2 o' clock. It was Hetty who took maximum time to dress up. Thus Mrs. Poyser said, ... "dizening yourself as if there was a wedding i'stid of a funeral?" Hetty came to church in her Sunday hat and frock, evoking as if she had been made of roses. There was just pink and white about her.

"The little percussion set off for church : Mrs. Poyser in her plain bonnet and shawl : Mr. Poyser in his Sunday suit of drab with a red and green coat, a green watch ribbon, and with a yellow silk handkerchief around his neck. Marty and Tommy, boys of nine and seven, were dressed in little tailed coats and knee-breaches. Totty, wearing her red and black necklace outside her tippet, was carried by Molly. Old Martin Poyser, aged seventy-five opened the gate for the family and watched them until they disappeared behind a bend in the hedge."

When Mr. Poyser and his family proceeded towards the funeral of Thias, they walked through the fields. Mrs. Poyser commented upon everything she observed. She passed remarks on everything that she saw on the way. She expressed her dislike for the short-horned cows as they have low butter fat in their milk, the legs and appearance of her daughter Totty. Dinah's and Hetty's attractive looks were discussed by her. Molly and the boys were behind, for they stopped continually to look at birds on the trees and hedges. Mrs. Poyser sent back Hetty to tell them to hurry up. Marty avoided his mother's scolding by telling her that they had found the speckled turkey's nest, for which he claimed the promise reward of half a crown.

Poysers were already late by the time they reached the village, a number of people were already gathered in the churchyard. Several of the farm labourers formed a group around the grave under the white Thorn, where the burial ceremony was going on, but Chad Cranage and the rough workmen kept away from it. Martin Poyser too joined the group which rest of his family members went inside the church.

Lisbeth and her sons went into the church after the funeral service, other men also followed them. "The old grey aoken pews, the buff-washed walls, the touches of crimson towards the channels and the crimson altar cloth, embroidered with golden rays by Miss Lydia's own hand, gave a pleasing appearance to the shabby interior of the church." The choir had two narrow pews to themselves, and Joshua Rann set among them as the principal singer and returned to his desk when the singing was over. Adam sat with his mother, instead of his usual place in the choir.

Hetty was not without a companion, for she held in her hand the wonderful pink and white plant given by Mr. Craig. She is heartless and frivolous. She was preoccupied with the thought that Arthur, whom she had not seen since their meeting in the wood would come into the church. Hetty's heart beats fast as the door swung open. But old Mr. Donnithorne followed by Miss Lydia and the servants entered. Hetty almost cried with disappointment as Arthur was not with them. Her tears began to fall as she knelt down. Molly offered her smelling salts, thinking she was tired and ill. But Hetty peevishly turned away from her and tried to control herself. She would have endured anything rather than to be laughed at. Adam admired the beauty of Hetty as he glanced at her on rising and his feelings for her seemed to blend with devotion the service inspired in him. The selfishness of Hetty is well brought out now as she thinks more of Arthur than of the dead father of Adam.

Joshua Rann was reading the funeral prayer which was impressive, for nature had poured some of her music into this honest, conceited soul and given him a fine sonorous voice and a musical ear. The singing of the funeral psalm entranced his sense of his own importance. Mr and Mrs. Poyser wailed to talk with Lisbeth and her sons after the completion of service. Hetty after receiving the white and pink plant from Mr. Craig, came to know a very important news about Arthur's absence. Soon the conversation turned to war with the French. Adam asked whereabouts of Arthur. Craig replied that he had gone to Eagledale for a bit of fishing, but would probably be back in a few days. This news helped Hetty to know that Arthur was not present in Hayslope. But she was equally puzzled and uneasy to learn that Arthur voluntarily had gone. She could not understand why he had gone away in this way. This chapter shows Hetty's frivolous and conceited nature.

CHAPTER - 19

Adam on a Working Day

When on the next morning Adam was marching towards his place of work at a country house about three miles off, he was lost in Hetty's thoughts. He felt the melancholy look on her face the previous day was a sign of sympathy.

Adam's interest in Hetty made him realise that his father's death proved lucky. It had brought the prospect of marriage nearer, but there were still difficulties in the way. He was not sure of Hetty's love for him. He doubt that his mother too would not approve his marriage even if Hetty loved him. He had not saved enough to furnish even a small cottage for himself for he had paid a large amount to secure Seth's release from the military. Adam thought he and Seth might carry on a little business for themselves, by buying a small stock of superior wood and making articles of household furniture. He made up his mind to meet Hetty that evening, for he felt a strong desire to be near her and speak to her.

Adam worked with all his energy and frequently sang out loudly some solemn psalm tunes. Adam was not a genius. But he was no ordinary character among workmen. He had to work very hard to learn to read and write and also to memorise the psalms he sang. He had read many Bartle Massey's book, such as Bunyan's *The Pilgrim's Progress*, but at present he had little leisure for study. In this chapter we get clear and deeper image of Adam.

CHAPTER - 20

Adam Visits the Hall Farm

Adam came back from his work and got ready to go to Hall Farm by a quarter to seven. Lisbeth repeatedly enquired Adam why he is wearing his best clothes to visit the Poysers. These questions annoyed Adam and he hurriedly went out. His mother asked him if he is angry. He tried to explain to her in a kindly manner that now he had grown up, she must cease treating him like a child.

On reaching the Hall Farm Adam found Mrs. Poyser in the dairy and chatted with her, while she gave him a basin of whey to drink. It was whey, "with a flavour so dedicate that one can hardly distinguish it from an odour, and with that soft, gliding warmth that fills one's imagination with a still happy dreaminess." Mrs. Poyser asked Adam to convey a message to Hetty, that she must sent in Totty. Totty was gathering red currants and Adam went through the large farm house garden. He was attracted by Totty's cheery-stained face, so kissed her and sent her in to her mother.

As Hetty felt that someone was near her she startled violently and dropped her basket of red currants. On finding Adam, she blushed, and his heart beat with happiness. Adam helped her and as they worked together his heart was overjoyed with happiness and thus could not speak anything.

Hetty was lost in the thoughts of Arthur. Adam's arrival roused her thoughts. Hetty for the first time felt Adam's tenderness which soothed her. She wanted to be treated lovingly and soothed and consoled, for it was so hard to bear this long period of absence and apparent indifference after those happy moments of love.

When Adam finished his work, he took the basket and offered Hetty his arm. As both of them walked along Hetty asked him if he had ever been to Eagledale, and how long it took him to go there. Hetty attentively listened to his reply. She was equally glad to know that Arthur could quickly return if he wished as it was not a long distance.

Adam gave Hetty a beautiful rose, and she stuck it in her hair. The tender admiration in Adam's face was slightly shadowed by his disapproval of her love of ornament. He told her that a beautiful woman's face needed no ornaments or cosmetics. He gave her an example of Dinah Morris as she looked very attractive even in her plain Methodist cap.

Hetty and Adam entered the house, by this time everybody was back from work on the farm. Mr. Poyser and his father were seated. Mrs. Poyser had laid the cloth for supper. Hetty went upstairs to see Totty and the others were soon seated at the table. Molly came with some drinks, after some time. Her eyes were fixed on the vessels she carried. Therefore she unprepared for any rebuke and punishment. When Mrs. Poyser started to scold her for having taken so long time, she tried to hurry, her foot was caught in her apron and she fell with a crash. Mrs. Poyser continued to scold her, this made Molly very miserable. She wept and shed tears profusely.

Mrs. Poyser went to the cupboard. She took out a brown and white coloured jug, as she was already trembling with anger, and in a hurry, the jug fell down from her hands. There was an outburst of laughter which continued as Hetty, who seemed to Mrs. Poyser to be a phantom, came into view. She was dressed in a black gown of her aunt's with one of Dinah's high-crowned net caps on her head. The men were amused. But Mrs. Poyser was angry and ordered Hetty to go up and change her dress.

Somehow at the end of the supper, Mrs. Poyser regained her good humour. Adam stayed to talk for a while and Hetty sat near the window picking the currants. After biding good bye he went to see Bartle Massey. Everybody present there thought that Hetty would be lucky to get Adam as a husband. Because she would be able to ride in her own spring cart. Nobody could see the toss of her head indicating her scorn. To ride in a spring cart seemed to her to be a miserable alternative to splendid carriages which Arthur could offer.

CHAPTER - 21

The Night School and The School Master

In this chapter we are introduced to a minor character but an interesting one. His name is Bartle Massey who is the village school-master. He is painstaking and patient with his pupils. As Adam entered his house, he found that teaching was in progress. Massey was teaching his three most backward pupils—a stone cutter of twenty four, a brick maker, Brimstone, who had been a poacher but was now a converted Methodist anxious to learn to read the *Bible*; and a thin, wiry man who was a dyer, confident that he would save himself labour and expense if he could learn to read. Bartle Massey's face had a gentle, kind expression in spite of his formidable, irregular nose, wide brow, and grey, bristly hair. It gave him great pleasure to see these three big men painfully making out such simple sentence as "The grass is green." For such grown up pupils, he had no severe epithets and no rebukes.

When reading of lessons was over, two young boys of age between sixteen and eighteen came up with their sums. They were badly scolded for their mistakes and lack of progress : "Never come to me again if you can't show that your've been working with your own head instead of thinking you can pay for the men who work for you." Other students had their writing books to show in various stages of progress from pot-books to round texts, Jacob Story's 2's all had their tops turned, the wrong way, but he observed that it was a letter, "You hardly even wanted."

After completion of the teaching work the pupil went away. Adam put out the candles and followed Massey. He was lame but still quite active. They went into the kitchen. Massey's bitch Vixen welcomed her master. Adam was surprised to see two puppies there and remarked that he thought a family was against the law in Massey's home. "What's the use o' law when a man's once such a fool as to let a woman into his house?" said Bartle. Bartle explained that the birth of the puppies was the cause of his absence from church on Sunday. Thus it becomes clear that Bartle was a woman hater.

Then Massey had his meal. Adam noticed that the house and furniture were perfectly clean. When he had, had his supper at the Hall Farm, he looked on while Massey ate and talked about his favourite subject i.e., the shortcomings of women and the superiority of men. "I tell you there isn't a thing under the sun that needs to be done at all but what a man can do better than a woman, unless it's bearing children, and they do that in poor, make shift way." Adam doubt Bartle's view of women and marriages. He didn't know if they are based on his own experiences or not because nobody knew where he had lived before he came and settled in the village twenty years earlier.

After having their meal, they had a nice talk. Massey told Adam that Satchell, the Squire's inefficient estate foreman, had a paralytic stroke. He felt sure that Adam would one day get this job, but Adam explained that he was in the bad books of the Squire for he had given some offence to him. Miss Lydia, the Squire's daughter, had asked Adam to make a frame for a screen; he had taken a great deal of trouble over it; and she was much pleased with it. Later he asked her one pound thirteen shillings for it. But the Squire had said that it was worth no more than a pound. Then he told Lydia that he would make her a present of the screen for, "If I'm paid. I can't take a smaller price than I asked because that 'ud be saying like I'd asked more than was just". He had then taken his leave. In the evening the Squire's footman brought him one pound and thirteen shillings demanded by him. Since then, the Squire had not been very happy with him.

BOOK III

CHAPTER - 22

Going to the Birthday Feast

It was thirtieth of July, one of those half dozen warm days. It was Arthur's 21st birthday which was to be celebrated with due pomp and hospitality, suitable for the dignity of the heir to the estate. The bells rang merrily as if conscious of the joyfull event. No rain had fallen for a few days and the weather was perfect for that time of the year. Hetty too was preparing herself for the feast. She, admiring herself in her mirror, wore her evening frock of pink and white with real lace which her aunt had lent her. She unlocked the drawer that had her valuables. She took out a pretty small box lined with satin of white colour. It had a pair of gold and pearl earrings. She put them on for a while as she could not wear them outside her bedroom. Because these were presents from Arthur given to her the previous week. The locket presented to her by Arthur was also concealed by her. She suspends it from her chain of dark brown berries and would conceal it inside her frock. Hetty was not quite as fond of the locket as of the earrings though it was a handsome large locket, with enamelled flowers at the back and a beautiful gold border round the glass, which showed a light brown, slightly waving lock, forming a background for two little dark rings.

All the other members of the family were waiting when Hetty came downstairs. They all were dressed in their Sunday clothes. They set off in the covered cart and changed greetings on the way with many acquaintances for all Broxton and all Hayslope were invited to the birthday feast. The church bells had struck up again now a last tune, before the ringers came down the hill to have their share of the festival. The music played by the band of the Benefit Club could be heard as the Poysers arrived, a wagon full of old people including old Father Taft came and the guests were taken to a special table. The Poyser party wisely struck across the grass under the shade of the trees. The fine old remnant of the Chase is a plain square mansion built in the reign of Queen Anne and connected at one end with the ruins of an old Abbey, seemed asleep in the hot mid-day.

It made Hetty quite sad to look at it, as Arthur would be with the grand company, where he could not know her presence. At the time, Arthur, looking handsome in his blue frock-coat, was walking with Mr. Irwine in the cool cloisters of the old church, where the long tables were laid for the humbler tenants and farm-servants. They later went up the stone staircase to the gallery to see the dinner tables for the more important tenant.

When Mr. Irwine asked about Adam, then Arthur told Mr. Irwine and indirectly to the readers that the Squire intended to employ Adam as superintendent of the woods at a salary of a guinea a week. Adam accepted the proposal and Arthur had invited him to dine with the more important tenants, for he intended to announce the appointment to them. He wanted to ask them to drink to Adam's health. He wanted to create a special place for him in Adam's heart. He would thus honour Adam, and make him feel that he was a favourite with him.

The irony is best displayed as Arthur wanted to befriend him, but very soon they would come to blows over Hetty. Thus, their friendship would come to an end.

CHAPTER - 23

Dinner-Time

When Adam heard that he was to dine up-stairs with the large tenants, he felt uncomfortable. His mother and Seth were going to dine in the cloisters below. Adam told about his uncomfort to his brother. But Seth persuaded him to go up. Adam went alongwith Bartle as he was too shy to join the Poyser group on this public occasion.

Bartle Massey was called to settle the matter, of the President's election. He suggested that the fattest man should sit at the top and the second fattest at the bottom. It created a humourous situation. Martin Poyser was called upon to sit at the top as President. And Mr. Casson, landlord of the Donnithorne Arms, sat at the bottom end as Vice-President.

Casson actually disliked Adam and when he suddenly noticed his presence, and remarked, "Well, Mr Bede, you have never dined here before, as I remember." Adam replied that he was there as the Captain had invited him. Several people gave him a warm welcome.

Slowly the conversation turned to singing and music, and Bartle Massey remarked to Mr. Craig, who was praising Scotch tunes, that, "The Scotch tunes are just like a scolding nagging woman. They go on with the same thing over and over again and never come to a reasonable end."

Adam could see Hetty who was sitting at the next table. She appeared charming to him though she was pettishly annoyed with Totty, who persisted in putting her dusty shoes on her frock. Marry Burge hoped that Adam would reflect on the small value of beauty in a woman whose temper was bad. But Hetty saw many watching her and gave Adam one of her brightest smiles. Actually Hetty had no special intention behind the smile, but it was like wine to Adam.

CHAPTER - 24

The Health-Drinking

When the dinner was over and the great cask of birthday ale was brought up, Mr. Poyser moved aside and two chairs were placed at the head of the table. When the young Squire entered, with Mr. Irwine by his side, everyone stood up, and this moment of homage was very agreeable to Arthur. He carried a great deal for the good-will of these people and their show of respect was pleasing to him. Mr. Poyser, who knew that he was expected to make a speech, expressed slowly and deliberately the good wishes of the company to Arthur, on the occasion of his birthday. He told the young Squire how much he was esteemed for, "We've never known anything of you but that was good and honourable". He thanked him for the good dinner and called on the company to drink to his health. Later Arthur said, "I thank you all, my good friends and neighbours, for the good opinion of me, and the kind feelings towards me..." His conscience had pricked him during Mr. Poyser's speech, but he re-assured himself that no harm would come of his flirtation with Hetty. He thought when he would be alone with Hetty, he would certainly explain to her that she must not think seriously of him. This dilemma going inside Arthur's mind gives us a peep into his soul and reveals to us his inherent nobility.

Arthur thanked his guests for their good wishes. He told his future plans for betterment and asked to drink to the health of his grandfather, the present Squire. The toast was drunk with all the enthusiasm that was wanting to the last and it certainly was the most picturesque moment. Arthur then praised Adam Bede and announced his appointment as a manager of the woods; finally he praised Mr. Irwine and asked them to drink to his health.

Mr. Irwine in his speech thanked his parishioners for their expression of good will, and in the end praised Adam. When he had finished, Arthur stood up, and filling his glass, said, "A bumper to Adam Bede, and may he live to have sons as faithful and clever as himself." Adam was quite moved by this honour. But he felt no shyness or self-consciousness. In his speech, he thanked Arthur, without any trace of slavish flattery. People differed in their views about the speech. Some thought he seemed too proud and not thankful enough; others that his speech was straightforward, dignified and becoming.

Arthur walked around, speaking to mothers and patting children. But he did not dare go near Hetty. He just bowed to her as he passed by the opposite side of the table and she felt thoroughly miserable. Arthur, who had seemed so near, was separated from her, "as the hero of a great procession is separated from a small outsider in the crowd."

CHAPTER - 25

The Games

The great dance was not to begin until 8 o'clock, but there was music always at hand and those who wished to dance could do so on the grass outside.

Meantime, when the sun had moved off the great open space in front of the house, the games began. There were well-soaped poles to be climbed by the boys and youths, races, weight lifting and a donkey race. Soon after 4 o'clock, splendid old Mrs. Irwine, in her damask satin and jewels and black lace, was led out by Arthur, to her raised seat under the tent from where she was to distribute the prizes. Old Mr. Donnithorne followed with Mrs. Irwine; Mr. Irwine brought Miss Lydia; and Mr. Irwine came last with his pale sister Anne.

Mrs. Irwine in her speech said that it was the last celebration she was likely to see, unless Arthur decided to marry soon. She advised him to choose a handsome bride and one who could take care of him. She asked questions about the different tenants, and on seeing Hetty inquired about her. "She's a perfect beauty I've never seen anything as pretty since my young days. What a pity such a beauty as that should be thrown away among the farmers". Hetty blushed because she had heard herself praised but Arthur pretended not to hear about Hetty. Arthur was pleased because he valued Mrs. Irwine's opinion highly.

Now came the time for prize distribution. Bessy Cranage, red in the face from exertion, came up to receive her prize for the sack race. Bessy was wearing her earrings again and was decked out in whatever finery she could get. When Arthur heard that her prize was a gown of coarse cloth and a piece of flannel he asked his aunt if there was nothing more suitable for a young girl. "I have bought nothing but what is useful and substantial", said Miss Lydia. Bessy felt dejected as she saw the ugly, heavy, gown and Arthur made up his mind to give her some money as a present later on. Since Arthur had himself decided prizes for men, therefore they all were completely satisfied.

Wiry Ben proposed to amuse the company, before the gentry went to dinner with impromptu dance. Joshua Rann played for him on the fiddle. Ben was thoroughly absorbed in dance and looked like a dancing monkey. His antics aroused the amusement of the gentry, the admiration of Martin Poyser, and the scorn of Mrs. Poyser. Adam Bede hasn't had much fun.

CHAPTER - 26

The Dance

Arthur had chosen the entrance hall for the ballroom. It was large, airy and with the advantage of the wide door opening into the garden as well as other rooms. It had been decorated with green boughs and plants and the lights were charmingly arranged in coloured-paper lamps. The stairs of the stone staircase were covered with cushions to serve as seats for the children. Only the chief tenants were invited to the ball in this hall; the cottagers were to dance separately in the Abbey gallery. It was a pretty scene outside the house.

Seth and his mother left, but Adam, at Arthur's request, stayed on. Lisbeth grumbled at this; but when Adam offered to go home she insisted that he must stay to please the Captain. Then he hurried to join the Poyser group and Mrs. Poyser persuaded him to take part in the dancing. He asked Hetty for a dance and she promised him the fourth one.

They went to hall for the dance at 8 o'clock. Very soon Arthur entered in his regimental uniform, leading Mrs. Irwine to a dais. The old Squire before taking his seat next to her, walked round the hall and spoke politely to the tenants. But he was particularly civil to Mrs. Poyser, who immediately suspected that he must have some plot against her.

As the dancing began, Hetty's heartbeat fastened because Arthur proposed her for the dance. She was afraid that she would cry, if he gave no signs of his love for her, but as he took her hand he pressed it. The look she gave him caused him both pain and joy, for he was delighted as well as afraid. He felt that he could give three years of his youth for the pleasure of abandoning himself freely to his passion for Hetty. But he could not do so. He could never marry her as such was the distance between them.

When the third dance ended, Adam went to claim Hetty's hand for the fourth dance. Adam was waiting eagerly to dance with Hetty. While Molly went to fetch shawls and bonnets, Hetty was holding the sleeping Totty for a few moments. Adam offered to hold the child, and as he took her she awoke. The child struck out with her left fist at Adam's arm and with her right caught at the string of beads round Hetty's neck. The string was broken and the beads and locket were scattered on the floor. "My locket, my locket", Hetty said in a loud, frightened whispher to Adam. While picking it up, he saw the glass with light and dark hair beneath it. He turned it over and saw the enamelled gold back. Molly returned and Hetty took the locket with an air of indifference, as if it was of no importance.

They took their places for the dance, but Adam was puzzled and alarmed, and wondered if Hetty had a lover. How could she have a lover without his being aware of the fact? He did not even suspect that the lover could be Arthur, a person so well known to him. His pleasure in the dance had gone, and they were both glad when it ended. It was the real irony of the life.

Adam could no longer stay there, so he went back home with several possibilities in his mind. One of possibility could be that Hetty loved finery and had probably bought the locket herself. It was impossible that she should have a lover unknown to him. Her agitation might have been due to the fact that she knew Adam disapproved of finery and that she did not wish to displease him. Adam at least went to bed comforted, having woven for himself an ingenious web of probabilities.

Arthur and Hetty had one more dance during the course of which he said to her in low hurried tones, "I shall be in the wood the day after tomorrow at seven; come as early as you can". They both wished that the dance would last forever—Arthur telling himself that it was the last flirtation with Hetty he meant to indulge in.

Mrs. Poyser decided that it was time to go home. And Hetty had danced with the young Squire. Mr. Poyser was in his best mood. He complimented his wife on her dancing and said to Hetty, "It'll serve you to talk on, Hetty, when you're an old woman—how you danced with the young Squire the day he cam'o ge". Hetty indeed had enjoyed a lot with Arthur, but she is unknown to the tragedy that will be caused by Arthur.

BOOK IV

CHAPTER - 27

A Crisis

Nearly three weeks after the birthday feast the eighteenth of August was one of these days, when the sunshine looked brighter in all eyes. Adam was busy working in the workshop of Jonathan. He had accepted the job which Arthur had offered him but he continued to work for Burgess until some satisfactory person could be found to take place. He had high hopes of getting married to Hetty, because she had behaved very kindly towards him on the two occasions on which he had met her after the dance.

Adam wanted to meet Hetty. So one evening when he was told she had gone to Treddleston, he followed her and met her climbing over a stile quite out of the Treddleston road. She explained that she had gone out of her way because it was so pleasant to be out doors. When they reached the Hall Farm, Hetty begged Adam to come in and he could not refuse. Mrs. Poyser did not rebuke Hetty for coming late because Adam was with her.

Adam knew that Hetty on that particular day will be going to the Chase to sew with the Lady's maid. So he thought of doing maximum work by the evening. A few days later Adam was busy with some repairs at the Chase Farm, for which it was rumoured, the Squire had a small tenant.

It was nearly seven when Adam had finished his work, and on his way home he stopped at the Chase stables. Mr. Craig told him of the send-off that the servants planned to give Arthur who was leaving Hayslope in two day's time.

Adam decided to go through the Grove in order to shorten his way. While he walked along the broad, winding path, he noted the tall beeches and paused to examine one of them closely. For the rest of the life he remembered that moment; as he stepped away from the beech tree, his eyes fell on two figures about twenty yards ahead, standing opposite to each other with clasped hands, about to part; and while they were bending to kiss, Gyp gave a sharp bark. They separated with a start. Hetty hurried off and Arthur walked slowly towards Adam. Arthur looked flushed and excited and still under the influence of wine he had drunk at dinner. He felt confident that he could laugh the thing off and explain it away. He walked to Adam with carelessness.

Adam had not moved. Now everything became clear to him—the locket and Hetty' behaviour. Arthur did not notice the look on Adam's face and tried to explain the incident with a few casual remarks. Adam in harsh voice asked Arthur to stop and said "I mean, sir, that you don't deceive me by your light words." He knew that this was not their first meeting. "Well, sir, what then?" Asked Arthur. Adam blames him for being a selfish, light minded scoundrel who had filled Hetty's head with the thought of him so that she would never love a man whom she could marry and who would be a good husband to her. Arthur perceived that he did not have full knowledge of the affair and could still be deceived as to the true position. He admitted he was wrong in flirting with Hetty but that she would forget the whole thing as he was going away from the village.

Adam was filled with anger at the thought that he had been robed of Hetty by one whom he trusted, that after telling Arthur how deeply he loved Hetty. He threw off his coat and cap and challenged him to a fight.

Arthur's heart was beating violently. The discovery that Adam loved Hetty, was a shock which made him for the moment see himself in the light of Adam's indignation. Adam's words of hatred and contempt—the first he had ever heard—touched him to the quick. He begged Adam to go away and did his best to avoid a fight. But Adam provoked him with insults and soon they were fighting fiercely.

Arthur was no match to Adam, who was much superior to him in physical strength. Arthur fell down and lay motionless after receiving a blow from Adam. Adam was horror-struck, for Arthur appeared to him to be dead.

The Arthur-Hetty love affair means tragedy for all concerned. This chapter has been well titled for the fight is a crisis in the life of Arthur, Adam and Hetty.

CHAPTER - 28

A Dilemma

It was only after a few minutes Adam perceived a look of consciousness in Arthur's face. He was much relieved. He brought water from the brook in his basket and after a time Arthur was well enough to rise and he asked Adam to help him to walk to the Hermitage. When he opened the door, Adam was surprised to see a comfortable room with all signs of frequent use. He found some brandy, which he gave to Arthur. And then he decided to go to the Chase and bring some more brandy.

Both Adam and Arthur were relieved to be apart from each other for a short time. While Adam was away, Arthur rose feebly, lighted a candle and went round the room. He picked up a woman's little pink silk handkerchief and hide it deep down into a water-paper basket. Adam soon returned while slowly drank brandy and water. They sat in an uneasy silence. After sometime Adam, apologized for his behaviour and harsh judgement and Arthur was in wretched position of being under compulsion to deceive Adam to the utmost. He said he forgave him, and offered to shake hands and be friends once again. But Adam said that Arthur must first explain his behaviour towards Hetty. Arthur tried to explain that there had been nothing serious in the flirtation. Adam was worried about Hetty, so he looked at things from Hetty's point of view. He insisted that she had been gravely wronged by Arthur's love making. He blamed him that he should have not made love to her, knowing well that he could never marry her. He was fully determined to do what was good for Hetty and asked Arthur to write to her a letter, telling her that he could not marry her, therefore she should put an end to her false hopes. Adam was firm that Arthur should write the letter though

Arthur tried to avoid the letter writing. "Either tell me she can never be my wife tell me you've been lying or else promise me what I've said".

Arthur promised to write the letter after an inward struggle. Adam later helped him to go home. Adam said that he would call the following day to take the letter, and himself deliver it to Hetty. But Arthur entered the house without answering his "good-night". In this chapter we come to know the strong and weak characterstics of Adam and Arthur.

CHAPTER - 29

The Next Morning

Arthur did not pass a sleepless night infact he slept long and well. He awoke the next morning much troubled and restless. The loss of Adam's respect that he had called him a scoundrel was a great shock to him. He had cheated one of his best friends. Adam had always been so respectful to him. He wanted to be reconciled to him, but felt he would never be forgiven.

Arthur was distressed for Hetty's sake too, and for his own because he must leave her. He knew that Hetty hoped that he would marry her, and he had never dared to tell her that he would never marry her, but had soothed her with tender hopeful words. Finally he was forced to write this letter, which seemed to him to be at one moment an act of gross cruelty and the next the greatest kindness he could do to her. In this agitated state of mind the four walls of his room seemed to him to be a prison. Finally he decided to go out for a ride.

After all his agitation, Arthur decided that the best course was to write the letter and thus make the way open for the marriage of Hetty and Adam. When Adam called at the Chase, in the afternoon, Pym handed to him the letter. He said that the Captain was too busy to see him and had written down everything he had to say.

Arthur had written a letter which was addressed to Adam and contained a sealed envelope addressed to Hetty. The note to Adam read, "I have written everything you wish I leave it to you to decide whether you will be doing best to deliver it to Hetty or return it to me". But later the reader comes to know that the letter was not written in the form in which Adam wanted it to be written. Actually, Arthur was a dual personality.

CHAPTER - 30

The Delivery of the Letter

The next Sunday Adam joined the Poysers on their way out of church. He had the letter in his pocket and was anxious to deliver it and to talk alone to Hetty. Hetty, not knowing that a fight had taken place in the wood, felt confident that she could persuade Adam not to do anything she did not want him to do, and to attain this end, she showed him some favour and this encouraged him. Hetty felt very unhappy, the parting with Arthur was a double pain to her. But she hoped to see him again on Christmas, when he was likely to come back.

Adam returned to the Hall Farm with the Poysers, and, after tea, followed Hetty and the children into the garden. When they were alone, Adam told Hetty that he must speak to her as it is his duty to act in her best interests when he saw a gentleman, who could not marry her, and did not even think of marrying her was making love to her. Adam said "He's been trifling with you and making a plaything for you." Hetty burst out 'Yes, he does care for me; I know better nor you'. Everything was forgotten but the pain and anger she felt at Adam's words.

Hetty felt a revival of hope at the mention of a letter which Adam had not read. She took the sealed letter and put it in her pocket. Adam engaged the Poysers in conversation as much as possible. He wanted to help Hetty, so that Hetty could be more at ease and they may not notice her excitement. He was delighted to see that she showed great self-command. He did realize that she was in the hope that Arthur's letter would have something different from that Adam had said. She hoped that Arthur must have assured her that he would soon marry her.

Adam pressed her hand gently as at last he said good night. While walking towards home he devised excuses for her folly. He was bitterly jealous; and in proportion as his love made him lenient in his judgement of Hetty. His bitterness found expression in his anger towards Arthur. He met Seth and walked away with him. Seth gave Adam a letter from Dinah to read, when Adam actually asked about Dinah to him. Their mother Lisbeth met them at the door with her usual angry remark of annoyance. Adam went up to his room. He read Dinah's letter by candle light. Dinah wrote of Divine Love, of sorrow and of sacrifice. She also gave news of her work and informed them that she had been called to Leeds. She sent kind messages to Lisbeth. When Seth went upstairs. Adam then asked him his opinion about the letter "I don't know what I should have thought of her and her letter if I'd never seen her" said Adam. "I dare say I should have thought a preaching woman hateful. But she's one as makes everything seem right she says and does, and I seemed to see her and hear her speaking when I read the letter." Again in this chapter Hetty's and Dinah's point of view are contrasted.

CHAPTER - 31

In Hetty's Bed Chamber

It was no longer light enough, so Hetty carried one candle with her as she went up to her bedroom soon after Adam had gone and bolted the door. Now she would read her letter. It had a faint scent of roses and kissed it, as it gave her Arthur's presence. Her heart began to flutter and her hands to tremble as she broke the seal. She read slowly, although Arthur had taken great pains to write clearly.

He told her that he really loved her and that he would never forget their love. But it would have been better if they had never known happiness together. It was his duty to ask her to have him as less as possible because she would never be happy with him and would be much better off married to a man of her own status. He is bound to his own duties and responsibilities and since they could not marry, they must part. He wrote to her in a very kind tone and also gave her an address to which she might write if it were necessary and if she were in any trouble. He begged her forgiveness and assured her that he would always remain her affectionate and devoted friend.

After reading the letter Hetty was convulsed and began to shiver. She wrapped a warm coat around her and took up the letter again. Tears blinded her eyes and she could read with difficulty. She thought of Arthur's cruel behaviour. Her dreams shattered which broke her heart. She sobbed until she was completely exhausted with crying. Then she threw herself on bed and went to sleep. She was unable to adjust with reality.

She awoke with a sense of misery and deep anguish and realized that she must conceal her suffering from her aunt and uncle. She opened her treasure drawer and looked at her trinkets. Then she read the letter again and crushed it in anger. She hated the writer of the letter, whom she actually loved, but who was so cruel. She tried to reconcile herself and tried to prepare herself for the future. She could no longer stay there. After washing and dressing herself neatly, she recovered sufficient self-control to hide her feelings.

That evening Hetty told her uncle that she wanted to take up service, thus asked him to allow her to take up the position of a lady's maid. Mr. Poyser expressed that he did not wish a niece of his to go into service and would like her to stay at the farm until she had a good husband. Old Martin remarked bitterly that Hetty took after her mother, who had married the worthless Sorrel against his wishes.

Mrs. Poyser came in as Hetty began to cry and she too joined the discussion. She stated that she would never allow Hetty to take the position of a lady's maid. While sitting alone in the room Hetty gave a thought over her uncle's words. Because she knew the meaning of a good husband for his uncle meant Adam Bede : The possibility of marrying Adam presented itself to her in a new and more favourable light. She did not care what she did as long as it made a change in her life, and she felt sure Adam still wanted to marry her. She did not think about herself i.e. whether she is worthy enough for him. She is so selfish and superficial that she bothers only for her own happiness and not for others.

CHAPTER - 32

Mrs. Poyser "Has Her Say Out"

The next Saturday evening there was much excited discussion at the Donnithorne Arms concerning a smart man in top boots, said by some to be a farmer who had entered into an agreement with the Squire regarding the tenancy of the Hall Farm, and that the Poysers were to be shifted to some other unproductive farm.

A day or two later the old Squire called at the Hall Farm and Mrs. Poyser felt that something unusual was in the wind for his visit was a rare event. She invited him into the house and sent Hetty to fetch Mr. Poyser. Mrs. Poyser was complemented for her clean kitchen by Mr. Squire. He then asked her to show her the dairy and declared it to be a well-managed dairy, neat and clean with everything at the right place.

When Mr. Poyser arrived the Squire told him that he was considering letting the Chase Farm to a Mr. Thurle. But there was too much dairyland and too little plough land to suit Mr. Thurle. He hoped that Mr. Poyser would be prepared to take an extra pasture and supply milk, cream and butter to the Chase, and allow Mr. Thurle to save his corn land.

Mrs. Poyser was frank and open lady. But Poyser was astute enough to see through the whole business. Mrs. Poyser made it clear that she would not dream of taking on extra dairy work and working herself to death so that money could go into other folks' pockets. The Squire tried to pacify her and to get his way by talking to Poyser, but Mrs. Poyser continued angrily to voice her objections. The Squire then changed his tactics. He now held out a veiled threat that when Poyser's lease expired it would not be renewed, and the Thurle would be ready to take on both the farms. Mr. Poyser was alarmed at the possibility of having to leave the old place where he had been born and bred. Whereas Mrs. Poyser was confident to have her say out, at least for once, no matter what the consequences.

Mrs. Poyser said that she felt sorry for Thurle if he wished to live in a house, "with all the plagues of Egypt in it; with cellars full of water; a rotten floor and rats and mice everywhere". Poyser was the only tenant who could put up with such things. "You run away from my words, sir," she continued as the Squire walked out, "we're not dumb creatures to be abused and made money on by them as have got the lash'i their hands". She then proceeded to tell him how much he was disliked in the village.

The Squire thus cut a sorry figure. He rode off, well-aware that his servants making fun of him at his back.

Mr. Poyser was scared of the consequences which were likely to follow from the Squire's displeasure but Mrs. Poyser said," I've had my say out, and I shall beth' easier for it all my life." Mrs. Poyser seem to be more practical and straight forward than her husband. Her power of tongue had great influence on the people.

CHAPTER - 33

More Links

The barley was all carried at last and the harvest suppers went by without waiting for the dismal black crop of beans. Time passed, but Mr. Thurle did not come to the Chase Farm. It was widely known that Mrs. Poyser had frustated the Squire's plans. It had been humorously commented by the novelist, "the news that Napoleon had returned from Egypt was unexciting by comparison and the repulse of the French in Italy was nothing compared to Mrs. Poyser's repulse of the old Squire." Apart from Mr. Poyser's occasional forebodings, things went on much as usual in the Poyser household. Mrs. Poyser thought she noticed a great improvement in Hetty. She had lost desire to go out and spoke little. She did not mind giving up her lessons in needle work at the Chase. Hetty responded better to Adam. When ever Adam came to the Hall Farm she seemed to be in good spirits. It shows that she was responding to his love.

Adam himself watched her at first with trembling anxiety, which gave way to surprise and delicious hope. Adam was surprised at Hetty's behaviour. He became more and more hopeful of marrying her. She always smiled when she used to see him when he came to the farm. Still, when he looked at her again and again with a close look he observed some change. There was something different in her eyes, in her expressions and her moments. Adam saw something colder, harder and less child-like in her face. As time went on, he was sure that Hetty's heart was turning to him at last. This softened his feelings towards Arthur a little.

It seemed at the beginning of November Jonathan Burge, finding it impossible to replace Adam, had at last made up his mind to offer him a share in the business. Adam saw an opening into a broadening path of prosperous work. He went home full of happy visions. He would be able to make a separate house for himself and provide for his mother in the old one. If Dinah married Seth, Lisbeth would be more content to live with them and apart from Adam. The chapter now opens a prosperous way for Adam's life.

CHAPTER - 34

The Betrothal

It was a dry Sunday and really a pleasant day for the second of November. Mrs. Poyser did not go to church, for she had suffered from cold. Mr. Poyser stayed at home to keep her company. Hetty and the boys went to church. Adam was bold enough to join them after church. Adam behaved now much like determined lover. He offered Hetty his arm. She took it smilingly, although she had little love for Adam in her heart. Adam longed to spoke to her of his love. But he decided to be patient. Therefore he spoke of his prospects instead and told her that Mr. Burge had offered him a share in his business. Hetty too had often heard it, hinted that Adam would have the partnership if he would marry Mary Burge. Her eyes filled with tears at the thought of losing the one person on whom all her hopes now rested.

Adam when saw her tears, realized what she was thinking of. Trembling with joy he took her hand and said, "I could afford to be married now, Hetty—I could make a wife comfortable but I shall never want to be married, if you won't have me." Hetty smiled and got relief and Adam could hardly believe in the happiness of that moment. When he asked her if she loved him. Hetty put her face against his, for she wanted to be caressed and loved again, and feel as if Arthur were with her. She might have agreed to marry Adam.

Arthur might have been un faithful to her, but she still had her grand dreams.

The Poysers were delighted to learn of their betrothal and that evening, seated in front of the fire. Hetty felt happy and contented in the midst of all this love. Plans for the future were discussed and Mr. Poyser suggested that Easter would be the best time for the wedding. Mrs. Poyser supported the statement 'Ay, to be sure. Christian folks can't be married like cuckoos."

CHAPTER - 35

The Hidden Dread

Adam and Hetty would be married in March was lastly decided. Two new rooms were added to the old house, for Lisbeth had cried so piteously at the thought of Adam's leaving her and living in a separate house, that he was obliged to ask Hetty if she would consent to live with the old lady. Hetty agreed for her mind was oppressed with a greater burden than the problem of living with Lisbeth. On seeing Hetty sometimes unhappy, Adam became worried. But she assured him that she was quite happy and satisfied. Adam thought that she was probably over-worked as Mrs. Poyser had been ill through January. Therefore he did not pay much attention to the matter.

One day in February, Hetty in her red cloak and warm bonnet went to buy some things from the town of Treddetston. She turned through a gate on the road and went down a field path, her dark eyes were blank and desolate like those of one who is homeless and unloved. Hetty went on till she came to a pond with some water weeds growing round it and sat down on the grassy bank. She had often thought of suicide and had then thought of this pool in the dreary nights of the previous month. And she now looked at it earnestly. She had no courage to jump into the cold water. There was only one thing to do—to go away to some place where she could not be found. Hetty had upto now, rejected the idea of writing to Arthur, but in her desperation she decided that she would go to him at Windsor.

Hetty visited Treddleston, made her purchases, and on return home, asked Mrs. Poyser if she might go to see Dinah and persuade her to come back for the wedding. The Poysers and Adam thought that this was an excellent plan and that as the weather was pleasant she should better go at once.

At three o'clock that day, Hetty was travelling by the coach that was to take her to Leicester. She was dimly aware that this long journey might be taking her towards the beginning of fresh trouble and misery. But she was still hopeful that Arthur would act honourably once he knew that she was going to be the mother of his child. This 'new hope' gives the title to next chapter as "The Journey in Hope".

BOOK V

CHAPTER - 36

The Journey in Hope

Hetty left Hayslope in a coach, sad and lonely, with the prospects of a long journey before her. The burly old coachman, seeing such a pretty young woman among the outside passengers, invited her to come up and sit beside him. His questions frightened her, for she thought he might know something about her. When the coach stopped at the inn at Stoniton, Hetty hastened away with her basket to another part of the town.

Hetty had no experience of a journey and did not know the needs of a traveller. She had thought herself large enough provided with three guineas in her pocket. But when she found how much it cost her to get to Stoniton she became cautious. She sought a cheap lodging for the night and asked the landlord how she might get to Windsor, as she could not afford to go any further by coach.

The landlord adviced her to start in the morning to Ashby. She did the same in hope to a cart which would take her on, at least for part of the way. After walking four miles her courage sank. She was overcome with fatigue, hunger and misery, for she had taken only bread and milk in breakfast. Moreover, she was not used to such an outdoor exertion. It began to rain and Hetty sat down on the top of a stile, sobbing hysterically. The rain continued, so Hetty collected herself and walked on to look for shelter. Presently she heard the rumble of wheels behind her and a covered wagon approached. Hetty waited for it and the sight of a small white dog sitting on the front of the wagon encouraged her to ask the driver to take her towards Ashby, as she was on the way of Windsor to her brother, who was a soldier. She offered to pay, but the driver said he would take her to Leicester without charging anything. Hetty climbed up and lay on the wool-packs. It was lunury to her and she slept away the hours. Late at night they reached Leicester and the second day of her journey was over.

In the morning she found her way to a coach office to ask about the road to Windsor and see if it would cost her too much. The elderly clerk at the office wrote down for her the names of the chief places she must pass through. This was the only comfort she got in Leicester, for the men stared at her and made her feel most miserable. Soon she started her journey again and met on the way a carrier's cart which took her to Hinckley. With the help of the drunken driver of a chaise she was in the heart of Warwickshire before nightfall, Hetty was still hundred miles from Windsor. She went to Stratford-on-Avon and it was not till the fifth day that she reached Stony Stratford. Her body was aching too with these days of fatigue and anxiety, they had made her look more pale and worn than all the time of hidden dread she had gone through at home.

By now Hetty's weariness and impatience had become too strong for her economical caution and she determined to take the coach for the rest of the way, though it should cost all her remaining money. After paying her fare for the coach to Windsor, she was left with only a shilling. As she got down at the Green Man Inn of Windsor at twelve o'clock on the seventh day, she was faint and hungry. The coachman asked for a tip. But when he saw her distress he refused the shilling she offered him. As she held out the shilling, she lifted up her dark tear filled eyes to the coach man's face and said, "Can you give me back six pence?" "No, no", he said gruffly, "never mind-put the shilling up again". The landlord of the Green Man stood near enough to witness the scene. He was a good natured landlord. He kindly told Hetty to come in. He took her to his wife and asked her to take care of Hetty. Hetty started shedding tears with grief fast. The land lady brought bread, meat and beer. Hetty ate eagerly. The landlady was touched by her youthful beauty and her miserable plight as she noticed her ringless hand and also her family way. The novelist says "The landlady sat opposite to her as she ate, and looked at her earnestly. No wonder: Hetty had thrown off her bonnet, and her curls had fallen down : her face was all the more touching in its youth and beauty because of its weary look, and the good woman's eyes wandered to her figure, which in her hurried dressing on her journey she had taken no pains to conceal; more over, the stranger's eye delects what the familiar, unsuspecting eye leave unnoticed." "Why, you're not very fit for travelling", she said, glancing while she spoke at Hetty's ringless hand. "Have you come far?"

Hetty explained that she was tired and had come a long way, and taking out the paper on which Arthur's address was written, she asked the landlady to direct her to the place. While she was speaking, the landlord came in, took the paper and read the address.

He told her that the place had been shut up for a fortnight and asked whom she wants to meet. She said that she wanted to meet Captain Donnithorne. He said that he knew him and he had gone to Ireland with the Loamshire Militia, a fortnight ago.

As this terrible news Hetty fainted, and the landlord and his wife carried her to the sofa.

"Here's a bad business, I suspect", said the landlord as he brought in some water.

"Ah, it's plain enough what sort of business it is," said the wife. "She's not a common flaunting drat chell, I can see that. She looks like respectable country girl, and she comes from a good way off, to judge by her tongue. She talks something like that ostler we had that from the north : he was as honest a fellow as we ever had about the house they're all honest folks in the north".

"I never saw a prettier young woman in my life", said the husband, "she's like a picture in a shop-winder. It goes to one's heart to look at her." "It'ud have been a good deal better for her if she'd been uglier and had more conduct," said the landlady, who on any charitable construction must have been supposed to have more 'conduct' than beauty "But she's coming to gain. Fetch a drop of more water."

In this chapter, together with the next one, forms the very core of the novel. It is a clever piece of psycho-analysis, and it gives us a peep into the anguished mind and heart of Hetty.

CHAPTER - 37

The Journey in Despair

Hetty was too ill through the rest of that day for any questions to be addressed to her. But then sleep and rest had brought back the strength necessary for the keenness of mental suffering. By the next morning she was well enough to ponder as to what she should do next. It was impossible for her to enter into any service, there seemed nothing but beggary in store for her, and she thought with horror of the hardship and shame to which she was doomed.

Her state of mind was miserable. "It was impossible for her to enter into any service if she could obtain it : there was nothing but immediate beggary before her. She thought of a young woman who had been found against the church wall at Hayslope one Sunday, nearly dead with cold and hunger and tiny infant in her arms, the woman was rescued and taken to the parish. The parish ! You can perhaps hardly understand the effect of that word on a mind like

Hetty's, brought up among people who were somewhat hard in their feelings even towards poverty, who lived among the fields, and had little pity for want and rages as a hard inevitable fate such as they sometimes seem in cities, but held them a mark of idleness and vice—and it was idleness and vice that brought burthens on the parish. To Hetty, 'the parish' was next to the prison in disgrace; and to ask anything of strangers-—to beg—lay in the same far-off hideous region of intolerable shame, that Hetty had all her life thought it impossible she could ever come near. But now the remembrance of that wretched woman whom she had seen herself, on her way from church, being carried into Joshua Rann's, came back upon her with new terrible sense that there was very little now to divide her from the same lot. And the dread of bodily hardship mingled with the dread of shame for Hetty had the luxurious nature of a round soft coated pet animal."

How she yearned to be back in her safe home again, cherished and cared for she had always been. Her aunt's scolding about trifles would have been music to her ears now : she longed for it : she used to hear it in a time when she had only trifles to hide. Could she be the same Hetty that used to make up the butter in the dairy with the Gueldre roses peeping in at the window—she, a runaway whom her friends would not open their doors again, lying in this strange bed, with the knowledge that she had no money to pay for what she received, and must offer those strangers some of the clothes in her basket?

It was then she thought of her locket and earings and seeing her pocket lie near and spread the contents on the bed before her. There were the locket and earnings in the velvet lined boxes, and with them there was a beautiful silver thimble Adam had given her. These ornaments and the gold rings in her ears were surely worth some money. But it would not be enough. She looked through her bag again to see if there was anything of value she might have forgotten. She must have enough money to get away from Windsor, and if there was nothing else she could do, she might find courage to dive into some pond on the way.

While searching her bag she saw the name "Dinah Morris-Snow field" written on a piece of paper. Hetty remembered Dinah's kindness. But she shrank from confession of her sin even to her, although she thought of going to Dinah as a possible alternative, if she could not commit suicide.

The good landlady was amazed when Hetty came downstairs, neatly dressed and looking nice. Hetty explained that she had been overtired after the long journey which she had undertaken to fir out her brother who had run away from home. Her family, she lie thought Captain Donnithorne might know something about him. A breakfast Hetty brought out her ornaments and asked the landlo if she could get some money for them. At his wife's suggestions h offered to advance to her the three guineas she needed, and sa that if she wished to do so she could redeem them when she g home.

The kind landlord did not accept any money from her for h food and bed, and at eleven o'clock she set off in the coach that w to take her twenty miles back along the way she had come. Het felt that no one could deliver her from the evils that would mal life hateful to her and no one, she said to herself, should ever knc her misery and humiliation. No, she would not confess even to Dina She would wander out of sight, and drown herself where her bo would never be found and no one should know what had happen to her.

When she got off this coach, she began to walk again, and ta cheap rides in carts and get cheap meals, going back the way s had come without any distinct purpose. She often sat for hours und the hedgerows, looking before her with black, beautiful eyes, wo dering if there would be anything worse after death than she dread in life. Hetty was one of those people who, inspite of regular churc going, had never absorbed a single Christian idea or Christian feelir

She chose to go to Stratford-on-Avon again, where she had go before by mistake; for she remembered some grassy fields. Whe she arrived hungry in urgent need of food and rest. She had l Windsor five days ago. She was wandering about, avoiding spee and questioning looks as much as possible. Eventually she reach the fields and began to search for a pool. At last she found one, hidd under the darkening sky, and sat down beside it. She collected so stones to make the basket sink, but she felt there was no hurry she had all night to drown herself in. She took the three buns s had in her basket and ate them eagerly. After eating lavishly s fell asleep.

When she awoke it was deep night and she felt chilled. She w frightened of this darkness. She took up her basket and set out find a hovel of furze that she had seen near a sheepfold. She h difficulty in locating it, but at last found the shelter. It was smelling and close, but it was warm and there was straw on t ground. Hetty sank down and shed tears of hysterical joy that s

faithful love. He couldn't bear to blame her : she never meant to cause him this dreadful pain. The blame lay with that man who had selfishly played with her heart—had perhaps even deliberately lured her away.

At Oakbourne the ostler remembered Hetty, but said he had lost sight of her after she left the coach. After much delay, Adam found the coach man who had driven Hetty to Stoniton, but after that he could find no trace of her movement. So there was nothing for Adam to do but go home. He was forced to the conclusion that Hetty had gone to Arthur, or that she had run away to avoid marrying him.

The heart sick Adam reached home early on the Wednesday morning. Seth was shocked at the ghastly sight of Adam, who fell on his neck and sobbed. After a time he told Seth that he believed Hetty had run away to avoid marrying him. The dialogue between the two brothers fully brings out the anguish in Adam.

"God have mercy on us, Addy", he said, in a low voice, sitting down on the bench beside Adam, "What is it?"

Adam was unable to speak : the strong man, accustomed to suppress the signs of sorrow, had felt his heart swell like a child's at this first approach of sympathy. He fell on Seth's neck and sobbed.

Seth was prepared for the worst now, for even in his recollections of their boyhood, Adam had never sobbed before. "Is it death, Adam? Is she dead?" He asked in a low tone, when Adam raised his head and was recovering himself.

"No, lad; but she's gone—gone away from us. She's never been to Snowfield. Dinah's been gone to Leeds ever since last Friday was a fortnight, the very day Hetty set out. I can't find out where she went after she got to Stoniton."

Seth was silent from utter astonishment : he knew nothing that could suggest to him a reason for Hetty's going away.

"Hast any notion what she's done it for." He said at last.

"She can't ha' loved me : she didn't like our marriage when it came night—that must be it," said Adam. He had determined to mention no further reason.

"I hear mother stirring", said Seth, "Must we tell her?"

"No, not yet," said Adam, rising from the bench, and pushing the hair from his face as if he wanted to rouse himself. "I can't have her told yet; and I must set out on another journey directly, after I've been to the village and th' Hall Farm. I can't tell thee where I'm going, and thee must say to her. I'm gone on business as nobody is to know anything about. I'll go and wash myself now." Adam moved towards the door of the workshop and again came back. Seeing calm, sad glance at Seth's eyes he said, "I must take all the money out O' the tin box, lad; but if anything happens to me, all the rest 'll be thine, to take care o' mother with".

Seth was pale and trembling : he felt there was some terrible secret under all this. "Brother", he said, faintly — he never called Adam "brother" except in solemn moment— "I don't believe you'll do anything as you can't ask God's blessing on."

"Nay, lad", said Adam, "don't be afraid. I'm for doing nought but what's a man's duty."

Later, Adam set off to the village, intending to make secret arrangement to follow Hetty to Ireland. He met Martin Poyser and told him that he could trace Hetty no further than Stoniton. Mr. Poyser was much upset and jumped to the conclusion that she had gone to try to get a place as a lady's maid. Adam encouraged his supposition and begged him to be kind to her if she returned. He said to Mr. Poyser, "It was better it should be so", he said, as quietly as he could, "if she felt she couldn't like me for a husband, better run away before than repent after. I hope you won't look harshly on her if she comes back, as she may do if she finds it hard to get on away from home."

"I cannot look on her as I've done before," said Martin, decisively. "She's acted bad by you, and by all of us. But I"ll not turn my back on her. It'll be a hard job for me to tell her aunt. Why did not Dinah come back as yet? —She'd ha' helped to pacify her aunt a bit."

"Dinah wasn't at Snowfield. She's been gone to Leeds this fortnight; and I couldn't learn from the old woman any direction where she is at Leeds, else I should ha' brought it to you."

Adam then shook hands with Poyser, asked him not to disclose the news to anyone for sometime, and then left him. They were true honest men, and misfortune now made them fast friends. Adam then decided that if he were to set off on the long journey to Ireland it would be wise to confide in Mr. Irwine before he left, and to seek his advice.

CHAPTER - 39

The Tidings

Adam at once started for Bronton where Mr. Irwine lived. Mr. Irwine was busy when Adam arrived and he had to wait for a few minutes before he was shown into the study. Adam noticed a strange expression on the clergy's face and also an open letter lying on the table. Adam at once started telling his painful story and also informed about Arthur's role in it. On hearing about Arthur, the Rector became greatly agitated. Adam went on to tell him what he knew about the love affair between Hetty and Arthur; of the fight in the wood and also about the letter he had forced Arthur to write. As Adam told the story; "Mr. Irwine remembered the morning Arthur had come to breakfast, and realized that then he must have wanted to confess his infatuation for Hetty. It was a bitter remembrance to him now—that morning when Arthur breakfasted with him, and seemed as if he were on the verge of a confession. It was plain enough now what he had wanted to confess. And if their words had taken another turn....if he himself ahead been less fastidious about intruding on another man's secrets....it was cruel to think how thin a film had shut out rescue from all this guilt and misery. He saw the whole history now by that terrible illumination which the present sheds back upon the past. But every other feeling as it rushed upon him was thrown into abeyance by pity, deep respectful pity for the man who sat before him, already so bruised, going forth with sad blind resignedness to an unreal sorrow, while a real one was close upon him, too far beyond the range of common trial for him ever to have feared it. His own agitation was quelled by certain awe that comes over us in the presence of a great anguish; for the anguish he must inflict on Adam was already present to him. Again he put his hand on the arm that lay in the table, but very gently this time."

As Adam finished his story, Mr. Irwine gave another sorrowful news to Adam. He gives the news to him that Hetty was in prison at Stoniton. The constable who had arrested her had just been to see him. When Adam said, "For what", the Rector replies "For a great crime—the murder of her child."

Adam almost shouted and was thrown into a frenzy at the news. He refused to believe that Hetty could be guilty of child murder. On being enquired by Adam about the whole story, the Rector gave and showed him the letter he had received from the magistrate in front of whom the girl had been taken. She denied everything and would not give her name, but it seemed certain that she was Hetty.

Adam became very angry with Arthur and his one desire was to make him share Hetty's sham and misery. "It's his doing," he said, "if there's been any crime, it's at his door, not at hers. He taught her to deceive—he deceived me first. Let'em put him on his trial—let him stand in court beside her, and I'll tell how he got hold of her heart, and 'ticed her t' evil, and then lied to me. Is he to go free, while they lay all the punishment on her....so weak and young?"

"The image called up by these last words gave a new direction to poor Adam's maddened feelings. He was silent looking at the corner of the room as if he saw something there. Then he burst out again, in a tone of appealing anguish.

"I can't bear it .... O God, it's too hard to lay upon me—it's too hard to think she's wicked.

Mr. Irwine told him that Arthur was on the way home as the old Squire had sent for him ten days before. It would be of no use for him now to go to Ireland to take vengeance on him.

The Rector then persuaded him to ride with him to Stoniton, where Hetty was at the time. He advised him to help Hetty.

CHAPTER - 40

The Bitter Waters Spread

Mr. Irwine returned from Stoniton in a post-chaise that night. The first news that Carrol gave him was that old Squire Donnithorne had been found dead in bed at ten o'clock that morning. Adam himself had not come back from Stoniton, for though he shrank from seeing Hetty, he could not bear to go to a distance from her again. Before ten o'clock on Thursday morning the home at the Hall Farm was a house of mourning for a misfortune felt to be worse than death. As Mr. Irwine had the unpleasant task of breaking the news about Hetty to the Poyser family and the Hall Farm, Mr. Poyser and his father felt the sense of dishonour keenly. Their grief can better be imagined than described in words. Mr. Irwine was struck with surprise to observe that Mrs. Poyser was less severe than her husband. Mrs. Poyser said "We'd better ha' sent for Dinah, if we'd known where she is." The only address he could suggest was that of Sarah Williamson, Methodist preacher, Leeds.

Very soon the news of Hetty's trouble spread through the village and after calling on Mr. Irwine to ask about Adam, Bartle Massey decided to shut up his school and go to Stoniton to look after Adam until the trial was over. Bartle promised Mr. Irwine that he would be tactful in his remarks about Hetty. He went off to make his arrangements which included taking his bitch Vixen with him.

The title of the chapter reveals us that the "bitter news" had been spread in the Hall Farm.

CHAPTER - 41

The Eve of the Trial

It was ten o'clock on Thursday night. Bartle and Adam were seated in their upper room in a dull Stoniton street. With the light of the one dip candle Bartle is pretending to read, while he is really looking over his spectacles at Adam Bede, seated near the dark window. Adam's face was thin, his eyes sunken and he had not shaved. It was ten o'clock when Mr. Irwine arrived and he informed them that he and the jail chaplin had been with Hetty. Adam inquired whether she had consented to see him, but the Rector replied that she shrank from seeing anyone and answered 'no' to all the questions. Her heart seemed shut against her fellow-creatures. Mr. Irwine advised Adam against seeing Hetty. He said, "I don't like to advise you against your own feelings, Adam, if they now urge you strongly to go and see her tomorrow morning, even without her consent. It is just possible notwithstanding appearances to the contrary, that the interview might affect her favourably. But I grieve to say I have scarcely any hope of that. She didn't seem agitated when I mentioned your name; she only said 'no' in the same cold, obstinate way as usual. And if the meeting had no good effect on her, it would be pure, useless suffering to you—severe suffering I fear. She is very much changed."

Adam asked if Arthur had arrived, and was told he had not. Adam blamed Arthur for Hetty's disgrace and misery. The Rector did his best to calm Adam and to turn his thoughts away from vengeance. He told Adam, "Adam, he will know—he will suffer, long and bitterly. He has a heart and a conscience : I can't be entirely deceived in his character. I am convinced—I am sure he didn't fall under temptation without a struggle. He may be weak, but he is not callous, not coldly selfish. I am persuaded that this will be a shock of which he will feel the effects all his life. Why do you crave vengeance in this way? No amount of torture that you could inflict on him could benefit her".

"No—O God, no", Adam groaned out, sinking on his chair again, "But then, that's the deepest curse of all...that's what makes the blackness of it...it can never be undone. My poor Hetty...she can never be my sweet Hetty again...the prettiest thing God had made—smiling up at me...I thought she loved me...and was good."

Adam's voice had been gradually sinking into a hoarse undertone, as if he were only talking to himself; but now he said abruptly, looking at Mr. Irwine.

"But she isn't as guilty as they say? You don't think she is sir? She can't ha' done it."

"That perhaps can never be known with certainty."

Adam was silent; the last words had called up a vivid image of the past, and Mr. Irwine left him to his thoughts, while he spoke to Bartle about old Mr. Donnithorne's funeral and other matters of an indifferent kind. Then he told that Martin Poyser had come to Stoniton. Dinah had not yet come to the farm, so they were afraid that the letter had not reached her. Mr. Irwine wished that Dinah should have come, for she might have persuaded Hetty to open out her heart. The jail chaplain is harsh in his manner. But Adam responded negatively as he was sad.

CHAPTER - 42

The Morning of the Trial

At one o'clock the next day, Adam was alone in his dull upper room where his watch was counting the long minutes. He had no knowledge of trial. He groaned in his suffering. "O, God", Adam groaned, as he leaned on the table, and looked blankly at the face of the watch, "and men have suffered like this before......and poor helpless young things have suffered like this before.....and poor helpless young things have suffered like her.... Such a little while ago looking so happy and so pretty ...issing'em all, her grandfather and all of 'em and they wishing her luck. O my poor, poor Hetty.....dos't think on it now?"

Adam stared and looked round towards the door. It was Bartle Massey on the door. He told him all that had been happening at the trial. Things were going slowly because there was a great deal of cross-examination by the counsel for Hetty's defence. The chief evidence had been given by the doctor. Everyone present in the court had sympathy for Martin Poyser. Hetty appeared to be very frightened and there were a lot of foolish, curious women, fashionably dressed, sitting near the judge. They kept putting up their glasses, staring and whispering. After that Hetty stood like a white image, staring down at her hands, and seeming neither to hear nor see anything. She didn't speak when they asked her whether she was "guilty" or "not guilty". But when she heard her uncle's name, there seemed to go a shiver right through her and when they told him to look at her, she hung her head down, and covered and hide her face in her hands

Mr. Poyser's voice trembled and was scarcely able to speak. So they spared him as much as they could. Mr. Irwine did all he could to help him. Things seemed to be going against Hetty because inspite of the doctor's evidence she kept on denying that she had had a child. Mr. Massey told, Adam, "Yes, my lad, yes : the truth is the best thing to tell. It must come at last. The doctors' evidence is heavy on her—is heavy. But she's gone on denying she's had a child from first to last : these poor silly women things—they've not the sense to know it's no use denying what's proved. It'll make against her with the jury. I doubt, her being so obstinate : they may be less for recommending her to mercy, if the verdict's against her. But Mr. Irwine'll leave no stone unturned with the judges—you may rely upon that, Adam".

"Is there nobody to stand by her, and seem to care for her, in the court?" said Adam.

Mr. Irwine replied only the jail chaplains stand with Hetty.

"There's one man as ought to be there" said Adam. He pulled himself together and said he would go, for it was cowardly of him to keep away. Nerved by this active resolution, he took some bread and wine. He began to look more like his former self.

CHAPTER - 43

The Verdict

Adam Bede's tall figure was suddenly seen, being ushered to the side of the prisoner's dock. In the broad sunlight among the sleek shaven faces of other men, the marks of sufferings in his face were startling. But Hetty did not see him. She was standing with her hands crossed and her eyes fixed on them. She seemed to Adam to be the corpse of the woman he loved.

A woman was in the witness-box, a middle-aged woman who spoke in a firm distinct voice. She said that she was a widow named Sarah Stone and that she kept a small shop in Stoniton. She said the lady in the witness box looking ill and tired, with a basket on her arm, had come to her house on Saturday evening, the twenty-seventh of February, to ask for lodging when she said that it was not a lodging house, the girl began to cry and said that she was too tired to go further. And her prettiness, and her condition, and something respectable about her clothes and looks and the trouble forced Mrs. Stone to help her. "She had no money to pay for the coach or to purchase food and drink. She had been obliged to sell most of the things out of her basket; but she'd thankfully give a shilling for a bed. I saw no reason why I shouldn't take the young woman in for a night. I had only one room, but there were two beds in it and told her she might stay with me. I thought she'd been led wrong, and got into trouble, but if she was going to her friends, it would be a good work to keep her out of further harm."

The witness then stated that in the night a child was born and she identified the baby clothes were shown to her as those in which she had dressed the child. She had asked Hetty her friends' name, but she said she would later write to them herself. In spite of trial through which she had just passed, Hetty had gone up and dressed herself. Towards evening she seemed flushed and had a strange look in her eyes. So Mrs. Stone decided to fetch an acquaintance who was an experienced woman. She left Hetty sitting by the fire in the kitchen with the baby on her lap.

She had to wait for the woman for sometime. When they returned after one and half hour, both Hetty and the baby were gone. She had taken her cloak and bonnet, but had left the basket and the things in it. Mrs. Stone was frightened and angry that she had gone but had no reason to report the matter to the police because Hetty had every right to go from her home.

The effect of this evidence on Adam was electrical, it gave him new force. Hetty could not be guilty of the crime—her heart must have clung to her baby—else why should she have taken it with her? She might have left it behind. The little creature had died naturally and then she had hidden it; babies were so liable to death—and there might be the strongest suspicion without any proof of guilt His mind was so occupied with imaginary arguments against such suspicions, that he could not listen to the cross-examination by Hetty's counsel, who tried, without result, to elicit evidence that the prisoner had shown some movements of material affection towards the child.

A labourer named John Olding was the next witness. He lived two miles out of Stoniton. He told how, on the Monday at about one o'clock he was going towards Hetton Coppice and saw Hetty, in a red cloak, sitting under a haystack. She looked white and seemed a bit crazy. As he walked through the coppice he heard a strange cry. He looked round but could find nothing. But when he came back the same way after an hour, he had another look and saw something odd under a nut bush. It was the hand of a baby. The body was hidden under turf and timber choppings from which the hand was coming out. When he took the baby home, his wife said that the child was dead. So he told the constable and they went to report to Justice Hardy. The next morning Olding and another constable went to the spot where they had found the child. Hetty was still sitting there against the bush. She cried out when she saw them. But she did not try to move. She had a big piece of bread on her lap.

Adam had given a faint groan of despair while the witness was speaking. He had hidden his face on his arm. It was the supreme moment of his suffering : Hetty was guilty and he was silently calling to God for help. He did not hear Mr. Irwine give evidence regarding Hetty's unblemished character in her parish and the virtuous habits in which she had been brought up.

The judge addressed the jury and they retired to consult among themselves. The decisive moment was not far off. All eyes, except Adam's were trying to look at Hetty, who stood like a statue of dull despair.

At last Adam lifted up his head as the judge addressed the jury and they retired to consult among themselves. The decisive moment was not far off. All eyes, except Adam's were trying to look at Hetty, who stood like a statue of dull despair.

It was not very long when jury came to their decision. There was silence while the jurymen's names were called and the prisoner was made to hold up her hand. The jury were asked to give their verdict. They found Hetty "guilty" of child-murder. There was no recommendation for mercy to the criminal and the sympathy of the court was not with the prisoner. The judgement was an expected one.

The judge put on his black cap and spoke, "Hester Sorrel", The blood rushed to Hetty's face then drained back again. At the words, "and then be hanged by the neck till you be dead", she gave to a piercing shriek. Adam held out his arms to her, but his arms could not reach her, and she fainted and was carried out of the court.

CHAPTER - 44

Arthur's Return

When Arthur lànded at Liverpool, he received the letters from his Aunt Lydia announcing his grand-father's death. Pity softened his death, his own real life was beginning. He would be able to show the Loamshire people with a fine country gentleman he was. He would be spoken of as a first-rate landlord and happy faces would greet him everywhere. He would see to it that the Rector was paid much more than at present, and his aunt would be made as comfortable as possible.

Mr. Irwine, in one of his letters to Arthur had mentioned that

Adam and Hetty were to be married in March. So Arthur's mind was at ease about Hetty. He would do a great deal for them to make up for any suffering that he might have caused to Hetty. But Arthur thought she could not have felt much if she had so soon decided to marry Adam. His mind still had the memory of her charm and beauty.

When Arthur reached the Chase he was not surprised to see the servants looking grave and sad. He went in and was greeted by the lawyer and his aunt Lydia, who was the only person in the house who knew nothing of Hetty's troubles.

When he went up to his room he saw many letters and packets lying on his dressing table. But he attended to his toilet before looking at them. The top letter was from Mr. Irwine, marked "To be delivered as soon as he arrives".

Arthur opened the letter and started reading it. When he came to the words, "Hetty Sorrel is in prison and will be tried on Friday for the crime of child-murder," he started from his chair and his whole frame was convulsed with violent throbs. He read no further but rushed from the house, had his horse saddled and set off at a gallop for Stoniton.

This sudden reaction shows that he is not bad at the core of his heart. He had acted wrongly, but he is not a scoundrel.

CHAPTER - 45

In the Prison

Near sunset that evening, Dinah Morris arrived at Stoniton jail and asked an elderly gentleman who was standing at the entrance if she might be allowed to go in to Hetty Sorrel. She had just heard from her uncle that Hetty had been condemned to death.

The chaplain recognised Dinah, for he was the gentleman on horse back who had stopped to hear her preach on Hayslope Green. He was a Magistrate, Colonel Townley so he was able to take Dinah into the prison. After speaking to the jailer, he told Dinah that if she wanted she might spend the night with Hetty, but that no light would be allowed in the cell. Perhaps God would enable her to open out the heart of the obstinate criminal.

As the jailer opened the door of the cell the light from his lantern fell upon Hetty sitting on her straw bed with her face buried in her knees. The door was closed and Dinah called to her softly. Hetty started but did not look up. Dinah spoke again and presently Hetty rose and was soon clasped in Dinah's arms. Hetty clung to Dinah and they sat down together.

Dinah thought suffering and fear might have driven Hetty out of her mind and she did not speak for some time. But she then began to feel the Divine presence more and more and tried to comfort Hetty with the assurance that, although she could not save her from death a day later, she would not desert her. She spoke of God's presence and begged Hetty to clear her heart of all falsehood and open it out to Him. They knelt together, holding hands, and Dinah prayed earnestly for Hetty's spiritual salvation.

Hetty was touched. She burst out sobbing and threw her arms round Dinah's neck, saying, "I will speak.....I will tell.....I won't hide it any more." At first her sobs were too violent, but presently she was able to whisper her tragic story to Dinah. God had opened out her heart.

She told her to her futile journey to Windsor; of her thoughts of suicide; of her agony of mind and body, and fear of shame; of the unexpected birth of the baby and her thought that if she could get rid of it she could return home; of how she saw a hole under the nut tree like a grave and how she put the baby there and partly covered it with grass and pieces of wood hoping that some one would find it and take care of it. She saw a man in a smock who frightened her and she went to a village to get something to eat, but she could not get the baby's crying out of her head. She slept in a barn, but the baby's crying kept waking her and she went back to the place in the wood where she had buried it. When she saw it was dead, she was struck dumb like stone, with fear and horror, and was unable to move. Then they came and took her away.

She shuddered, was silent for sometime and then said, "Dinah, do you think God will take away that crying and the place in the wood, now I've told everything?" asked Hetty.

"Let us pray, poor sinner : Let us fall on our knees again and pray to the God of all mercy," answered Dinah.

This was the tragic tale of poor Hetty. She had sinned, but now she confessed and this was the only way for her to get God's mercy.

CHAPTER - 46

The Hours of Suspense

On Sunday morning, when the church bells in Stoniton were

ringing for morning service, Bartle Massey re-entered Adam's room, after a short absence, and said,

'Adam, her's a visitor wants to see you.'

Dinah had came to see Adam and asked him to come to the prison to say farewell to Hetty because Hetty wished him to forgive her. Adam trembled with emotion and said that he could not come to say good-bye to her as long as there was any hope of pardon. He asked Dinah to tell Hetty that he forgave her from the bottom of his heart but would come to her at the very last, when all hope was gone. Dinah hurried back to the prison and Bartle tried to comfort Adam. But they could not sleep that night.

The cart set off at half-past seven. In ten minutes from that time, Adam was at the door of the cell. Adam went to the prison, but there was no news of pardon or reprieve. He waited for half-an-hour more, before he could bring himself to let Dinah know that he was there.

It was so dark that Adam could not see her when he first entered the cell. But very soon he saw Hetty's face through the dimness—it was marble, now with pallid, quivering lips and eyes that looked at him mournfully. She looked as if she had come from the dead to tell him of her misery. She trembled when she saw the change in Adam, and when Dinah told to speak to him. She also begged him to forgive her. Adam answered with a half-sob that he had done so long ago. His tears fell and Hetty asked for a parting kiss. Adam took the blanched wasted hand she put out to him, and they gave each other the solemn unspeakable kiss of a life-long parting. She asked him to tell Arthur that she was trying to forgive him.

At this moment there was a noise at the door of the cell, for the last preparations were being made and Adam could stay no longer. He was too agitated to see more—even to see Mr. Irwine. He departed silently and went to his chamber in loneliness, leaving Bartle to watch and see the end.

In this chapter Adam was deeply moved by Hetty's misery and for the first time we can see both of them expressing love for each other simultaneously.

CHAPTER - 47

The Last Moment

A large crowd was waiting at the place where Hetty was to be hanged on that clear, grey morning, when the fatal cart with the two young women Dinah and Hetty reached. All Stoniton had heard of Dinah Morris, the young Methodist woman who had brought the obstinate criminal to confess, and there was as much eagerness to see her as to see the wretched Hetty. Hetty was terrified at the sight of the crowd and Dinah told her to look at her eyes. As the cart stopped, there was a vast yell, they clasped each other in horror and Hetty shrieked in terror.

But it was a shout of sudden excitement as the watchers saw a horseman, riding desperately like a mad man. He came through the crowd at full gallop.

It was Arthur Donnithorne, carrying in his hand the hard-won release from death for Hetty. Her sentence had been reduced to transportation.

CHAPTER - 48

Another Meeting In the Wood

It was evening of Squire Donithorne's funeral. Arthur came to the Grove for a lonely walk, in order to consider his future. Adam also came at that very time. They were both drawn to the place by common memories. Adam had resolved to go to the grove for the last time. He had made up his mind that, like the Poysers, he would leave the neighbourhood. He had decided not to see Arthur again, for as Arthur himself had seen Hetty, there was no need to deliver her message—her forgiveness—to him. Presently the two met and Adam noted the signs of suffering on Arthur's face. Arthur was the first to speak. And when he heard that Adam meant to leave Hayslope, he persuaded him to come to the Hermitage so that they could talk things over. It had not been entered into since the night of their quarrel, long back.

Arthur told Adam that he also intended to leave the Chase and go into the army. But Adam made it plain that nothing Arthur could do could lessen the sorrow and suffering he had caused. Arthur begged Adam to remain at Hayslope. Mr. Irwine would have full authority to manage the estate in the way he liked, so they would be under someone whom they liked and respected.

Arthur then talked to him of his own suffering, "Haven't I loved her too. Didn't I see her yesterday? Shan't I carry the thought of her about with me as much as you will? And don't you think you would suffer more if your's been in fault?" Adam was moved by his tale of suffering and offered to shake hands with him. With this act of forgiveness and reconciliation there was a strong resurgence in both men of old boyish affection. Arthur said that he would never have wronged Hetty if he had known that Adam loved her. He had struggled against temptation and had never meant to harm her. "But I was all wrong from the very first, and horrible suffering has come of it." Arthur was truly and sincerely repentent.

Adam asked about Hetty and Arthur said he felt it would drive him mad to think of her looks and what she had said to him. He regretted that he could not get a full pardon for her.

There was no saving her from the wretched fate of transportation "I can do nothing for her all those years : and she may die under it, and never know comfort any more."

After that they spoke with admiration of Dinah, who had promised to stay with Hetty till the last moment, till she went from country. Arthur asked Adam to give Dinah his watch and chain. "In remembrance of the man to which she is the one source of comfort." He would like to think that she was using it. Adam promised to do so and also that he could to restrain the Poysers from leaving the village. Adam left the Hermitage, feeling that sorrow was more bearable now that hatred was gone.

As soon as the door was closed behind him, Arthur went to the waste-paper basket and took out the little pink silk necker-chief. It was Hetty's and he had concealed it there. Now he wanted to take it away with him as memoriam of the woman he had loved and wronged.

This second meeting in the wood and the Hermitage parallels the first meeting of the two. But how different and with what different results. Instead of quarrel there is forgiveness and reconciliation.

BOOK VI

CHAPTER - 49

At the Hall Farm

On an autumn afternoon in 1801, more than eighteen months after the parting of Adam and Arthur, Mrs. Poyser, dressed in mourning for her late father-in-law, was talking to Dinah and trying to persuade her not to leave the Hall Farm and go to Snowfield. Dinah said she felt called to continue her work there. The invitation to stay was temptation to be resisted, "lest the love of the creature should become like a mist...shutting out the heavenly light."

Their discussion was interrupted by the arrival of Adam Bede. Dinah blushed faintly when she saw him and he said that he had come to ask her to stay the night with Lisbeth, who was ill. Mrs

Poyser prepared tea and Mr. Poyser joined them. The question of Dinah's return to Snowfield again came up for discussion, and Adam, seeing that she was much disturbed by the discussion said, "I can't find fault with anything Dinah does'....but if she thinks well to go, I wouldn't cross her, or make it hard to her by objecting."

Tears came into Dinah's eyes and she hurried upstairs to get her bonned. When she came down again, Totty sang out, "Dinah was saying her prayer and crying ever so."

When the good-bye was said, Dinah and Adam left the Hall Farm together.

CHAPTER - 50

In the Cottage

Adam did not ask Dinah to take his arm when they got out into the lane. As he had observed that she never walked arm-in-arm with Seth. As Dinah and Adam walked along together, they discussed her work and her conviction that she was called away from the Hall Farm to preach at Snowfield, Adam said he regretted there was no hope of her marrying Seth as he would have considered it a blessing to have had her as a sister-in-law. He was surprised to notice that Dinah's eyes were bright with suppressed agitation and that her cheeks flushed. He thought his remarks had displeased her and so he apologized. Dinah asked him, if he received any news of Arthur, and was told that Mr. Irwine had heard from him. He wrote that he did not want to return home, even if the war with France ended, for he felt old and broken. And unable to make plans for the future.

Lisbeth was delighted to see Dinah, who sat and talked to her while Seth and Adam worked in the new room which had been built nearly two years ago. Adam had not outlived his sorrow, Adam had but became more sympathetic and gentle towards others, particularly to Seth, his mother and the Poysers. As for Dinah, all she said and did seemed right to him.

Dinah and Seth came downstairs the next morning about five o'clock. Seth came down to prepare the breakfast. Dinah began cleaning the house. So when she went into the new room she noticed the dust lying thick on Adam's paper. She heard footsteps outside. She thought it was Seth and so called out : "Seth is your brother wrathful when his papers are stirred ?" Dinah was startled and shaken with intense emotion when Adam answered her. He came in and helped her in cleaning the room. As they worked together he noticed that she avoided looking at him. He asked if he had done anything to displease her.

Dinah looked at him earnestly and assured him that he had not. He told her how much grieved he was at the thought of parting from her and she answered that she must leave Hayslope because of manifold temptations and weaknesses of the flesh that threatened her there.

Commenting on the scene between the two the novelist writes, "This is a simple scene, reader. But it is almost certain that you, too, have been in love—perhaps, even, more than once, though you, may not choose to say so to all your feminine friends. If so, you will no more think the slight words, the timid looks, the tremulous touches, by which two human souls approach each other gradually, like two little quivering rain streams before they mingle into one—you will no more think these things trivial than you will think the first detected signs of coming spring trivial, though they be put a faint, indescribable something in the air and in the song of the birds, and the tiniest perceptible budding on the bed grow branches. Those slight words and looks and touches are part of the soul's language; and the finest language, I believe is chiefly made up of unimposing words, such as "light", "sound", "stars", "music"—words really not worth looking at, or hearing in themselves, any more than "chips" or "sawdust" : it is only that they happen to be the signs of something unspeakably great and beautiful. I am of opinion that love is a great and beautiful thing too; and if you agree with me the smallest signs of it will not be chips and saw dust to you : they will rather be like those little words, "light" and "music" stirring the love winding fibres of your memory, and enriching your present with your most precious past.

Thus, the scene becomes clear that the two Adam and Dinah—were in love, conscious of their love and gradually coming together. And preparing themselves for future partnership.

CHAPTER - 51

Sunday Morning

Dinah spent the following day with Lisbeth. Lisbeth was unhappy over Dinah's decision to leave Hayslope and expressed her wish that Dinah should marry one of her sons. The same evening, after Dinah's departure, Lisbeth confided in Seth that she was sure that Dinah secretly loved Adam, "And he might be willing to marry her if he knew she's fond of him, but he'll ne'er think of it if somebody doesn't put it into his head".

Seth begged his mother to speak to Adam regarding this matter on Sunday in his absence, when he goes to the church. She further told Seth that she knew that Adam loved Dinah as well. Adam was quite surprised and deeply moved when Lisbeth spoke to him. He now remembered the many little things and incidents which seemed to confirm his mother's remarks. He then rose and went out into the fields. The idea that Dinah was in love with him had overwhelmed him. Dinah was bound up with the sad, unpleasant memories of his past that haunted him and his love for her had emerged out of that past.

He wanted to be sure first that his brother Seth who had been in love with Dinah no longer entertained the hope of marrying her. He wanted to ascertain this and tried to find out by some tactful questions. Seth realised that Adam was interested in marrying Dinah. So he encouraged his brother to go ahead and propose marriage to her.

Adam rejoiced at the suggestion and decided to see her that very afternoon and propose to her.

CHAPTER - 52

Adam and Dinah

Around three o'clock Adam went to Hall Farm and knocked at the door. He was well aware of the fact that none of the family would be at home at that time except Dinah. The other family members would be at the church that time. Dinah was rather surprised when she opened the door to find Adam standing there. They went inside. Dinah enquired about Lisbeth's health. After some time Adam took both her hands and said, "Dinah, I love you with my whole heart and soul. I love you next to God who made me."

Dinah turned pale and trembled with painful joy. Her hands which were in Adam's turned death cold. Her eyes were filled with tears as she told him that they must part as they must submit to another will". She expressed her fear that her love for him was diverting her from the path of God. She feared that her soul might lose its freedom if it became enslaved to an earthly emotion of love. She admitted that she should and must choose between Adam and God, the Redeemer of all. Adam tried his best to persuade and convince her that it would be right for her to marry and assured her that he would allow her every freedom to continue her mission to serve God.

To this Dinah replied that she will wait for a clearer guidance from God before taking any decision.

Both of them then went out into the field and had a lengthy

conversation : "Dinah", said Adam mournfully, "you can't love me so well as I love you, else, you'd have no doubts. But its natural you shouldn't; for I'm not so good as you. I can't doubt it's might for me to love the best thing God's ever given me to know."

Dinah protested and said that her love for Adam is not weak. This love will give her the strength and not hinder her to seek to obey the uttermost, i.e. God. On this Adam assured her that he will speak nothing to disturb her.

They walked towards the fields, where they would meet the family coming from the church. Adam asked her to take his arm and she accepted willingly. Nothing, not even the uncertainty of the issue of their marriage could lessen the sweetness from Adam's sense that Dinah loved him. He thought he would stay at the Hall Farm all that evening. He wished to be near her and spend time with her as long as he could.

The Poyser family were surprised when they saw Adam and Dinah walking hand in hand. They discussed the possibility of Adam being in love with Dinah. Mrs. Poyser dismissed the prospect of marriage between Adam and Dinah as she felt that Dinah would "never marry anybody if he isn't a Methodist and a cripple". Adam was invited to the 'Harvest Supper' on the coming Wednesday, and he agreed to come.

CHAPTER - 53

The Harvest Super

As Adam was going homewards, on Wednesday evening, he saw in the distance the last load of barley being taken to the yard-gate of the Hall Farm and heard the chant, "Harvest Home." Adam was optimistic of seeing Dinah that evening at the Poyser's Harvest Supper. By the time he finished his work and dressed up in his best clothes, it was already seven o'clock. His heart was full of loving emotion and he dreamed of accompanying her to Oakburn and to talk to her on the way.

The Poyser's home was reverberating with the clatter of knives, pewter plates and tin cans when Adam entered. Voices did not accompany the clattering sound of the crockeries, as the farm labourers were too busy eating the excellent roasted beef to talk. Martin Poyser, the host took great delight in serving these farm labourers who generally satisfy their hunger with cold dinner and drank beer from wonder bottles. Tom Saft the Jester among the farm labourers was at the party. Kester Bale, an old man with a close leather cap full of winkles in his sun tanned face was also at the party. He was "one of those invaluable labourers who can not only turn their hand to everything, but excel everything they turn their hand to." Alick, the shephard sat opposite his master. He was not on very good terms with Old Kester Tim, the good tempered Wagoner did not get along with Alick as he had grudges against him concerning corn. Then there was the thresher Ben who on more than one occasion secretly carried away his master corn in his pockets.

After everyone had finished their dinner and the cloth drawn, it was time for the actual ceremony of the evening—the harvest song in which every man was supposed to join. They sang "Here's a health into our master". During the first and second quatrain of the song, no wine was served though it was a drinking song. Alick's can was filled with wine and he was bound to finish it before the chorus, "Then drink, boys, drink" ceased. The next turn was that of Kester, who had to drink wine and pass to the next on line. So everyman in his turn had to drink under the stimulus of the chorus.

After the chorus everyone voted for solo music. Tim, the wagoner was requested but he was too shy to oblige. Young David blushed and didn't sing.

While everyone were laughing and enjoying the party, a serious conversation had taken place at the head of the table. Adam learned from Mr. Poyser that Dinah had left for Snowfield the previous day. Adam was hurt and disappointed. Then there had been a serious discussion on the subject of women between Bartle Massey and Mrs. Poyser which led to a heated argument between the two. Their verbal duel was interrupted by a noise from the lower end of the table. David was singing "My love's a rose without a thorn", with Tim trying to outsing him and Old Kester joining in and trying his best to outdo the other singers.

Everyone was making merry, singing loudly and enjoying. Adam was about to go. He rose to say good night to everyone. Bartle Massey unable to bear the dim put his fingers in his ears and joined Adam. As they walked together for home, they had a discussion about the nature of Mrs. Poyser. Adam tried to defend her and said that her tongue was sharp but her heart was good. "I don't say the apple isn't sound at the core, but it sets my teeth on edge" said Bartle Massey.

CHAPTER - 54

The Meeting on the Hill

Although Adam was rather disappointed to know about Dinah's departure for Snowfield, he later seemed to understand. He drew hope rather than become discouraged in Dinah's hurry to go away. May be she was fearful lest the strength of her feeling towards him should hinder her from waiting and listening faithfully for the ultimate guiding voice from within. Yet he became impatient to see her again. "I wish I'd asked her to write to me, though, disturb her a bit, perhaps. She wants to be quite in her old way a while. And I've no right to be impatient and interrupting her with my wishes. She told me what her mind is; and she's not a woman to say one thing and mean another. I'll wait patiently".

Adam was hungering for the sight of Dinah. He had a mental debate whether to go to Snowfield to meet Dinah or not. Would Dinah be displeased with him if he goes? But she had never forbidden him to go! At last his heart won over his mind and he decided to go to Snowfield. On the second Sunday of October he set off for Snowfield on Jonnathon Burge's horse. The journey brought back painful memories for him. He rode along in that Sunday morning with vivid recollection of his past. His feeling towards Dinah, the hope of passing his life with her, had been the distant unseen point towards which that hard journey from Snowfield eighteen months ago had been leading him. He realised that his love for Dinah was the outgrowth of that fuller life which had come to him from his acquaintance with deep sorrow.

It was more than two o'clock in the afternoon when Adam reached the grey town on the hill side and looked searchingly towards the green valley below. He learned that Dinah had gone to preach at Sloman's End, a hamlet three miles off. He took a hasty meal in an inn and set off for Sloman's End. As he came nearer he heard the sound of voice singing a hymn. He thought that perhaps that would be the last hymn and decided to wait for Dinah at the top of the Hill where they would be able to talk freely away from all inquisitive eyes.

She took longer time to come than he expected. After waiting for at least an hour, he saw a little black figure coming from the grey houses. When Dinah approached nearer, Adam rose from sitting position. At that moment, she paused for a while and looked back at the village. Adam called out her name twice. At first she didn't turn round. But at the second call, she turned towards him with a look of yearning and love in her mild grey eyes. "She did not start against at the sight of him; she said nothing, but moved towards him so that his arm could clasp her round".

They walked together in silence, warm tears rolled down their cheeks. Adam was content and said nothing. Dinah was the first one to speak.

"Adam", she said, "it is the Divine will. My soul is so knit with yours that it is a divided life I live without you. And this moment, now you are with me, and I feel that your heart is filled with the same love, have a fullness of strength to bear and do our heavenly Father's will, that I had lost before".

Adam paused and looked into her sincere eyes. "Then wel'll never part any more, Dinah, till death partners".

They kissed each other with deep joy.

The author George Eliot gives a comment that—'what greater thing is there for two human souls, than to feel that they are joined for life to strengthen each other in all labour, to rest on each other in all sorrow, to minister to each other in all pain, to be one with each other in silent unspeakable memories at the moment of the last parting?'

CHAPTER - 55

Marriage Bells

In a little more than a month after that meeting on the hill at Sloman's End, Adam and Dinah were married on a rimy morning in departing November. It had been the most talked about and much thought of event in the village. All Mr. Burge's men had a holiday, and all Mr. Poyser's. There was hardly anybody in Hayslope who did not come to the church to see Adam and Dinah get married or who did not wait near the church gate to greet the newly wed couple as they came forth. Mrs. Irwine and her daughters were waiting at the church yard gate in their carriage to shake hands with the bride and the groom. Dinah was dressed in a grey Quaker frock and wore a grey Quaker Bonnet. Three couples followed the bride and the groom : first Martin Poyser looking bright and cheerful, led the brides maid Marry Burge; then followed Seth, serenely happy with Mrs. Poyser on his arm and lastly Lisbeth with Bartle Massey. She wore a new gown and bonnet, too busy with her pride in her son and in her delight in possessing one daughter-in-law she had desired.

Bartle Massey, the women hater, who was against marriage in

general, marriage of a sensible like Adam in particular, had consented to attend the marriage at the earnest request of Adam.

Behind the last couple came Mr. Irwine, glad at heart over Adam and Dinah's wedding. He had seen Adam in his worst moments of sorrow and was happy for him now to see him in wedlock.

People shook hands with the bride and the groom and showered them with blessings.

'That's a bit of good news to cheer Arthur, said Mr. Irwine to his mother, as they drove off. 'I shall write to him the first thing when we get home'.

Epilogue

The time was towards the end of June 1807. The workshop in Adam Bede's timber yard had been shut for more than half-an-hour. The workshop belonged to Jonathon Burge's earlier. Dinah and her two children, Lisbeth aged four and Adam two, were waiting eagerly for Adam's return alongwith Seth. Their home was now the pleasant house on the side of the timber yard. All of them have a very hearty conversation. Dinah says excitedly that she has seen Adam coming. Seth asks where Adam was as he carried young Addy over his shoulder and all of them walked on into the adjoining field. From their conversation it becomes clear that Lisbeth Bede, Adam's mother was no longer alive. Arthur Donnithrone had come to Hayslope after a long absence. Adam on that day had gone to meet Arthur. We also come to know about Hetty's death from their conversation.

When Adam reached, he received a warm welcome by his children and wife. Adam told Dinah about Arthur's illness. Arthur had been ill for quite sometime and the doctors hoped that he would soon be well again in his own country. He asked about Dinah and would be coming to visit her the following day. Adam further mentioned that he told Arthur that Dinah did not preach anymore. The second Wesleyan Conference had forbidden women to preach.

He told them how Mr. Irwine was delighted to have Arthur home again and had promised to take good care of him. Adam remained silent for a while and said that it was very 'cutting' when he and Arthur saw one another. Arthur had never heard about Hetty till Mr. Irwine met him in London. He never received his letters. He was fully of remorse and repented that he could do nothing to her. He lamented that Hetty had suffered enough on his account and he thought of the time when he would have been able to ease her pain. He agreed with a remark that Adam had made to him long time back—that there are some wrongs that can never be made up for. Just at that time the Poysers arrive to talk things over, and Adam goes inside to have some rest.

"The Epilogue" is crucial and necessary part of the novel. Through "the Epilogue", the novelist conveys her message. The message is contained in the words of Adam spoken to Arthur and repeated again in the Epilogue, "There is a sort of wrong that can never be made up for." Those who yield to temptation have to suffer, and have to pay a heavy price. This truth is borne out by the suffering of Arthur and Hetty.

CHAPTER - 21

CHARACTER ANALYSIS OF *ADAM BEDE*

CHARACTER ANALYSIS OF ADAM BEDE

Likeness between Adam Bede and Robert Evans

Adam Bede, the protagonist of the novel *Adam Bede* is a close pen-portrait of the novelist's own father, Robert Evans. There are close resemblances between the characters of the two. Adam Bede is a carpenter by profession, and lives in his humble house with his parents—Lisbeth and Thias Bede—and his brother Seth Bede.

An Elevated Personality

The novelist presents Adam Bede as an elevated personality. He is exceptional in many respects. His extraordinary physical strength is stressed in the very beginning of the novel. As George Eliot tells us, "he is a large-boned, muscular man, nearly six feet high, with a back so flat and a head so well poised that when he drew himself up to take a more distant survey of his work, he had the air of a soldier standing at ease. His sleeves rolled up above the elbow showed an arm that was likely to win the prize for jeals of strength; yet the long supple hand, with its broad finger-tips, looked ready for works of skill. In his tall stalwartness Adam Bede was a Sanon, and justified his name; but the jet-black hair, made the more noticeable by its contrast with the light paper cap, and the keen glance of the dark eyes that shone from under strongly marked, prominent and mobile eyebrows, indicated a celtic blood. The face was large and roughly hewn, and when in repose had no other beauty than such as belongs to an expression of good-humoured, honest intelligence."

An Honest and Proficient Craftsman

Adam Bede's physical strength is combined with his honest and proficient craftsmanship. The protagonist is a dedicated workman. He is an accomplished craftsman who takes pleasure in his work and in life. He works with sincerity and lives happily. His dedication towards his work can be cited. When Adam Bede finds that a coffin which has to be delivered the next day has not been completed by his father, he immediately sets to work on it even though he is tired after the days hard work. He does not even care to take his food. He works for the coffin all night and has it ready for delivery the next morning. When his mother contends that he should first have his food and then begin his work, he furiously pushes her aside and says, "It's the talking about having supper when here's a coffin promised to be ready at Bronton by seven o'clock tomorrow morning, and ought to ha' been there now, and not a nail struck yet. My thewat's too full to swallow victuals." As a craftsman he realised that whatever he does should be well-done and the work should be done on time.

It is because of his dedication, honesty, skill and capability, that he is widely respected, valued and honoured. Thus Arthur makes him the manager of the woods, and gives him a place of honour during the celebration of his 21st birthday. Jonathan Burges is keen to make him a partner in his business and the Poysers feel that Adam Bede would make a better husband to Hetty. They feel honoured when he courts her and is betrothed to her.

Patient and God-fearing

Adam Bede is presented as a tolerant and God-fearing man. In matters of religion he stands for conformity, for remaining within the folds of the established church. When the other workmen laugh at his brother Seth Bede for his being a Methodist, he explicitly tells them that though he would follow the teachings of the established church and go to the church regularly, but he does not like that anybody should laugh the religion of others. Adam opined that everybody is free to practise their own religion. It does not trouble him that his brother Seth is following a different religion. The protagonist is thus patient and God-fearing. He is not a fanatic and believes that everybody should seek God according to their own understanding.

Regarding his own practise, Adam follows the religion of his father. The former believed in the virtue of hard work; work is his religion, work is worship for him. He is honest in his dealings with others and expects others also to be equally honest with him. Thus, he is not awestruck by Lydia Donnithorne, the Squire's sister and insists on a fair price for the screen he has made for her.

His Physical Prowess : Positive Innocence

Adam is sincere and hard-working, and he also has the physical ability to hold his own against iniquity done to him. As R.T. Jones points out, Adam represents, "a positive, and active innocence", as compared with his brother Seth who represents "Passive innocence." Adam will not intentionally hurt anybody, but he will not hesitate to hurt someone, if he is convinced that he deserved it. As the protagonist tells Mr. Irwine that he will not strike anybody except a miscreant, and he does strike Arthur and lays him flat on the ground because he has acted like a scoundrel towards Hetty. Arthur is a military man, but nevertheless Adam thrashes him, and compels him to write a letter to Hetty and confess to her the fact that he can never marry her, and so their affair should come to an end.

His Love of Knowledge

Despite his hectic work Adam labours hard to acquire a bit of knowledge. It had cost him a great deal of trouble and stamina to work overtime in order to get the mastery of his pen, to write plainly and spell fairly-well, and to learn his musical notes. He had read his Bible and several books such as the *Pilgrim's Progress*. Had he enough time in his hand Bartle Massey would have lent him more books to read. Among his workmen Adam certainly stands out for he knew the importance of education.

His Love of Hetty

Adam's intense attachment towards Hetty is the only flaw in his character. Love blinded him to Hetty's true nature. He overlooked her behaviour and her faults, except her vanity towards finery : when she stuck a rose in her hairs, "The tender admiration in Adam's face was slightly shadowed by reluctant disapproval." Hetty's love of journey was just the thing that would most provoke his mother, and he himself disliked it as much as it was possible for him to dislike anything that belonged to her. "Adam's suffering at the time of Hetty's trial was almost too much to be borne, and affected him for the rest of his life. He shrank from witnessing her agony, but forced himself to stand by her.

No doubt, Adam ultimately transferred his love to Dinah, but the memories of Hetty which they have in common, do much to bring them together. During Hetty's trial Adam and Dinah, the two principal characters get to know each other ultimately, and love found its way into their hearts. "And Dinah was so bound up with the sad memories of his first passion, that he was not forsaking them, but rather giving them a new sacredness by loving her. Nay, his love for her had grown out of the past : it was the noon of that morning." Adam's affection for Hetty had been tender and intense, but his love for Dinah was fitter and more precious to him, for it was the outgrowth of that fuller life which had come to him from his acquaintance with distress. "It's like as if it was a new strength to me", he said to himself, "to love her, and know as she loves me. I shall look t'her, to help me to see things right. For she's better than

I am —there's less O'self in her, and pride." Indeed, Adam's love for Dinah made him a stronger and judicious man.

The Basic Flaw : Habit of Moralising

Adam's sense of his own "righteousness", his vanity that he had clarity of vision, and can understand everything clearly while others cannot is the chief drawback in his character and the novel shows his gradual purgation and inner illumination and accomplishment of self-knowledge. In this context we may quote the views of Joan Bennett, "It is evident that the author intended self-righteousness to be the flaw in his character which is partially, if not wholly, purged by the suffering he undergoes in the course of the story. Adam, before the tragic climax in the prison, is a prig and forfeits some of the reader's sympathy in consequence. But the author deliberately draws him as a man who is too apt to moralize on all occasions. He preaches to his mother when she nags at him for putting on his best clothes to visit Hetty.

'Nay, nay, Mother', said Adam, gravely, and standing still while he put his arm on her shoulder, 'I'm not angered. But, I wish for thy own sake, thee'dst be more contented to let me do what I've made up my mind to do. I'll never be no other than a good son to thee as long as we live. But a man had other feelings besides what he owes to's father and mother; and thee oughtna' to want to rule over my body and soul. And thee must make up thy mind, as I'll not give way to thee where I've a right to do what I like. So let us have no more words about it."

Self-righteous, Harsh and Unsympathetic

Adam's sense of his own 'righteousness' makes him arrogant and harsh. He is less accessible to compassion than his brother Seth. As George Eliot tells us, "the idle tramps always felt sure that they could get a copper from Seth, they scarcely ever spoke to Adam." He is impatient of any failing or drawback in others. He is critical of his father's habit of neglecting his work and going out for drinking; he is furious and agitated when his mother insists that he should have his food before beginning work on the coffin. His brother, Seth, too understands that it is futile to prevail upon him, for he always abides to what he says.

It is the sense of his own 'righteousness' which makes him so arrogant and unsympathetic to the failings of others. Many critics have called him a 'prig' and "mouster of goodness". Thus, Henry James writes, "My chief complaint with Adam Bede himself is that he is too good. He is meant, I conceive, to be every inch a man;

but to my mind, there are several inches wanting. He lacks spontaneity, he is too stiff-backed He lacks that supreme quality without which a man can never be interesting to man-the capacity to be tempted."

His Education and Sanctification

Adam Bede's inclination towards moralising is a part of the novelist' conception of his character. The reader who has respect for the protagonist, but only a limited admiration is being affected as the novelist meant that he should be. This idea holds true for the novelist allows Adam finally to discover, as the result of suffering, that his own self-righteousness had marred his relation with his parents, with Arthur Donnithorne and even with Hetty. His intense grief in his dealt upper room outside her trial is combined with mortification. It is there that he first begins to realise his own drawback.

The second scene in the novel with Arthur in the wood, in which the reconciliation takes place, is important to his self-discovery and purgation. The conduct of both men is convincing throughout the scene and the barriers, inherent in the nature of each, are very gradually overcome until at last, after a silence of minutes, Adam says. 'It's true what you say, sir : I'm hard, it's in my nature. I was too hard with my father, for doing wrong. I've been a bit hard t' everybody but her. I felt as if nobody pitied her enough, her suffering cut into me so; and when I thought the folks at the Fam were too hard on her, I said, I'd never be hard to anybody myself again. But feeling over much about her has perhaps made me unfair to you. I've known what it is in My life to repent and feel it's too late : I felt I'd been too harsh to my father when he was gone from me—I feel it now, when I think of him. I've no right to be hard towards them as have done wrong and repent.'

Finally, when Adam discovers his love for Dinah he realises what has been amiss in himself : 'It's like as if it was a new strength to me,' he said to himself, "to love her, and know as she loves me. I shall look t' her to help me to see things right. For she's better than I am—there's less o'self in her, and pride. I've always been thinking I knew better than them as belonged to me, and that's a poor sort O'life when you can't look to them nearest to you to help you with a bit better thought than what you've got inside you already.'

The marriage of Dinah and Adam is justified because it enables the novelist to put final touches to Adam's education and sanctification.

parlour and always wear white stockings; to have some large, beautiful ear-rings, to have Nottingham lace round the top of her gown and something to make her handkerchief smell nice." It can be pointed out that her dreams of such luxuries are appropriate to her nature and George Eliot's account of such dreams adds to the realism of her character. If she had dreamed of running the affairs of the Donnithorne estate and of the village Hayslope, and of being applauded for her intelligence, judgement and discretion, then we might well have regarded her fantasies as dangerous and absurd.

Fallacious Softness : Core of Hardness

Hetty is beautiful, but her beauty is fallacious. She has the softness, and loveliness and fertility of Loamshire, but also its core of hardness. The protagonist of the novel, Adam is deceived by her apparent softness, but her aunt Mrs. Poyser is able to see through it and apprehend the core of hardness that lies within. She was aware of Hetty's beauty and admired it too, but she also saw her faults: "She's no better than a peacock, as'ud strut on the wall, and spread its tail when the sun shone, if all the folks in the parish was dying", Mrs. Poyser complained to her husband. The ruthlessness which Mrs. Poyser had observed in her niece came to the fore during Hetty's flight : 'A hard and even fierce look had come in the eyes, though their lashes were as long as ever, and they had all their dark brightness. And the cheek was never dimpled with smiles now. It was the same rounded pouting, childish prettiness, but with all belief in love departed from it—the sadder for its beauty, like that wondrous Medusa-face with the passionate, passionless life." She could not comprehend how anyone could be fond of middle-aged people and children. Hetty found children bothersome. Though she was provided shelter by her uncle Martin Poyser, she was not very attached to him; and she was also annoyed by Totty. She is so insensitive and self-centered that, moved by her instinct of self-preservation, she could even kill her own child.

A Self-Centred : Flirt

Hetty is presented in the novel as vain and coquettish. She knew that Adam was the best and most appropriate among all her suitors but she did not reciprocate his love for her for she had no wish to marry him. She was aware of Adam's poverty and knew that after her marriage he would be unable to provide her with the fineries which she loved, and of which she always dreamed. But, Hetty was also clever enough not to loose any of her admirers. She took care to rekindle his admiration and encouraged him if he stayed away from her for any length of time. She never intended to marry Adam because he was impoverished, and having the innocence of "young frisking things" of a kitten or of a "young star-browed calf", she was quite oblivious to the sterling qualities of his head and heart. The protagonist, Adam Bede "could not more stir in her the emotions that make the sweet intoxication of young love, than the mere picture of the sun could stir the spring sap in the subtle fibres of the plant." The novel further informs us that she is a pretty creature of sensuous delight, who could hardly sympathise with Adam's troubles and grieve over the death of Thias Bede : "Young souls, in such pleasant delirium as hers, are as unsympathetic, as butterflies sipping nectar; they are isolated from all appeals by a barrier of dreams—by invisible looks and impalpable arms" She turns to Adam and accedes to marry him, when she had given up all hopes of Arthur's return to her. Hetty was now aware of Adam's progress in his business, that he was on the way to prosperity, and that he would be able to offer her the comforts she yearned for. She thinks of her own happiness, of the gratification of her own desires, and no thought of Adam's happiness enters into her head, so selfish and ungenerous is she.

Her Love for Arthur

Hetty's love for Arthur leads to her doom and her tragic end. Her first meeting with him intoxicates her and takes her to a world of dreams and fantasy. Henceforth, she thought more of Arthur Donnithorne than of Adam whose love for her was genuine. George Eliot comments, "Bright admiring glances from a handsome young gentleman, with white hands, a gold chair, occasional regimentals, and wealth and grandeur immeasurable—those were the warm rays that set poor Hetty's heart vibrating and playing its little foolish turned over and over again." She was the daughter of a simple farmer and to her a gentleman with a white hand would make her future bright. When Hetty realised that Arthur reciprocated her love for him her appreciation of her own beauty met a further boost. The scene in her bed-chamber showed her triviality. Dinah's pious talk disturbs her, not because she had the diffidence of a luxurious, pleasure-seeking nature which shrinks from the mention of pain.

Her Agony and Distress

Though Hetty shrinks from the mention of pain and agony distress lay in store for her. She was destined to face sufferings and anguish and her beautiful dreams ended in tragedy, "The parting with Arthur was a double pain to her : mingling with the tumult of passion and vanity, there was a dim, undefined fear that the future might shape itself in some way quite unlike her dream." Hetty's girlish happiness died on the night that she received Arthur's letter of farewell. "There is no despair so absolute as that which comes with the first moments of our first great sorrow."

Hetty so far had not undergone pain and suffering but henceforth agony and distress was to be her lot. The two chapters of the novel Journey in Hope, and Journey in Despair is a poignant record of the heart-rending grief of the 'innocent' Hetty. She was driven to take a drastic step and deliberation of suicide occurs to her for fear of disgrace and dishonour. She had no guiding principle to follow, for although she had attended church regularly, she had not imbibed a single Christian doctrine. Exhausted with her wanderings to Windsors and back to Stoniton, she prematurely gave birth to her child in the house of a stranger, Sarah Stone. The next evening, feverish and almost insane she went out and tried to escape from her ignominy by abandoning her child in the woods. But, the cry of her child haunted her and she returned—only too late. Facing the public contempt of her trial and the knowledge that she was reproached by all, Hetty "shut her heart against her fellow—creatures." The Methodist preacher Dinah was the only one to reach out and help her. The former convinced Hetty of God's Mercy and removed her dread of eternal regret beyond the grave.

Her Love of Life

On learning of her unpardonable mistake Hetty contemplates suicide. George Eliot tells us that as she wanders alone from her house she often thinks of suicide : "Soon she is in the Scottlands, where the greasy land slopes gradually downwards, and she leaves the level ground to follow the slope. Farther on there is a clump of trees on the low ground, and she is making her way towards it. No it is not a clump of trees, but a dark shrouded pool, so full with the wintry rains that the under boughs of the elder bushes lie low beneath the water. She sits down on the grassy bank, against the stooping stem of the great oak that hangs over the dark pool. She has thought of this pool often in the nights of the month that has just gone by, and now at last she has come to see it. She claps her hands round her knees and leans forward, and looks earnestly at it, as if trying to guess what sort of bed it would make for her young round limbs.

No, she has not the courage to jump into that cold watery bed, and if she had, they might find her they might find out why she had drowned herself. There is but one thing left to her : she must go away, go where they can't find her.

Her Destitution

U.G. Knoepflimacher has pointed out that throughout Hetty journey away from home arrival imagery has been used to bring out her helplessness, her ordeal as well as her passionate desire for life and the instinct of survival. During her flight, the fugitive meets a cart with a dog travelling on it, "a small white-and liver coloured spaniel", and for the first time Hetty feels "as if the helpless timid creature had some fellowship with her". In the next chapter of the novel Hetty clings to life "only as the hunted, wounded beauty clings to it." After her futile attempt at suicide she stumbles into the straw of a sheep fold. Her joy that she was alive caused her to break out in hysterical joy over the fact 'that she was still on the familiar earth". "The very consciousness of her own limbs was a delight to her : She turned up her sleeves, and kissed her arms with the passionate love of life." The sheep, the humble surroundings and, above all, her approaching motherhood, are inconsequential to Hetty. They merely accentuate her narcissism. The next time we hear of her is through the Mouth of Rector Irwine, informing the protagonist of the novel, Adam that she is accused of having murdered her child.

Hetty's Chastisement : Unacceptable and Offensive

Hetty's grief and agony is out of all proportion to her guilt. What befalls Hetty is not nemesis—the punishment of an exceptional, abominable crime, or of excessive and unnatural arrogance. Walter Allen opines, "One cannot help revolting against what seems her creator's vindictiveness towards Hetty." Hetty's sensuality is beautifully rendered : everyone in the novel who meets her feels it and so does the reader. But, for George Eliot it seems to be an unpardonable mistake, something in itself condemnable. George Eliot, we learn from her biographers, was perhaps over-conscious of what she analyzed as her own ugliness and it sometimes appears that in her fiction she had to mortify women beautiful as she herself was not. The novelist, could not, one feels, forgive sexual passion. V.S. Pritchett comments, "The drawing of Hetty is neither observation from life nor a true recasting of experience by the imagination; it is a personal fantasy of George Eliot's. George Eliot was punishing herself and Hetty has to suffer for the "Sin" George Eliot had committed, and for which, to her perhaps unconscious dismay, she herself was never punished."

Her Innocence

After Hetty learns of her impending motherhood she thinks of suicide as the only alternative. But, she does not have the courage to take her own life and so she wanders along. We may ask—why does she wander alone, and what does she think is likely to turn up and set her free from her present anxiety, despair and grievance? She cannot return home and holy matrimony with Adam is ruled out. But, Arthur can be forced into marrying her, for she has in her possession Arthur's letter, in which he asks her to correspond with him, "if any trouble should come that we do not foresee," and it constitutes evidence, of his accountability for her present condition. Arthur's letter indeed says that he cannot be her life-partner but situations have changed. We cannot suppose her not to comprehend the persuasive force of such a letter supported by her pregnancy. But, if we conceive that she does understand the seriousness of the matter and still does not make use of the letter, we must give her credit for a positive innocence that reflects back on her earlier behaviour. We can now believe that what Hetty has wanted all along has not been marriage at any price with Arthur. All that she has done for Arthur has been for affection (of which she has been starved at home); Arthur's warmth and comforting fondness, without which the marriage and Nottingham lace she has dreamed of, hold no charm for her when Hetty decides to go and meet Arthur, it is for affection, not marriage under hardship that she goes. But, the novelist does not give Hetty the credit for this innocence; and her comment at the end of the chapter, as Hetty sets off for Stoniton is unfair : "But Hetty's tears were not for Adam, not for the anguish that would come upon him, when he found, she was gone from him forever." They were for the misery of her own lot, and why should they not be so? Hetty's is the primary misery in the novel; the others are lesser sorrows that derive from it. It is more appropriate for Hetty to weep for her own lot and not for Adam's grief.

Hetty : Figure of Suffering Humanity

George Eliot has been so harsh with Hetty that we rightly agree with R.T. Jones, "Hetty is not absolutely innocent, but the consequences of her guilt are so vastly disproportionate to her responsibility that she remains, in our recollection of the novel as a representative of suffering humanity.' "No wonder Man's religion has much sorrow in it," says the novelist, "no, wonder he needs a suffering God". Within the novel *Adam Bede* Hetty represents the agony of mankind of which the crucifix ('an image of a great agony—the agony of the Cross') is an appropriate venerable reminder.

CHARACTER ANALYSIS OF MRS. POYSER

A Perpetual Figure of Amusement

Mrs. Poyser, the wife of Martin Poyser, a farmer by profession is among the immortals of literature. Like Shakespeare's Falstaff in Henry IV she is extremely witty and her verbal resourcefulness, has amazed all readers of *Adam Bede*. She is a minor character in the novel as she exercised little influence on the course of action. But the novel owes much of its charm and attraction to her. She pervades the novel and once we have made acquaintance with her we remember her throughout the novel.

Physical Features

Mrs. Poyser is described as being neither old nor shrewish but, "a good looking woman, not more than thirty eight, of fair complexion and sandy hair, well-shapen, light-footed : the most conspicuous article in her attire was an ample checkered linen apron, which almost covered her skirt and nothing could be plainer or less noticeable than her cap and gown, for there was no weakness of which she was less tolerant than feminine vanity, and the preference of ornament to utility. Her tongue was not less keen than her eye, and whenever a damsel came within earshot, it seemed to take up an unfinished lecture, as a barrel organ takes up a tune, precisely at the point where it had left off."

Her Wit and Intelligence

Mrs. Poyser has been highly praised for her wit and intelligence. In this context a critic comments "She has that combination of shrewish remark and homely wit with genuine kindness and racy style which is so attractive in Samuel Weller. Mrs. Poyser, in her way, is as amusing as Mrs. Gamp or Mrs. Nicklelby, and much more sensible. The devoted housewife's intelligence shines throughout the novel. Her sensibleness is a subject either, spoken by herself or quoted by any character in the novel or mentioned by the novelist. On one occasion George Eliot, unable to express herself in her own words, introduces Adam Bede to express the thought in his words, and the protagonist, finding his own language inadequate is obliged to fall back upon the expression used by Mrs. Poyser, whom accordingly he quoted." "You're mighty fond of Craig, says Mrs.Poyser to her husband, 'speaking of certain Scottish gardener, but for my part, I think he's welly-like a cock as thinks the Sun's rose o' purpose to hear him crow.' This is Mrs.Poyser's style, a good caustic remark and effective when it is necessary to scold her husband and to control her nieces.

A Devoted Housewife

Mrs. Poyser was a devoted housewife. She actively performed her family chores and was well known for the cleanliness of her kitchen and dairy. "Mrs. Poyser's environment is the farmhouse of the Hall Farm, and it is full of evidence of hard work." When we are first introduced to her in the novel, she is, as we might have expected, busy. She is ironing the clothes, and finding time, while the iron cools she engages herself to the work in the dairy and kitchen, to supervise the work of Hetty and Nancy. Her administration of the dairy work made her interested in the cattle and Mr. Poyser spoke highly of her discriminatory power in the matter of short horns. Mrs.Poyser's only drawback was her excessive love for her children. She adored Tolty and spoiled her, and could not fathom Hetty's lack of affection for her child.

An Outspoken and Straight Forward Person

Mrs. Poyser thoroughly liked a battle of words and usually defeated her opponents, as in her encounters with Bartle Massey and Squire Donnithrone. Once she launched herself in any conversation, she always sailed along without any awe or fear of the gentry. The confidence she had in her own ability of exposition was a motive force that overcame all resistance. Thus, she was not intimidated to tell the old Squire what she thought of him and enjoyed "having her say out" for once while Mr. Poyser waivers and is fearful to speak out, Mrs. Poyser is shrewd enough to see through the nefarious scheme of the churlish old Squire and boldly has her say without any fear of consequences. She dilates at length over the truthless drawbacks of the Hall Farm and makes herself out to be a martyr who drudges along the Farm with hardly profit enough to make both ends meet. The readers thoroughly praise her boldness, her verbal ability as well as enjoy the discomfiture of the old squire. The other characters in the novel—Molly, Nancy and Tim, grinning not far from him, also enjoy it, and so does the groom, who grins behind his back. Even Mr. Poyer is also delighted at his wife's straight forwardness despite all his fears of being turned at an early date, "leaving their roots behind."

Her Verbal Ability

There are innumerable examples of Mrs.Poyser's verbal ability. Once on a lovely afternoon, Molly, the maid, having completed her whole work asks her permission submissively, if she may sit down to her spinning work says George Eliot, as if herself enjoying the outburst, "But this shameless conduct, according to Mrs. Poyser, shrouded a secret indulgence of unbecoming wishes, which she now dragged forth and help up to Molly's view with cutting eloquence. And as for spinning, why, you've wasted as much as your wᴧgei' the flan you've spoiled learning to spin. And you've a right to feel that, and not to go about as gaping and as thoughtless as if you were beholding to nobody. Comb the wool for the whittaws, indeed. That's what you'd like to be doing, is it? That's the way with you that's the road you'd all like to go, headlongs to ruin. You're never easy till you've got some sweetheart who is as big a fool as yourself : you think you'll be finely off when you're married. I dare say, and have got a three-legged stool to sit on, and never a blanket to cover you, and a bit o'oat cake for your dinner, as three, children are snatching at." Poor Molly is confounded and can do nothing but weep.

Her Humanitarianism

Mrs. Poyser is not only 'sharp of eye' and 'sharp of tongue' but she also possesses the qualities of humantarianism. She is highly respected and if her tongue is sharp, her heart is tender, as Adam says of her at the end of the novel. Her continual ragging goes on to show her concern for the welfare of others and is not just a matter of habit. Regarding Dinah she says, "I've talked to her for an hour on end and scolded her too, for she's my own sister's child, and it feels good to me to do what I can for her," Mrs. Poyser's prayer might well be, "Bid her, therefore, that she helps me", and it would perhaps not be, as selfish as it sounds. It is a curious way of showing attachment but she means well by those she rebukes.

Her Ability in Handling Difficult Situations

Like Falstaff Mrs. Poyser has the ability to disengage herself from unpleasant situations, and wriggling out of dilemmas, may be of her own creation. The following example would be sufficient to bring out the point. Mrs.Poyser's maid servant, Molly once enters the room with her arms full of jugs, jars and mugs. But, unfortunately her leg gets caught in the apron which has come untied. She slips and falls down with a crash. This gives Mrs.Poyser an opportunity to indulge in one of her usual rant and poor Molly gets a sound drubbing. Mrs. Poyser then goes to the cupboard and takes out another jug. Just then Hetty comes, dressed like Dinah, and looking like a spirit in the dress. Mrs. Poyser is alarmed and breaks the jug. We would imagine that she would be astonished and speechless, taking into account the sharp rebuke she has just administered to poor Molly. But, there is no relief from Mrs. Poyser's incessant jabber. She is able to handle the situation with perfect ease—"Did ever anybody see thee like?" She said, with a suddenly lowered tone, after a moment's bewildered glance round the room. "The jugs are bewitched, I think. It's then hasty glazed handles—they slip o'er the finger like a snail."

"Why, thee'st let thy own ship fly i" thy face", said her husband, who had now joined in the laugh of the young ones.

"It's all very fine to look on and grin", rejoined Mrs. Poyser; "but there's times when the crockery seems alive, an' flies out of your hand like a bird. It's like the glass sometimes will crack as it stands. What is to be broke will be broke, for I never dropped a thing i' my life for want O' holding it else I should never ha' kept the crockery all these years as I bought at my own wedding."

Having handled this difficult situation with deftness Mrs. Poyser turns to Hetty to admonish her and send her back to change her dress. There is no repressing Mrs.Poyser, and no knowing what she will say next.

Her Poetic and Imaginative Faculties

Mrs.Poyser has rich poetic and imaginative faculties her enriched poetic faculties are shown by her use of similes and metaphors. Mrs. Irwine admired Mrs. Poyser, for as she said to her son, "I like that woman even better than I like her cream cheese. She has the spirit of three men, with that pale face of hers; and she says such sharp things too....her tongue is like a news—set razor. She's quite original in her talk, too, one of those untaught wils that help to stock a country with proverbs." We may state a few examples to show her wit and wisdom. She says : "Folks must put wi'their own kin, as hey put up with their noses—it's their own flesh and blood." Another example is when she says, "I am not one O'those as can see the cat i'the dairy an' wonder what she's come after." Yet, another example is when she says, "The men are mostly so slow, their thoughts overrun them, an' they can only catch them by the tail. However, I am not denying women are foolish, God Almighty made them to match the men." She further adds, "Some folks tongues are like the clocks as run on striking, not to tell you the time of the day, but because there is something wrong in their own inside." All these things said have the ring of a proverb.

Comparison with Her Husband

Mrs. Poysers kind heartedness is brought out when we compare her reactions to Hetty's disgrace with those of her husband. Mr. Poyser is unforgiving and deserts Hetty in her hour of need. The former says, "I'm willing to pay any money that is wanted towards trying to bring her off, but I'll not go nigh her, nor ever see her again by my own will. She' made our bread bitter to us, for all our lives to come....'. While the old grandfather weeps at her predicament, Mr. Poyser remains unmoved. Meanwhile, Hetty, we recall is likely to be executed. With this in mind, our sympathy with Mr. Poyser is limited when we weep for his own uprooting: 'Ah, there's no staying i' this country for us now, said Mr. Poyser, and the hard tears trickled slowly down his round cheeks. His wife, Mrs. Poyser is much less severe in her judgement than her husband. When old Mr. Martin says that they are dishonoured for ever, and that even their children would be jeered for being related to a murderess, Mrs. Poyser comes to Hetty's rescue and remarks, "It'll be their own wickedness, then. But there's one above 'will take care o'the innocent child, else it's but little truth they tell us at church. It'll be harder nor ever to die and leave the little nuns, an' nobody to be a mother to'em." These lines speak of the greatness of her soul, the largeness of her heart, and of her kind humble nature.

Conclusion

Mrs. Poyser may not hold an important place in the novel so far as the evolution of the plot is concerned, but it is she alone who provides the much needed dramatic relief in the novel. She plays a significant role to dispel the tragic gloom and the tensions generated by the ordeal and miseries of Hetty whose story forms the kernel of the novel. Mrs. Poyser, with her shrewdness, her untiring energy, her acrimonious speech and her generous heart is one of George Eliot's finest creations. While many critics admire her, Henry James alone is critical of her. The latter writes, "Mrs. Poyser is too epigrammatic; her wisdom smells of the lamp, I do not mean to say that she is not natural, and that women of her class are not often gifted with her homely fluency, her penetration, and her turn for forcible analogies. But, she is too substaned; her morality is too shrill—too much staccato. She too seldom sustained into the common place. Yet it cannot be denied that she puts things very happily. Mrs. Poyser has something almost of Yankee shrewdness and angularity." The last two sentences show that even a critic like Henry James has not been able to escape her magic spell.

CHARACTER ANALYSIS OF ARTHUR DONNITHORNE

His Physical Features

Arthur Donnithorne is the grandson of the Squire of Hayslope and heir to the estate. He is a charming young man who is affectionately called by different names—"the young squire", "the heir", and "the captain". He was held in high esteem by his people and though he was only a captain in the Loamshire Militia, to the Hayslope tenants he was a captain of prominent rank. The novelist writes about his physical features that he was "brown-locked, clear-complexioned young Englishman whom you have met with in a foreign town, and been proud of as a fellow countryman—well-washed, high-bred, white-handed, yet looking as if he could deliver well from the left shoulder, and floor his man". Thus, Arthur Donnithrone comes across as a youngman, cultured and refined and of considerable physical adroitness and physical charms.

A Conceited Person

The novel presents Arthur as a benevolent, amiable and an open-hearted man. His nature was impressionable and he found delight in others good opinion of him. But, apart from all his good qualities Arthur was also a conceited person. He would, no doubt confess his wrongdoings, but he had a confidence that his wrongdoings were all of a generous, kind, passionate and warm-blooded nature. He was good-natured and all his ideas of the future, when he would rule his estate, were made up of a prosperous, happy tenantry, idolizing their landlord, who would be an epitome of a perfect English gentleman. Thus, he tells the Rector, Reverend Adolphus Irwine that when he comes of age and inherits the estate he would do a lot for the good of his tenants particularly for Adam, "When I was a little fellow, and Adam was a strapping lad of fifteen, and taught me carpentering, I used to think if ever I was a rich sultan, I would make Adam my grand-vizier. And I believe now, he would bear the exaltation as well as any poor, wise man in an Eastern Story. If ever I live to be a large acred man instead of a poor devil with a mortgaged allowance of pocket-money. I'll have Adam for my right-hand. He shall manage my woods for me, for he seems to have a better notion of those things than any man I ever met with; and I know he would make twice the money out of them than my grandfather does, with that miserable old satchel to manage, who understands no more about timber than an old carp."

Not a Customary Miscreant

Arthur may be considered a miscreant a deceiver, a culprit who seduces an innocent girl Hetty. But, it may also be pointed out that the absence of the novelist's psycho-analysis of Arthur deprives us of a peep into the complex working of his mind, and the way in which he gives in to temptation, despite his best efforts. Comments R.T. Jones, "The innocence that Arthur represents consists in cultivating friendly relations with everybody; never willingly doing harm to anybody; and being willing to make amends for any harm he may accidentally do. This 'innocence' is a matter of intentions, of meaning well and meaning no ill, and is necessarily presented in descriptions of his thoughts rather than in actions. Without the account of his intentions, his actions, objectively regarded, would be almost indistinguishable from those of calculated villainy." We may consider the following lines : 'Do you always come back this way in the evening, or are you afraid to come by so lonely a road?' 'oh, no, sir, it's never late; I always set out by eight o'clock, and it's so light now in the evening. My aunt would be angry with me if I didn't get home before nine.'

'Perhaps Craig, the gardener, comes to take care of you?' A deep blush overspread 'Hetty's face and neck. "I'm sure he doesn't : I'm sure he never did; I wouldn't let him : I don't like him", she said hastily, and the tears of venation had come so fast, that before she had done speaking a bright drop rolled down her hot cheek. Then she felt ashamed to death that she was crying, and for one long instant her happiness was all gone. But in the next she felt loan arm steal round her, and a gentle voice said—'Why, Hetty what makes you cry? I didn't mean to vex you. I wouldn't vex you for the world you little blossom. Come, don't cry : Look at me, else I shall think you won't forgive me.'

Arthur had laid his hand on the soft arm that was nearest him, and was stooping towards Hetty with a look of coaxing entreaty...."

This shows that Arthur was man of good intentions and not a customary miscreant.

His Absence of Self Control

Young Arthur suffers from a lack of self control. No doubt, he has concern for the welfare of others, but all his good intentions become futile due to his absence of self-control. Despite all his good intentions, he cannot withstand a temptation. He was well aware of proprieties of behaviour and was unhappy with himself, annoyed and ashamed when he did wrong. Arthur cared for Hetty but he was not imprudent enough to wish to marry her. When he learnt that Adam loved Hetty, he was astounded. Had there been a possibility to make an atonement of his mistake, Arthur would have made it, but he did not learn the extent of the wrong he had done to Hetty until it was too late to make amends. We can only wonder whether he would have risen above his social prejudice in order to do what was right, had he known the truth in time. He did not wish to be unkind to others and did thoughtful acts, for he liked to have appreciative eyes beaming on him. Despite the agony that Arthur had to undergo in order to severe his relationship with Hetty, he felt that it would be a sensible act not to come in Adam's way. He had, however not washed his hands-off Hetty and had told her to write to him if she was in trouble. The result of Arthur's shortcoming was the tragedy that destroyed Hetty's life and his own. He made whatever reparations he could, but apart from saving her from execution, he could do little to help Hetty. To the last he wished to help her in some way, but unfortunately she died in exile.

His Penitence

Henry James, opines that the delineation of the character of Arthur is not commencing. He feels that there is something vague and indeterminate about his character. He writes, "I would, rather have him either better or worse. I would rather have he had a little more premeditation before his fault, or a little more repentance after it, that is, while repentance could still be of use. Not that, all things considered, he is not a very fair image of a frank-hearted, well-meaning, careless, self-indulgent young gentleman : but the author has in his case committed that error which in the case of Hetty she avoided the error of showing him as redeemed by suffering. I cannot but think that he was as weak as she. A weak woman, indeed, is weaker than a weak man; but Arthur Donnithrone was a superficial fellow, a person emphatically not to be moved by a shock of conscience into a really interesting and dignified attitude, such as he is made to assure at the close of the book." In other words, Arthur's repentance at the end of the novel falls to carry conviction according to the learned critic, Henry James.

His Deceptiveness

The novelist's account of Arthur shows how the later becomes a victim of deceptiveness both of himself and of others. The novel goes on to show how an affable character like him can degenerate.

His Innocence : Its Ironic Treatment

George Eliot's treatment of Arthur is an accomplished demonstration of the inadequacy of a very common mode of 'innocence' that consists of a general wish to please others and a belief that one never means any harm to anybody. It is this account that can endear us to return again and again, not only for what it demonstrates but for the way in which it does so R.T. Jones comments, "A familarity with George Eliot's ironical treatment Arthur's innocence is an antidote for complacency."

Psycho-Analysis

If the portrayal of Arthur's character had been that of "conventionally abominable Squire's son setting out to captivate the village maiden, he could hardly have made a better start. Yet, the novelist allows us to look at this scene—with the additional knowledge that there is no prospect of Arthur's marriage to Hetty—and still remain assured that he means no harm to her. For we have seen how Arthur has tried not to allow himself to meet Hetty : "If he lunched with Gawaine and lingered chatting, he should not reach the Chase again till nearly five, when Hetty would be safe out of his sight in housekeeper's room; and when she set out to go home, it would be his lazy time after dinner, so he should keep out of her way altogether." His mistake is to underestimate the strength of his impulse to meet Hetty; this fact becomes implicit in his apparent belief that after dinner, laziness will be an adequate deterrent. Arthur goes, but returns early and George Eliot's generalisation serves to make the return intelligible to us and at the same time to make us aware of a common inconsistency which we may recognise in ourselves, "It is the favourite stratagem of our passions to shame a retreat, and to turn sharp round upon as at the moment we have made up our minds that the day is our own."

Artifice of Passion

The 'stratagems of passion incorporated in the novel is seen with illuminating clarity when Arthur, after luncheon, is unable to 'recall the feelings and reflections which had been decisive' in his decision to avoid Hetty. The novel throws light on his conscious thoughts, and the self-deceptions and disfigurations of truth that we see in them, make, so to speak, a chart of the subconscious force of his impulse to see Hetty. It is in such accounts of inducement, conscious and unconscious, that Arthur is delineated. Our recognition of his good intentions, self-deceptions and weakness of will makes the portrayal real and acceptable to us.

His Genuine Repentance

The genuineness of Arthur's repentance cannot be doubted. By staying away from Hayslope, he made it possible for the Poysers and the protagonist Adam Bede to remain in their native place. His repentance was sincere and heart rending as he said to Adam, "I was all wrong from the very first, and horrible wrong had come of it. God knows, I'd give my life if I could undo it." His words are pathetic and carry a ring of honesty. It was right on the part of Adam Bede to be reconciled with Arthur Donnithorne.

comforts the afflicted; and the scene in which she prepares Hetty for death is created with a sureness of imagination that shows itself both in Dinah's approach and in Hetty's response." When Dinah talks about 'Misery after death' and 'a friend to take care of you after death—in that other world', the theology of hell and salvation is too explicitly present for the words to be taken in a double sense. But they are fully justified, by their effect on Hetty : her gradual acceptance to receive solace from Dinah. Hetty is moved not because of the religious consolation that Dinah offers, but because of the tender care which Dinah showers upon her. What helps Hetty to open her heart, enables her to talk about the misfortune she has endured and makes her approachable to the affection others bestow upon her, is not the religious dogma that Dinah offers, but the tender affection that Dinah expresses in offering it. Dinah undeniably has a gift for soothing others-a gift based on generous compassion and the application of Christian doctrine as its medium.

Her Devotion to Others

R.T. Jones rightly points out that Dinah's innocence takes the form of active and positive devotion to others. Dinah is a woman of kind disposition. She is a great comforter, and she is agonised at the Misery of others. Her ways are gentle, affectionate and sweet. That is why she was much adored by all who knew her—old and young, rich and poor alike. Even Hetty liked her even though their temperaments were different. Dinah provided great solace to others in trouble, for she seemed guided to say and to do the right thing. "She was never left to herself, but it was always given her when to keep silence and when to speak." Her goodness extended to cleaning and cooking well enough to please even Lisbeth.

Her Acceptance of Adam

Dinah faithfully performs the role of a 'preacher woman' while at the same time in her capacity as a married woman she sincerely performs her role. Adam is fortunate to Marry her; in comparison Seth has advantages only as a disciple. But here again one wishes the Biblical ideas were followed, otherwise they suggest self-deception. For Dinah's mode of speech implies adherence to a Divine authority of a kind that would favour Seth, the harmless contemplative person, while her choice for the flesh shows her allegiance to something more like Darwin's principle of natural selection, which prefers the active and materially practical Adam.

"The pretty preacher woman is domesticated in the end. Are we to see this as reduction of Dinah's exceptional destiny to mere commonplace domesticity? It seems that we do share some of Seth's regret that Dinah has to give up preaching; but the final effect of the close of the novel is that Dinah has exchanged an impressive but eccentric role for the higher destiny of full participation in the common lot of humanity."

Her Drawback

Dinah's use of Christian doctrines, Christian myth and Christian theology is commendable as long as she is comforting others. Her delivery of Methodist principles established a friendly relationship with her people and enables her to speak with authority. But, her use of Methodist language and Christian terminology sound rather contradictory and unnatural when she has to deal with her own private feelings. When she gets the offer of marriage proposal from Seth she refuses the proposal using Biblical terminology, "I've not turned a deaf ear to your words, Seth, for when I saw as your love was given to me, I thought it might be a leading of Providence for me to change my way of life and that we should be fellow helpers; and I spread the matter before the Lord....And when I've opened the Bible for direction, I've always lighted on some clear word to tell me where my work lay. I believe what you say, Seth, that you would try to be a help and not a hindrance to my work; but I see that our marriage is not God's will—He draws my heart another way....." The religious language comes too easily for a preacher like her but it gives a false air of Biblical authority to Dinah's own wishes. Her decision not to give in to Seth's proposal of marriage is indeed painful to him, "for it seems to shift the responsibility for her decision from herself to another Authority, another will, almost as if to imply that, left to herself, she would have accepted him." Dinah's decision has been taken by her awareness of her feelings towards Seth, and opening the Bible at random for direction has been merely a self-deceiving approval of her own decision. Dinah does not want Seth to be her life partner. One wishes, that she wanted it so, with that admirable simplicity that she often displays, instead of going contrary to her Biblical teaching.

Similarly, when Adam proposes her hand in marriage, she still uses the same Biblical terminology : "Yes, Adam, My heart is drawn strongly towards you; and of my own will, if I had no clear showing to the contrary, I could find my happiness in being near you, and ministering to you continually...." But, the above quoted lines come immediately after descriptions of her physical reactions : "Dinah's lips became pale, like her cheeks, and she trembled violently under the shock of painful joy. Her hands were cold as death between

Adam's. She could not draw them away, because he held them fast....tears were trembling in Dinah's eyes, and they fell before she could answer."

Assessment by Various Critics

Dinah has been criticised by a number of critics. R.T. Jones is of the opinion that her employment of Methodist terminology even in her personal relations is a sham and also bewildering. Another critic holds that Dinah is too good to be true. Her problem as a fictional character is that she is an all English girl as much as Adam is an 'all English boy.' Her goodness exceeds the bounds of modern literary taste, always returning good for evil, "walking the second mile', speaking in stilted, semi-biblical rhetoric, and in general acting like an employee of God instead of like a human being. She, too, begins to show her humanese only at the end of the book, and it takes a more humane Adam to awaken her humanity." Still another, critic, Joan Bennett is critical of her and writes, "if the characterization of Dinah partially fails to produce the effect intended, it is not because she is too virtuous but because of the author's treatment of her subject. It is in part because she intervenes too much, explicitly guiding the reader's response by her own comments, and it is in part the result of Dinah's semi-biblical idiom. Doubtless that idiom is a faithful record of the speech of Aunt Samuel and other Methodists, but it is none the less, a self-conscious and irritating mode of speech. When Dinah"s conversation is set beside Lisbeth Bede's in a scene in which George Eliot's excellent ear for dialogue probably catches the tune of each with equal fidelity, Lisbeth sounds natural and wins the reader's sympathy, where as Dinah sounds priggish and stilted"

A Balanced Appraisal

Though the portrayal of Dinah's character has met with criticism we endorse the appraisal made by Henry James. The latter's estimate of her character is more balanced and affectionate. Henry James writes, Dinah Morris is apparently a study from life and it is warm praise to say, that in spite of the high key in which she is conceived, morally, she retains many of the warm colours of life. But I confess that it is hard to conceive of a woman so exalted by religious fervour remaining so cool headed and so temperate. There is in Dinah Morris too close an agreement between her distinguished natural disposition and the action of her religious faith. If by nature she had been passionate, rebellious, selfish, I could better understand her actual self-abnegation. I would look upon it as the logical fruit of a profound religious experience. But as she stands, her heart and soul go easily, hand in hand. I believe it to be very uncommon for what is called a religious conversion merely to intensify and consecrate pre-existing inclinations. It is usually a change, a wrench, and the new life is apt to be the more sincere as the old one had less in common with it. Dinah Morris hears so many indications of being a reflection of facts well-known to the author and the phenomena of Methodism appear to be so familiar to her—that I hesitate to do anything but thankfully accept her portrait."

CHARACTER ANALYSIS OF SETH BEDE

A Foil (Reverse) to Adam Bede

Seth Bede is the younger brother of Adam Bede and an important minor character in the novel. He has an insignificant influence on the course of action, but throughout the novel he has been portrayed as a foil to his brother Adam Bede.

His Physical Delineation

From the very beginning of the novel Seth is compared with the protagonist, Adam as regards their physical appearance and also as workmen. We are informed that Seth is, "nearly as tall; he has the same type of features, the same hue of hair and complexion; but the strength of the family likeness seems only to render more conspicuous the remarkable difference of expression both in form and face. Seth's broad shoulders have a slight stoop; his eyes are grey, his eyebrows have less prominence and more repose than his brother's and his glance, instead of being keen, is confiding and benignant. He lacks the hardness of Adam and so, "the idle tramp always felt sure that they could get a copper from Seth, but they scarcely ever spoke to Adam." Adam is harsh to his parents, but Seth is more gentle, more understanding, more patient of the shortcomings of others, and more forgiving. While Adam is workaholic and works all night on the coffin which has to be delivered the next morning, it is Seth who consoles his mother and prays with her.

An Unorganised Craftsman

Unlike Adam, "Seth is an unskilled craftsman. He forgets to put the panels to the door, and announces that his work is completed. He also forgets his tool-box. Both the brothers are different from each other. While Adam is capable of working the whole day and night without food, Seth cannot take the same trouble. In their religion too, the two brothers are different. Seth is a Methodist, a dissenter, while Adam is a conformist, one who goes to the church regularly, and for whom the faith of his father is well enough.

A Passive and Ineffective Character

Both the brothers represent two different types of innocence. The protagonist represents an innocence which is active, dynamic and militant; Seth's innocence is passive and ineffective. In this context R.T. Jones comments, "While Adam exemplifies a positive and active righteousness, his brother Seth might remined us that the word 'innocent ' is derived from the Latin *no cere* 'to hurt', with a negative prefix. Adam though he does not knowingly wrong anybody, does not hesitate to hurt; it is Seth who is constantly careful not to hurt anybody. His pacific and soothing manner, backed by a good deal of quiet strength, is displayed in the first chapter and summarised by wiry Ben in the second : 'Seth's the lad for me, though he was a Methody twice O'er. I'm fair bear wi' Seth, for I've been teazin' him iver sin' we've working' together, an'he bears me no more malice nor a lamb. An' he's a stout hearted feller too, for when we saw the old tree all a fire is comin' across the fields one night, an' we thought as it was a boguy, Seth made no more ado, but went up to't as bold as constable....'

"Seth's meekness has nothing of fear in it; there is nothing paradoxical in the description of him as bold. But, for all goodness, Seth does not strike us as likely to prove a powerful and effective force for good as events in the novel unfold. He has already been characterised in the first chapter by the story of the door that he thinks he has finished making, while infact he has neglected to fit the panels into it. Thus, in such a village as the novel presents, is the kind of story that gives rise to local proverbial expressions, "Like Seth Bede's door."

"With his absent minded unreliability as a craftsman dramatised so vividly and so early in the novel, Seth must strike us as unlikely to be a decisive force in the novel. Neither his harmlessness nor his Methodism can be held accountable for his lack of concentrated application to the practical task in hand.

His Geniality and Love of Dinah

Seth's geniality and his love of Dinah is of the kind that William Blake described in the first stanza of *The Clod and the Pebble*:

> Love seeketh not itself to lease
> Not for itself hath any care,
> But for another gives its ease,
> And builds a Heaven in Hell's despair.

When Seth's proposal of marriage to Dinah has been gently rejected, he is resolving, as he now walks homeward under the solemn starlight, to supress his grief, to accept things as they come his way. His grief becomes all the more pathetic because his offer of marriage, far from being a selfish demand, was from the start an offer of dedication and service, "to give you more liberty—more than you can have now, for you've got to get your own living now, and I'm strong enough to work for us both."

A Docile and Resigned Character

However, much we may admire Seth's gentleness of character, his meekness and selflessness, his too ready acceptance of Dinah's refusal of marriage makes us feel that she has been right to reject him. Seth's innocence is not of a kind that decisively influences any train of events; he neither initiates action nor wholly matters the activities in which he is engaged. As a carpenter he forgets to put the panels on the door, and leaves his basket of tools behind. Further, as a Methodist, Seth is at the end of the novel an incompetent dissident with respect to the second Wesley conference's prohibition on women preachers. And, as an example of timidity and humility, he lacks the driving power.

In the sequence of events, Seth is almost inconsequential. His function in the novel is to act as a foil to Adam. The protagonist's capacity for sympathy which has been achieved with difficulty is more to be admired, and because it is based on experience and a habit of systematic thought, is more effective than Seth's.

"The fact that Seth, the rejected suitor, can live with Adam and Dinah without this ever occurring to anybody (including the reader), that the arrangement might be a dangerous or imprudent or improper one, and without Seth's seeming to find it in the least disturbing, tells us a great deal about Seth". "To talk by Dinah's side, and be tyrannised over by Dinah's and Adam's children, was uncle Seth's earthly happiness".

REV. ADALPHUS IRWINE

His Role in the Novel

Mr. Irwine, the Rector of Broxton, Vicar of Hayslope plays a crucial role in the development of action in the novel. He has a close friendly relation with the major characters in the novel and he is like a thread that links one character to the other. As a dignitary of the established church and as the close friend of Arthur Donnithorne the Squire's nephew and the future Squire, he enjoys immense prestige and authority.

External Appearance

Mr. Irwine's character has been portrayed by the novelist to the minutest detail. "In his ample white surplice that became so well, with his powdered hair thrown back, his rich brown complexion, and his finely cut nostril and upper lip; for there was a certain virtue in that benignant yet keen countenance, as there is in all human faces from which a generous soul beams out".

Noble and Large Hearted

He was good looking and very generous. He had a very measly income that amounted to no more than seven hundred pounds a year. He had to look after his mother and his unmarried disabled sisters. Seeing no other way to maintain, he sacrificed his happiness and remained a bachelor till the age of forty eight. He did not want any acclaim for the sacrifice he made by his renunciation of matrimony. He was one of those large-hearted sweet-natured persons who never held a grudge against anyone. He even forgives his mother's hardness towards his daughters. Mr. Irwine may not have been the perfect theologian, but he had the clarity which is found lacking even in profoundest of theologians. He was not harsh on other people's failings. He was admired by everyone at the church. He was not only a Vicar but also a kind of friend, philosopher and guide to his people. Arthur often used to confide in him and received valuable advices and suggestions from him. But he was not quick to discern their faults and remained in the dark about Arthur's weaknesses in spite of the close ties between them.

His Religious Fervour

Mr. Irwine's attitude to the church and his religious duties are well brought out by contrast with that of Dinah Morris, the Methodist preacher. One critic R.T.Jones marks the contrast between Mr. Irwine of regular church and Dinah, the Methodist and says that Mr. Irwine's redeeming features are qualities of character that seem to survive in spite of his ecclesiastical functions and have in themselves very little to do with a religious vocation. Dinah sometimes seems to speak seriously and earnestly about trivial things. On the other hand Mr. Irwine surprises the reader with lightness with which he speaks of his religion and its sacrament. When his mother beat him at chess. "Ah! you witch-mother, you sorceress. How is a Christian man to win a game of you? I should have sprinkled the board with holy water before we began. You've not won that game by fair means, now, so don't pretend it."

A Dutiful Son

Mr. Irwine has to look after his two unmarried sisters and a mother. While performing his duties towards his family he could hardly do justice to his parochial duties. In the description given by the novelist in the fifth chapter where he is introduced in the novel, the impression created by the house in one of ease and comfort one important aspect of that environment is perhaps his devotion towards his mother. The mother seemed to lack Christian values. She has been described in pagan splendour by the author : 'stately', 'magnificent' and 'splendid. There is no doubt about the fact that Mr. Irwine is dedicated primarily to her service.

His Tolerant Nature

One of his admirable qualities is his power of tolerance. Joshua Rann, the parish clerk of Hayslope comes to report methodist activity in the parish. Instead of reacting firmly as expected of a Vicar of a regular church, he casually advises to let the matter take its own course.

Even his mother agrees that he is very tolerant in nature.

"It is really insolent of that man, though, to call you an "idle Shephard", and a "dumb dog," said Mrs. Irwine : "I should be inclined to teach him a little there. You are too easy-tempered, Danphin."

"Why, mother, you don't think it would be a good way of sustaining my dignity to set about vindicating myself from the aspirations of will maskery? Besides, I'm not so sure that they are aspirations. I am a lazy fellow, and get terribly heavy in my saddle : not to mention that I'm always spending more than I can afford in bricks and mortar, so that I get savage at a lame beggar when he asks one for six pence. Those poor lean cobblers, who think they can help to regenerate mankind by setting out to preach in the morning twilight before they begin their day's work, may well have a poor opinion of me..."

Perhaps he does not take his duties towards the church as seriously as he should have.

His Role as a Cultured Gentleman

Mr. Irwine is a man of virtues. His deep knowledge of his parishioners, his cool temperament, impartial judgement, his lack of resentment at personal disparagement, his friendly co-operation with various individuals. These qualities which are attributed to him by the novelist are necessary to both—a clergyman as well as a squire. They eminently suit the tutor and his friend and disciple, Arthur

Donnithorne. These positive qualities or rather virtues enable him to play an effective role in the novel and also influence the course of events. He is a perfect gentleman who embodies great tolerance. He is somehow responsible for the tragedy of Hetty Sorrel. Arthur once came to him intending to confide in him about his affair with Hetty. Though he got some hints, like a true gentleman Mr. Irwine did not interfere taking it to be his personal matter and did not press him to confess. His timely intervention would probably have helped to avert the tragedy of Hetty. He did not try to enter into details as he had a conversation with Arthur, he was, too delicate, too soft to imply a friendly curiosity. He even changed the subject....“Evidently it is a hard vocation to be a priest, having the care of men’s souls and at the same time a gentleman, prohibited by delicacy from intruding into consciences of others.”

Wise and Discreet

The gentleman in Mr. Irwine stops him from extracting a confession from Arthur Donnithorne which proves fatal to Hetty. But his virtues are not alone responsible for the tragedy which might possibly have helped to avert the tragedy that was destined for Hetty and others. Once he comes to know about the tragedy he holds himself responsible and repents his inability to avert the sad consequences. His repentance and his handling of other parishioners as the news of Hetty’s arrest spreads like wild fire is really praise-worthy. He does not try to contradict Bartle Massey’s remark that ‘the sooner such women are put out o’ the world the better’; but he asks him not to speak ill of Adam. He reprimands Bartle Massey; “You must be careful what you say to him, you know. I’m afraid you have too little fellow-feeling in what you consider his weakness about Hetty”.

He uses his good will and wisdom to dissuade Adam from taking revenge on Arthur. He reasons with Adam and tries to change his mind to deter him from taking law into his own hands. In trying to reason with Adam, he does not take recourse to any religious arguments, but rather uses his practical common sense. He says :

> “It is not for us men, to apportion the shares of moral and retribution. We find it impossible to avoid mistakes even in determing who has committed a single criminal act and the problem how far a man is to be held responsible for the unforeseen consequences of his own deed is one that might well make us tremble to look into it. The evil consequences that may lie folded in a single act of selfish indulgence, is a thought so awful that is ought surely to awaken some feeling less presumtuous than a rash desire to punish....”

His Humanitarian Outlook

His experience as a man as well as a magistrate leads him to consider the human possibility of absolute justice very humbly. He upholds the view that one must not be too hard on sinners, everyone is fallible and liable to temptation. Himself being very humane, he expects his parishioners to adopt a humanistic approach to their fellow men who are prone to the weaknesses of the flesh.

PART - III

CHAPTER - 22

SELECT UNIVERSITY QUESTIONS AND ANSWERS

Q. 1. Hetty Sorrel is a perfect representative of Loamshire Hayslope world. Justify the above statement.

Or

Hetty's Narcissus Complex led to her tragedy. How far do you agree or disagree with this view?

Or

Write a note on the symbolic significance of Hetty Sorrel in the novel *Adam Bede.*

Or

Comment on the "Change of Nature-background in keeping with the changes in the career and fortunes of Hetty" in *Adam Bede.*

Ans. Hetty, a Representative of the Loamshire-Hayslope World

George Creeger is of the opinion that Hetty represents the rustic world of Loamshire and Hayslope in the best possible manner. Even the landscape, the nature background is presented by the novelist in keeping with her change in destiny. George Eliot's presentation of nature-background is strictly utilitarian, in the tradition of Hardy's *Tess of the D'urbervilles.*

Hetty, the rustic beauty with her narcissism and innocence also represents the fertility of the Loamshire world. The Hall Farm dairy, its gardens, the Grove of the Donnithorne estate—all have an individual aura, but all suggestive of fertility and growth. She is linked to all these places not only through her presence but also by parallel imagery. She is described in terms of vegetation, flowers and fruit in particular, of light-colour, warmth-coolness and moisture;

> "It is of little use for me to tell you that Hetty's cheek was like a rose petal, that dimples played about her panting lips, that her large dark eyes hid a soft roguishness under their long lashes, and that her curly hair, though all pushed back under her round cap while she was at work, stole back in dark delicate rings on her forehead, and about her white shell-like ears, it is of little use for me to say how lovely was the contour of her pink and white neckerchief, tucked into her low plum-coloured bodice or how the linen butter making apron...."

Her Fickleness

Hetty is a young girl of seventeen, full of exceptional physical charm and vivacity. She is aware of her physical beauty and its impact on others which makes her somewhat vain. She knows about Adam's weakness for her and knows that he was the most suitable match for her, yet she has no wish to marry him because he is too poor to afford the luxuries she dreams about. She secretly nurtures the wish to marry Arthur, as she was in awe of his social background and all that he could offer her would fulfil her dream. But yet she was not very indifferent to Adam which led him to believe that she was in love with him. She took care to rekindle his admiration and encourage him if he stayed away from her for any length of time. She is a pretty girl of sensuous delight who does not feel very deeply about Adam's trouble or about poor old Thias being drowned. "Young souls, in such pleasant delrium as hers, are as unsympathetic as butter flies sipping nectar..", George Eliot writes about her.

Her World of Dreams

Hetty was well aware of the fact that several men were attracted to her beauty. There was young Luke Briton of Broxton, a shabby silent youngman whom her uncle disapproved. Mr. Craig, the gardener at the chase, was head-over-heels in love with her. Then there was Adam whom her uncle considered a suitable groom as he had bright prospects. Adam did not interest Hetty or arouse any feeling of love in her heart. He was too poor to afford the luxuries she always craved for. When she saw that captain Arthur was showing interest in her, she was delighted at the thought of her long cherished dream being fulfulled by the captain. An illiterate, simple farm girl that she was, the gentlemanly Arthur had made a great impact on her. She was in awe of his manners and appearance, his courtesy and everything about him swept her off her feet. She knew that he can fulfil her dreams, her dream of all luxuries and finery—"To sit in a carpeted parlour and always wear white stockings, to have some large, beautiful ear-rings, to have Nottingham lace round the top of her gown and something to make her handkerchief smell nice." Her dreams are not inappropriate to her frivolous nature. The things that she craves for, she dreams about makes her character all the more realistic and convincing.

Her Innocence and Immaturity

In spite of her frivolous nature, Hetty had a child like innocence. The rich fertile and sheltered life of Hayslope had retained the child-like simplicity in Hetty. Hetty the simple farm girl who lived with her uncle and aunt had never known hardship in the real sense or undergone suffering in her rather carefree life. She had lived a sheltered life entirely free from the cares and worries of life. The occasional scoldings and rebukes are the only tough things that she had experienced. As a result she had not matured enough. She had grown up without maturity. Living a sheltered life she remained childish, immature enough to see reason and foresee the consequences of her own actions. She used to indulge in day dreams hardly giving a thought to the hard reality. She was fascinated by Arthur's rich gentleman like manner and dreamed of all the luxuries and fineries that he could offer. Lost in her world of dreams she fails to realise that Adam though poor has brighter prospects and is capable of giving her good life and keeps her happy. She is excited when Arthur gives her his attention and dreams of the kind of life she would lead and the finery she would wear after her marriage. She was not perturbed by the wide gulf between her and Arthur's social status.

Later on when she discovers her pregnancy, she leaves home with the hope of finding Arthur. She takes the content of Arthur's letter too seriously and for the first time in her life, the sheltered country girl ventures out to face the cruel world.

Her Narcissus Complex

A lively young girl of seventeen Hetty is quite aware of her physical charm. The fact that she had several admirers made her aware of her beauty all the more. On learning about Arthur's interest in her, she became more conscious about her looks. In the chapter, the two bed chambers, we get a fair idea about her narcissus complex. At night in her bed room she tried to look at her own reflection in the old mirror. As it was difficult to get a good view of her head and neck unless she sat down, she sat on the brass handles of the drawers which hurt her knees and she could not get near the glass comfortably, which did not deter her. George Eliot makes an ironic comment. "But devout worshippers never allow inconveniences to prevent them from performing their religious rites, and Hetty this evening was more bent on her peculiar form of worship than usual." When she saw her reflection, she was pleased and smiled, letting go off her ringlets. She felt prettier than any other woman in Hayslope and lovelier than any women, Arthur had seen or not. She took out a lace scarf from her drawer and a pair of large old earings. She admired her own beauty and thought of Arthur Donnithorne's love for her. She dreamt of her marriage with Arthur, ride in a grand coach, and gorgeous dresses for dinner etc.

Her Spiritual Intertia

Hetty's vain and frivolous nature leaves her spiritually inert. Dinah, the Methodist preacher realises about this early in the novel and tries to prepare Hetty for the possibility of pain in life, for the necessity of her adolescent dream-world, of growing up. She said to Hetty : "it has been borne in upon my mind tonight that you may some day be in trouble...." Dinah's concern and apprehension goes over Hetty's head and she asks—"But why should you think, I shall be in trouble?" Dinah's preaching has no effect on her soul, only her words "uttered with solemn, pathetic distinctness, affected her with a chill fear" and she cried not because Dinah's anxious pleading had brought realisation to her but because of a vague fear that something evile will befall her, grips her mind.

Dinah, seeing Hetty cry tried to soothe her with kisses but Hetty snubbed her telling her to go away.

Her Journey and Suffering

Little did Hetty realise, at the time of Dinah's pleading that very soon something is going to happen that would turn her whole world upside down. The frivolous and carefree, lovely Hetty was destined to face great pain and her lovely dreams ended in great tragedy. On discovering her pregnancy, she was driven to desperation and she even contemplated suicide. In her journey in search of Arthur she undergoes tremendous hardship and suffering. Throughout her journey, an animal imagery has been used to bring out her helplessness, her suffering and her passion for life. In her journey, for the first time she is exposed to the real world and realises that life in not a rosy picture seen through tinted glasses. Worn out with her wanderings to Windsor and back to Stoniton, she gave birth prematurely to her child in the house of a stranger. The very next evening feverish and half out of her mind, she went out and tried to escape from the shame of being an unwed mother by abandoning her child in the woods. She left the child but only to come back for it again as its crying haunted her. But it was too late. The child had died and she was convicted of murdering it. Facing the public disgrace of her trial and the knowledge that she was condemned by all, Hetty "shut her heart out against her fellow creatures". Dinah was the only person, who through her loving sympathy could reach out to her and convicted her to reveal the secret about her dead child by telling her of God's mercy.

Her Symbolic Stubbornness

Hetty is lovely, beautiful, but her beauty is deceptively soft. She not only has the softness, beauty and fertility of Loahmshire-Hayslope, but also its core of hardness. Everyone including Adam and Arthur are deceived by her apparent beauty and softness. Mrs. Poyser is the only person who sees though it and is able to perceive the core of hardness that lies beneath. The effect of Hetty's ordeal is to externalise the hardness that lies in the heart. Her tedious journey in search of Arthur results in giving birth to the child prematurely. At first motherhood softened her to some extent. To relieve herself from shame and social stigma she abandoned her child in the woods with the hope that she would return home and resume her life again in the sheltered cloistered life of Hayslope. But the woman in her was disturbed and she was haunted by the crying of the baby all night. She comes back again to her baby only to find its dead, still body. Committed with child murder, she is transformed almost into stone—emotionally. Mr. Irwine reports to Adam about her transformation that she has become a "pale, hard-looking culprit."

Most of the Loamshire world is shocked at the stubbornness of Hetty, how she has turned inhuman. They condemned her but were unwilling to help her or forgive her or even to comfort her. But Dinah the outsider from Stonyshire is the only person who is able to restore humane feeling in Hetty.

Q. 2. Adam Bede had regenerated into more genuine human being through the power of love. Comment on the above statement.

Or

Give your own views about the "Gradual shedding of Adam's hardness, pride and sense of self-righteousness".

Or

Consider the role of Mr. Irwine and Bartle Massey in the process of Adam"s regeneration.

Or

Adam gained enough education and had grown more mature through a process of suffering.

Ans. Adam a Perfect Man

Adam Bede the hero of the novel by the same title has been sketched by the novelist after her own father. He has been attributed with so many positive virtues that critics complain that he seems too good to be true. He has been presented as a perfect human being, the critics complain. But the truth is otherwise, though the novelist invests so much of her attention to project him as a human being of virtue, yet the character of Adam is not totally flawless. A deeper insight to his character reveals that he is proud, hard, self righteous with little sympathy for ordinary sinners. The novel, with its development in the plot traces the process by which he gradually sheds his false sense of learning—of his education, enlightenment and growth to maturity through a process of suffering and love—he ultimately becomes a complete man, a fully integrated personality. He is not a perfect man as often criticised but a very ordinary human being with his share of virtues as well as faults.

Self Righteous and Unsympathetic

Adam's sense of his own "righteousness" makes him stubborn and unsympathetic towards others. He is less accessible to compassion than his brother Seth. In the very first chapter of the novel we are told that, "The idle tramps always felt sure that they could get a copper from Seth, they scarcely ever spoke to Adam". Himself being a man of great strength, honest, diligent and a man of great integrity he is intolerant of any failing or weakness in others. He is critical of his father's habit of neglecting his duties and going out for drinking. He gets angry and irritated when his mother nags him to have his food while he was busy with his work. He holds on so stead fastly to his own self "righteousness" that he becomes cruel and unsympathetic to others. This becomes a flaw in his character.

Adam's Flaw : His Habit of Moralising

Adam's sense of self 'righteousness' makes him vain and egoistic. His belief that he has clarity of vision and can see everything clearly while others fail in this matter makes him all the more vain. He is a man of virtue, there is no doubt about it, he is honest, hardworking, possesses a strong moral character, a man of great integrity—and there lies his flaw. Being a man of strong moral integrity he finds fault with others very quickly. He does not harm anyone knowingly, but at the same time does not hesitate to hurt anyone. He is rather proud of his clarity of vision and his understanding: "I've seen pretty clear, ever since I could cast up a sum, as you can never do what's wrong without breeding sin and trouble more than you can ever see....". When he sees Arthur and his beloved Hetty together in the woods he was shocked beyond words. His confidence in his own righteousness gets a severe blow. He gradually realises the truth that one cannot foresee the consequences of his own wrong doing. Seeing Arthur and Hetty together in the woods shook him to the realisation that "how incomplete his mental seeing has been: He understood it all now—the locket, and everything else that had been doubtful to him a terrible scorching light showed him the hidden letters that changed the meaning of the past" ironically the woods incident where he catches both Arthur and Hetty red handed, marks the beginning of the process of his education and self-realisation.

Adam's Involvement with Hetty

His love of Hetty is the only weakness of otherwise virtuous Adam. Love blinded him to Hetty's faults and failings. The self-righteous man who is intolerant of other's failings, seemed to overlook her faults and constantly made excuses for her behaviour. He does not appreciate her love of finery but was too greatly attracted by her to accept that as her drawback. His dream of marrying Hetty was shattered when he saw her with Arthur one night in the woods. He blamed Arthur not Hetty and thought that Arthur was taking advantage of her innocence. Yet he had forgiven her and was ready to marry her. His suffering during Hetty's trial was too much to be borne and it affected him for the rest of his life. He shrank from witnessing Hetty's agony but, at the same time stood by her during her trial. Though ultimately Adam transfers his love to Dinah, but it is the memory of Hetty, which they have in common brings them together.

His Head Rules over the Matters of His Heart

According to critic George R. Creeger, Adam may be intelligent, diligent, trustworthy and loyal yet as a man he was very immature. This is because his head over-rules his heart. He is sincere, honest, hardworking but at the same time stern, wrathful, unyielding; stubborn and intolerant. He is essentially an emotionless person who threatens to shake anyone at the least provocation. In the very first chapter when wiry Ben teases Seth he threatens to shake him. Critics are of the view that there is an imbalance between the head and the heart in the character of Adam. Adam, when the novel opens is seen to be proudly in control of his own life losing patience over the lesser mortals, who are fallible to vices like his father. The purpose of the character of Thias Bede is to reveal the extent of the stubbornness and hardness of his son. The same is true of Arthur Donnithorne. Adam is especially hard and unforgiving towards these two. Although he repents later of his severity, the repentance is futile as it reflects no genuine increase in his capacity for sympathy.

His Learning Experience Through Suffering.

Adam was not fully involved emotionally at least with either his brother Seth or his father. Because of his emotional isolation, he can neither participate in their plight nor understand it. So it becomes necessary for Adam to get "his heart-strings bound round the weak and erring, so that he may share not only the outward consequences of their error, but their inward suffering". A similar emotional involvement exist before Adam and Hetty. The relationship is not based on reason but rather it is passion which overpowers him. As a result of his emotional involvement, Adam suffers and becomes humble enough to share the suffering of other people. He is shocked when he sees Arthur and Hetty together in the wood and is anguished at the thought, that Hetty plans to elope with Arthur to avoid their approaching marriage. He suffers all the more on learning about Hetty's arrest and that she was being tried for child murder. He suffers from deep spiritual anguish. His response to his suffering is quite different from Hetty's response. Hetty convicted of child-murder sank into passivity and inaction, refusing to divulge the truth or speak, she behaved as if she had been transformed into a stony statue. Quite contrary to Hetty, Adam moves towards the opposite direction, into violent retribution. Hetty who becomes hardened out of her selfishness is faced with a situation she cannot handle and is brought to a dead quiet. Adam, who on the other hand gets hardened out of his pride and self righteousness, lashes out at the world.

Adam's Regeneration Through the Power of Love

Adam through his suffering realises his folly. He finally discovers that his own self-righteousness had in a way strained his relationship with his father, mother and, Arthur Donnithorne and even Hetty. When a desperate Adam who was about to go in search of the missing Hetty is told by Mr. irwine about the news of Hetty's arrest and conviction, his world falls apart. He refuses to believe the allegation levelled against Hetty. He faces the greatest crisis of his life. At this moment there is the possibility of regeneration through a human agent who is capable of exercising the power of love. The suffering Adam underwent, seems to be a precondition for his regeneration. Mr. Irwine and Bartle Massey in the form of human agents help him to sail out of his misery. Both of them being very close to Arthur sense the possibility of potential violence in Adam and anticipating the fact that he may seek vengeance on Arthur for doing wrong on Hetty, they try to divert him. The Vicar Mr. Irwine uses the power of reason and tries to talk sense into Adam who was hell bent on teaching Arthur a lesson for bringing upon misery to poor Hetty. He argued that to injure Arthur would not help Hetty and that passionate violence would lead only to another crime. Though Adam agrees he was not ready for a full acceptance. The full acceptance in brought about by the universal women hater Battle Massey.

The Role of Bartle Massey in Adam's Regeneration

It is rather ironic that Bartle Massey, the women hater is able to bring about a symbolic awakening to "full consciousness" in Adam. The scene of this awakening takes place in Stoniton in what the novelist calls "an upper room", a "duel supper room". Adam, in this scene comes to comprehend the necessity of human compassion and forgiveness. A symbolic Lord's supper takes place there. Bartle Massey, before reporting the latest news of trial, says, "I must see to your having a bit of the loaf, and some of that wine Mr. Irwine sent this morning....I must have a bit and a soup myself. Drink a drop with me," Though at first his suffering continued to haunt him with the thought of revenge, gradually as Bartle speaks his hardness melts and he softens his stand. Finally he declares that he will go to the court and stand by Hetty. Bartle encouraged him to take another drink. After taking a morsel of bread and drinking more wine, the haggard and tired looking Adam stood upright again and looked like Adam Bede of former days again. His regeneration was complete.

Adam's Growth to Maturity

The novel traces the process of education through loss and suffering of Adam which leaves him a better and wiser man. Gradually Adam sheds all his pride in his self righteousness and clarity of vision and gains a sounder and more complex understanding of life. His suffering makes him conscious of his own follies. He has a better understanding of human nature now and realises that human beings are fallible to follies, that those who act wrongly may not be wicked in reality though they seem wicked. He decides to stand by Hetty, as an expression of his love for her as well as his newly perceived willingness to involve his life with the suffering of others. His awakening to human consciousness has two positive consequences. He is able to forgive Arthur and he becomes capable for a new love. All his suffering intimates him with the truth that "Love does not exist without sympathy, sympathy does not exist without suffering in common." Critics regard the Dinha Adam love affair and their ultimate marriage as an anti-climax. But Dinah and Adam had suffered in common, they share the painful memories of Hetty, such common suffering gives rise to natural sympathy which is the source of love. And hence it seems quite natural that both should come together and unite through the bond of marriage. This love leads to the fulfilment of his personality, and the process of his growth and maturity is completed. There is now a full integration of head and heart.

Q. 3. Write about the significance of the minor characters in *Adam Bede.*

Or

George Eliot has presented a cross-section of the Midland society in *Adam Bede*. Write a note on the minor characters in the light of the above statement

Or

The minor characters of *Adam Bede* present a comprehensive picture of Midland life and society. The farmers, clergymen, gardeners, school master, carpenters, milk-maids and in keepers all come out alive in the novel. Give your own views.

Ans. A Cross Section of Midland Society

In *Adam Bede* George Eliot has introduced a number of minor characters alongwith the major characters who appear every now and then. Though they are not sketched in detail, yet they come out alive with life and vigour and become an inherent part of the novel and share their own respective significance in the design of the novel.

The novelist fills up her canvas with all these minor figures and presents a complete picture of Midland life and society. These characters are drawn from various walks of Midland life. Farmers, clergymen, gardeners, school masters, carpenters, milk-maids and inkeepers all come to life in the hands of the novelist. They speak in the Midland dialect, sing and dance, gossip—and as a whole represent the midland society in its totality.

The Chorus of Rustic Characters

Though not sketched in detail these minor characters, are able to make an impression on the readers. They charm the reader with their rustic simplicity, humour and fun loving nature and leave a lasting impression on the minds of the readers. They are very realistic and in their eccentricities and grotesqueries may be compared to the minor characters of Thomas Hardy. The charms of these lively characters also play an important role in the novel. They contribute to the intensification of theme and character. The chorus also acts like a narrator and is used to make tragic statements by the author. It comments on the protagonist and throws enough light on the plight of the protagonist, thus enabling the reader to know more about him. The chorus also enlightens the readers by providing them information about the characters and family history. In this novel *Adam Bede,* the entire community of Hayslope plays the part of chorus.

Lisbeth Bede

The novelist has not invested as much attention in the minor characters as the major characters. Yet a glance at some of the figures shows that the novelist skillfully brings the characters to life with a few deft touches. Lisbeth Bede, mother of Adam is "an affectionate and querulous old woman, with her grey hair turned neatly back under a pure linen cap." She is devoted to her eldest son, Adam and is always concerned for him. Her over concern often irritates Adam and makes him behave rudely to her. She was anxious for him to have a sensible marriage and opposes any kind of marital alliance with Hetty. Though she disapproved Hetty for her vain and frivolous nature, yet she agreed later on as Adam was determined to marry her. She grows fond of Dinah and she is the one who eventually makes Adam realise his own deep affection for the Methodist preacher. She took pride in her son Adam and doted on him. She even insisted that only Adam and no one should make the coffin for her dead husband Thias.

Mrs. Poyser

Mrs. Poyser the wife of Martin Poyser, a rough and ready farmer, is one of the immortal creations of George Eliot. Like Shakespeare's Falstaff she is extremely witty and full of verbal resourcefulness. Though she is a minor character with little or no influence over the action, the novel would lose much of its charm and fascination without her. She is a rather good looking woman not more than thirty-eight years of age. She was never idle. A successful dairy women, a good housekeeper, a devoted wife and a mother, she was well known for the cleanliness her of kitchen and her dairy. She is witty and her witty remarks provide the much needed comic relief to the novel. She is known for her sharp tongue with which she subdues her husband, nieces and servants, but at the same time she also possesses a heart of gold. She pervades through the novel and makes a lasting impression on the reader's mind who too admires her.

Mrs. Irwine

Mrs. Irwine, the Rector's mother is a graceful and beautiful lady. She is also Arthur Donnithorne's godmother. She is a lively, exciting old lady with a rich toned complexion. She played chess with her son and having won a game insisted that they should play another despite her son's reluctance. George Eliot describes her as "a stately, beautiful old lady, with an aquiline nose, a firm, proud mouth and small, intense black eyes. She was carefully dressed and her small brown hand was laden with pearls, diamonds and turgnoises." She commands great respect from everyone. She dotes on her son but neglects her plain looking daughter. Her son is so devoted to her and the family that he made a sacrifice by remaining a bachelor as his measly income could not afford to feed an extra mouth.

Martin Poyser

Mrs. Poyser's jolly husband and Hetty's uncle, Martin Poyser is "the broadest man in the parish". He is the jovial tenant of the Farm House. His jovial, easy going nature is quite, in contrast to his shrewed sharp tongued wife. He comforts his orphan niece Hetty and behaves with her in a friendly manner whenever his wife reprimands Hetty for something or the other. He as per his nature was very soft on her and always protected her from the wrath and scorn of his sharp tongued wife. But ironically when the news of Hetty's conviction and trial was broken by Mr. Irwine, the kind hearted Martin Poyser was more severe on Hetty than his otherwise shrewed wife. He condemned Hetty for bringing disgrace to his family and was unwilling to forgive her for her offence. He said, "I'm willing to pay any money as is wanted towards trying to bring her off,....but I'll not go nigh her, nor ever see her again, by my own will. She's made our bread bitter to us for all our lives to come, an' we shall ne'er hold up our heads in this parish nor i' any other. The person talks O' folks pityin' us : it's poor amends pity' ll make us.'

Bartle Massey

Bartle Massey, the witty old school master of Hayslope, a man of ability and education has been turned out to be a woman hater by some earlier youthful experience. George Eliot describes him in the following manner.—"There were other people in the two parishes who derived dignity from their pocket, and of these Bartle Massey was one." A self proclaimed bachelor and a universal woman hater is however very patient with his rather backward pupils and loyal to his friend Adam. He even gave up his work to be with Adam and give him emotional and mental support during Hetty's trial. As a woman hater he contributes to the fun and humour of the novel. Ironically his pet is a bitch named Vixen. Adam jokeningly tells him that he should never have kept Vixen as his pet as she was a female against whom his deepest and bitter most hatred were reserved. When Vixen gives birth to two pups, Adam does not miss the opportunity to pull his legs and teasingly asked him if raising of a family was not against the rules of his house. Massey pleads that this was the consequence of his original sin of allowing a female to live in the house. A man of charismatic pride, he is a firm believer of men's superiority over women and believes that the only thing females are good at, is in bearing children. He says to Adam. "I tell you there's not a thing under the sun that needs to be done at all what a man can't do better than a woman unless its bearing children, and they do that in a poor, make shift way." His hatred for women and his comments on them makes him a comic and humourous character.

Bartle Massey Vs. Mrs. Poyser

An interesting battle of wit takes place between Bartle Massey and Mrs. Poyser on the subject of women. Both contradicted each other's view and it provides humour. Mrs. Poyser who has a strong belief in the superiority of the fairer sex over male of the species is not ready to accept Massey's contemptuous remarks about women and there follows a heated argument. She is contemptuous of Hayslope menfolk because she regards then as slow-witted. Though Mrs. Poyser and Massey contradict each other vehemently on the superiority or inferiority of women, there are so many points of resemblance between the two. Both of them are sharp witted and sharp tongued which enables them to put everything inimitably and forcefully. Ironically what looks like the greatest point of contrast between them is the greatest point of similarity, for both of them are equally contemptuous of the opposite sex. Both of them possess a heart of gold despite their sharp tongue and harsh language.

The Symbolic Significance of the Minor Characters

One critic has categorised the minor characters into two groups.

Characters like Mrs. Irwine, Squire Donnithorne and Martin Poyser symbolise the refined, polished, gentle exterior of Loamshire that conceals a hardness at the core. On the other hand characters like Mr. Irwine, Bartle Massey and Mrs. Poyser who have suffered themselves and are ready to sympathise with others fall in one common group.

George R. Creeger is of the view that Mrs. Irwine judges others externally. She has small intense black eye, very keen and sarcastic in expression that she almost looks like gypsy fortune teller who judges others by their appearance.

Squire Donnithorne in also very much like Mrs. Irwine, outwardly splendid, careful in his dress and very polite in his manners. Though he was polite, the farmers found out afterwards that his polishness was the sign of hardness. Once when he inquired about Mrs. Poyser's health showing elaborate civility, Mrs. Poyser whispered to her husband after he left " "I'll lay my life he's brewin' some nasty turn against us. Old Marry doesn't wag his tail so for nothing."

Mr. Poyser represents a third kind of hardness and the most important. Mrs. Irwine and Squire Donnithorne's hardness lies on the genteel fringe of the novel which is but expected. While Martin Poyser's hardness is quite unexpected as he gives no indication of external hardness at first. A good natured jolly fellow, an excellent husband, loving father, he never shows any kind of hardness towards anyone. He was totally opposite to his wife. But in him we can trace occasional signs of severity. His attitude towards his neighbour, Luke Britton was "as hard and implacable as the north-east wind". This in a way should prepare for his severe stand as regards Hetty. He exhibits a total lack of sympathy towards his once most loving niece. His severity and unforgiving stand takes us quite by surprise.

Then there are characters who have suffered themselves and are ready to sympathies with others, and forgive them for their follies. Bartle Massey, the woman hater with a mysterious past is a lame. Mrs. Poyser has been in precarious health since the birth of her youngest child. Though Mr. Irwine himself has not experienced suffering, he has seen the suffering of his sickly sisters and for whom he is invariably sympathetic. Furthermore he remained a bachelor to support his mother and sisters.

Because of their deep knowledge of suffering they are compassionate. Their worldly knowledge and intelligence are tempered with sympathy and love.

Mrs. Poyser herself agrees with Mr. Irwine that "her tongue is like a new set of Razor" or recalls the "freezing arctic ray" of her glance. Adam opines that "her tongue's keen, her heart's tender". Her sympathy for Hetty after the disgraceful incident in quite surprising and takes the reader aback.

The combination of keenness and mildness features in the character of Mr. Irwine too. The same can be said about Massey. As a teacher he condemns the erring youth but is patient and sympathetic to mature men and common labourer.

Q. 4. Write a note on the three suppers and their symbolic significance.

Or

"The first of these suppers is designed to remind Adam of his origin in Nature"—How far would you agree with this view?

Or

Give in your own words an account of George Eliot's artistic and philosophic intentions in the portrayal of Adam's growth.

Or

Write a note on the restoration of Adam's humanity and his regeneration.

Or

The novel abounds with religious and symbolic elements. Comment.

Ans. Influence of Christianity

George Eliot's novels are known for their intellectual and philosophical undertone. She was greatly influenced by Feuerbach whose religious views are reflected in her novels. She even translated his *The Essence of Christianity* in English. In his book Feuerbach brings out the religious significance of bread, water and wine which are all sacred. Water is an element of nature, it is the life source for all living things, a life force that gives life and vitality to everything that has life. Taking of water symbolises our affinity with nature. This is also symbolic of Christian ritual of Baptimism. Bread and wine though formed out of materials provided by nature, symbolises man's superiority over lower creatures. The lower creatures are incapable of transforming natural material to other objects. Hence in Baptimism only water is used for children, in the Lord's Supper wine is drunk and bread is taken by the mature and grown up all these symbolises manhood and men's distinction from animals. Hunger and thirst destroy man's humanity lowering him to the levels of animal. And taking of bread and wine restores to him his humanity. George Eliot delivers this religious belief symbolically through the three suppers which restore, to Adam his humanity, his mental and moral powers.

The Significance of the Three Suppers

According to a critic all the three suppers mentioned in the novel *Adam Bede* has symbolic significance. He is of the view that the first of these suppers is designed to remind Adam of his origin in nature, a concept represented by Feuerback through the symbol of water. The scene of the second supper stresses on Adam's inability to see that man must be distinguished from nature. In the third Supper however, Adam learns how to celebrate this "distinction" in a manner which will give a truly "religious import" to life. The most important of the three, this scene relies entirely on Feuerbach's allegoric treatment of the Lord's supper.

The First Supper

In the first supper scene the self-righteous, hardworking Adam completes the making of a coffin that his drunkard father had neglected. He ignores his mother's request to have his food and allows his hungry dog to eat his food. It was late evening when Adam called for a light and a draught of water. He asks for a second "drop of water" and admits that he is thirsty. Then Adam resumes his work with the coffin little realising that his drunken father has a watery death. His acceptance of the two sips of water indicates his acceptance of his father's drunkenness when, he later discovers Thias' body, sympathy sets in dissolving his hardness. The water is used as symbol and like the parallel between man and dog, it is intended to remind Adam of his origin, his affinity with nature, an origin that is common in all living beings be it animal or plant.

The Second Supper

The second scene of Supper is presented during Arthur Donnithorne's birthday party. Adam was not comfortable with the idea of dining upstairs with the tenants, at the thought of being exalted above his mother and brother who were supposed to dine below in the cloisters of the old church. If a man must bow down, he must also know how to rise above it. Adam's ignorance of this rule is manifested in their supper. Isolated from his kin, Adam sits upstairs at the Squire's table not drinking water, but the rich

Loamshire ale. He accepts the toast which Arthur, the seducer of his beloved makes in his honour. Ironically by this toast Arthur wishes him to have "sons as faithful and clever as himself". Arthur had promoted him to the post of manager of the woods. The irony becomes obvious here. Proud of his new capacity as the manager of the woods, still Adam is to learn that his full humanity can be attained through his distinction from nature. The incident in the woods, where he finds Arthur and Hetty together at night shocks him beyond words. This shocking incident forces upon him the suffering that every human being should undergo in order to elevate himself above the lower creatures.

The Last Supper

The last and the most significant supper in the symbolic sequence marks Adam's regeneration and growth to maturity. Adam goes to Stoniton, to witness Hetty's trial. Sitting upstairs in his dull room counting the long minutes. He was clueless as to what would be said by the witnesses on the trial. The author writes : "This brave active man, who would have hastened towards any danger or toil to rescue Hetty from an apprehended wrong or misfortunes, felt himself powerless to contemplate immediate evil and suffering" He kept brooding over Hetty's trial when Bartle Massey, the lame school master comes in. Bartle came to enlighten Adam about the proceeding in the court at the trial of Hetty and insisted that he should take a "bit of the loaf and some of the wine Mr. Irwine sent. Adam refuses and pushes away the cup. He asks Massey to tell him about the trial. Massey tells Adam about the pain and humiliation Hetty's uncle had to undergo at the court. Everyone in the court felt sorry for him when he sobbed out loudly. Massey requests him to sympathise with Martin Poyser and help him and said : "Drink some wine now and show me you mean to clear it like a man." Like an obedient child Adam obliged and took the cup to drink a little. He enquires about Hetty and on learning about her suffering and Mr. Irwine's emotional support to the Poyser family Adam exclaims : "God bless him, and you too Mr. Massey". This involuntary blessing reverses his earlier exclamation about Hetty : "God bless her for loving me". So Adam's regeneration is complete now. He sheds all his inhibitions and pride and accepts the fallible nature of humanity. Adam has become capable of signifying his 'distinction' from Nature in an act which in George Eliot's word is "a baptism, a regeneration, the initiation into new state." The new Adam promises to stand by Hetty at court and offer her emotional support. At this point Massey asks Adam to eat a bit and to have another sip for the love of him. Gaining stamina from his firm resolution Adam took a morsel of bread and drank some more wine. "He was haggard and unshaven, as he had been yesterday, but he stood upright again, and looked like the Adam Bede of former days. Adam's transformation to that "new awe and new pity" that lie at the core of George Eliot's religion of humanity is thus completed."

Q. 5. "Life not only contains sorrow; it needs sorrow in order that there may be love". Elucidate.

Or

Critics complain that the marriage of Dinah and Adam is an artistic fault. How far would you agree to this view?

Or

Dinah, the Methodist preacher also gains maturity and gets educated in the course of the novel. Comment.

Or

The Dinah Adam love story is significant as it marks Adam's maturity. Discuss.

Ans. Imbalance in Dinah's Character

At the very beginning of the novel, we get acquainted with the character and personality of the hero Adam Bede. He is honest, diligent, self righteous but lacks integrity and maturity. He is not a balanced personality as his head rules over his heart. But the same cannot be detected in Dinah at the very outset, when we are introduced to her in the novel. The balance of head and heart is missing in her, and as such she also lacks maturity. The novel traces how through her love for Adam, she is able to fill in the gulf between her head and the heart and in the process becomes a fully integrated and mature personality. Thus the criticism that the Dinah Adam marriage in an artistic fault loses its ground as it promotes the central philosophical and intellectual purposes of the novelist.

Her Detachment from Life

Dinah as portrayed by the novelist is a mild, compassionate and a true and selfless devotee of God. She is pure at heart but lacks genuine vitality. She scarcely seems to breathe in the minds of her enduring calmness. Confronted by a world, full of vitality and vigour, she retreats. According to a critic the cause of her retreat is the fear of selfishness and hardness resulting from too great abundance of world by goods. Implicit in her fear is a kind of unwillingness to become fully involved in life. Dinah, observes human condition with sympathy and compassion, but without deeper involvement. She is the personification of 'selfless', a word that is used most frequently to describe her by the author. "Selfless" is not only an antonym of the word "selfish", it not only means the opposite of 'selfish', it also means lacking in self. The lack of this sense of human identity is to make à person either less or more than human - a god, perhaps or a divinity.' She is haunted by the fear of being diverted from her chosen path to serve God. When Seth proposes to her professing his love she turns him down saying that "....I see that our marriage is not God's will—he draws my heart another way....". Her over involvement with the church and dedication to God makes her less humane and detached from life. She admits this withdrawal from life herself. She tells Mr. Irwine : "I'm too much given to sit still and keep by myself : it seem as if I could sit silent all day long with the thought of God overflowing my soul—as the pebbles lie bathed in the willow Brook. For thoughts are so great—aren't they, Sir? They seem to lie upon us like a deep flood; and its my besetment to forget where I am and everything about me, and lose myself in thoughts that I could give no account of, for I could neither make a beginning nor end of them in words".

Her Withdrawal

Her psychological state demands a complete withdrawal from life. And this withdrawal is characteristic of Dinah. Whenever any complicated or crucial situation arises or where ever life takes a paradoxical turn Dinah flees back to Stonyshire, the barren, sterile land under the "overreaching sky". When Adam professes his love for her, Dinah in spite of her tender feeling for him replies that she could return his love except for the fear that she would "forget to rejoice and weep with others", or even forget the Divine presence. She fears to express her feeling lest it hinders her ideals. Its ironical that her peace and joy is derived from having no life of her own. She is too detached, too uninvolved. She is scared to reveal her feeling. Her apprehension that her love for a particular person will make her forget Jesus makes her retreat. She is in a difficult situation and voices her doubts to Adam—"And think how it is with me, Adam—that life I have led, is like a land I have trodden in blessedness since my childhood; and if I long for a moment to follow the voice which calls me to another land that I know not, I cannot but fear that my soul might hereafter yearn for that early blessedness which I had forsaken, and where doubt enters there is not perfect love. I must wait for clearer guidance. I must go from you. Dinah refuses to acknowledge her love for Adam and retreats. Its a clear expression of the rejection of full maturity. She finds the land of Loamshire strange and returns to Stonyshire. Hetty is incapable of growing up and Dinah is afraid to."

Dinah Attains Maturity Through Love

Dinah is able to overcome her fear, but the novel does not enlighten the reader about the process of her maturity. Adam declares his love for Dinah and though she admits her tender feeling, she is afraid to reciprocate fearing it might divert her from the divine path she treads. She flees to Stonyshire and does not even stay to participate in the harvest supper and does not inform Adam. Adam though disappointed on learning about Dinah's departure, consoled himself with the hope that she did so for him only. Adam waits for several weeks and then gets impatient. Unable to endure the strain of separation from his beloved Dinah, he sets out for Stonyshire to meet her. As he leaves Loamshire and enters the grey treeless world of Stonyshire, his mind gets a flashback of the past, he is reminded of his sad past, his love for Hetty, her tragic incident, but in a different light. He is reminded of his past, but Adam being reborn again, possesses what George Eliot calls "a sense of enlarged being". The suffering that Adam undergoes on account of Hetty's incident, transforms him completely, making a humble and more mature man out of him. The self righteous Adam who refused to pardon his fellow beings for their fallible nature turns over a new leaf and emerges as a more mature and more humane person. He sheds his self pride gradually and accepts life as it is. He sees Stonyshire through Dinah's eyes, as it were, and his vision includes the barren land. His vision of the world enlarges and it includes the wonderful flooding light and the huge embracing sky.

Adam on reaching Stonyshire finds that Dinah has gone to preach. He waits for her return not at her home but on a hill top. Here in Dinah's own world Adam discovers a new Dinah. The power of love had transformed her enabling her to overcome her fears and apprehensions, she feels incomplete, a divided person without him. She accepts and reciprocates his love and is ready to become his wife. He takes her back to Loamshire. The marriage takes place not in the green and golden world of June but in the season of autumn which is symbolic of maturity. "On a rimy morning in departing November", when a tinge of sadness makes the weather as well as in the joy that accompanies the wedding, Adam and Dinah are married. It is quite befitting that a hint of sorrow should be present, because the world of Loamshire-Hayslope sorrow is not only a part of life, it needs sorrow so that there may be love. A hint of sorrow is required to enhance the fountain of love. So it is quite natural that they should come together and they are bound by their common suffering. Suffering gives rise to sympathy and love springs from sympathy. Love based on such sympathy is mature not based on passion alone and is fruitful and can be everlasting.

Conclusion

Dinah who was reluctant to get involved with life and retreated at the very thought of getting diverted from the divine path, at last faces the reality and overcomes her fear, she is domisticated in the end. But she is not reduced to a mere commonplace domesticity from a position of higher exceptional destiny. Rather it would be more appropriate to say that she gave up an impressive but an eccentric role to fully participate in life among the common lot of humanity. So Dinah takes a journey in which she undergoes suffering to understand the realities of life. She detached herself from the common human being in the fear that her involvement may divert her from her chosen path. But with suffering she grows mature like Adam and at last overcomes all fears that prevented her from participating in life.

Q. 6. Consider *Adam Bede* as a novel of psychological realism.

Or

"George Eliot's serious characters are envisaged exclusively in their moral aspect. They are portraits of inner man.....". Consider the novel *Adam Bede* in the light of the above statement.

Or

"Our deeds determine us, as much as we determine our deeds." How far this is true of *Adam Bede*?

Or

George Eliot skilfully makes a psycho-analysis of the character in the novel *Adam Bede*.

Ans. George Eliot : A Pioneer of Psychological Novels

George Eliot can be heralded as one of the pioneers of the modern psychological novel. She through her novels attempted to present the inner struggle of the soul to reveal the inner motives. She tries to critically analyse the motives, impulses and hereditary influences that are responsible for human action. Browning, the Victorian poet presented the inner struggle of man through his dramatic monologues while George Eliot did the same thing through her novels. The technique followed by Browning in his poetry is that he generally stops when he finishes his story telling and either lets his readers draw their own conclusion or gives them his own conclusion in a few striking lines. But George Eliot follows a distinct technique, very characteristic of her own. She explains the motives of her character in minute detail and never forgets to impart the moral lesson to be learnt from them. She traces the development of a soul, either the gradual growth or decline of moral power, which interests her immensely. Her heroes and heroines belong to a world that is radically different from the world of Dickens and Thackery. The characters of Dickens and Thackery when we meet them, are already formed and we can predict how they would act or react under given circumstances. But in George Eliot's novels the characters develop gradually as we come to know them. They are not static characters but dynamic, full of life and vigour. They are real human beings, fallible in nature having positive as well as negative qualities, they grow from weakness to strength and vice versa according to the works they do and the thoughts that they cherish.

The Struggle of the Inner Mind

According to critic A.E. Baker, Eliot's sphere was the inner man, she exposed the internal clockwork. Her characters are neither passive nor do they stand still. They make their own history, continually changing or developing as their motives issue into acts and acts become part of the circumstances that condition modify and purify or demoralise the will.

George Eliot's ability of psycho-analysis, her understanding of mental processes that regulate human action finds expression in *Adam Bede.* Eliot analyses the working of a human mind, the motives that impel a character to act or react in a particular manner. She analyses and dissects the soul of her characters and exposes to the reader their inner self. The novel makes an interesting reading especially those parts where the souls of his character are laid bare for the benefit of the reader. George Eliot has probed so deep into the hearts of men that most critics have considered *Adam Bede* "finest psychological novel". Eliot has been awarded the distinction of leading the movement of psychological trends in novels. What makes *Adam Bede* the forerunner of psychological novels is that Eliot has depicted her major character from inside, probing deep inside their mind and soul not like her contemporary novelists who depicted their characters externally.

Diagnosis of Causes and Motives

Eliot makes a thorough analysis of the mind and heart of her characters with a view to take the readers to a journey to the soul of man and woman. As for example in the chapter "A Journey in Hope.", Eliot gives more time to the psychological dissection of Hetty's heart and mind than in the physical description of her hectic journey in search of her love. The preceding and the immediate following chapter similarly probes into the working of the mind of Adam and Hetty. The chapters depict the inner activity, in the minds of the characters though there is sufficient activity for the plot to carry on. It is seen that in each chapter only a single major episode or action, or sometimes a part of one action is dealt with, but at the same time the analysis of the causes of the action goes on throughout uninterrupted.

Eliot is an expert in her psychological approach. Sometimes she simply allows the readers to scan through the character's brain to know in detail the working of the mind and sometimes even lets the readers perceive what the characters themselves do not anticipate. For example, shortly after Thias Bede's death, his wife Lisbeth stays alone with her dead husband's body. After completing the ritual of cleansing and purification of the chamber where the dead body lay, she sank down into a chair in the kitchen and mourned. Had it been another time Lisbeth's thought would have been preoccupied with Adam's welfare. She would have been anxious; "Where is Adam?" But the sudden demise of her husband had restored in her affection she had held twenty six years ago. She had forgotten about his faults as "we forget the sorrows of our departed childhood, and thought of nothing but the young husband's kindness and the old man's patience." This gives a fair indication of Eliot's brilliant psychological insight.

In Eliot's novels, the readers get an opportunity to share the thoughts of the characters. As for example, when Adam accidently witnesses the scene where Arthur and Hetty were embracing in the woods, Hetty hurries away, and Arthur with deliberate carelessness leads towards Adam. Arthur Donnithorne looked flushed and excited; he had tried to make unpleasant feelings more bearable by drinking a little more wine than usual at dinner today and was still enough under its flattering influence to think more lightly of this accidental encounter with Adam. He thought, "After all, Adam was the best who could have happened to see him and Hetty together. He was a sensible fellow and would not bable about it to other people. Arthur felt confident that he could laugh the thing off and explain it away."

Arthur Donnithrone : A Psychological Study

Eliot's mastery of psychological insight enabled her to portray complex personalities in a much better way than her predecessors. Critic David Cecil says that Eliot draws the characters from the inside out, starting with central principle and in this process is able to show how it reveals itself in the most apparently inconsistent manifestations can give to the most varied coloured surface of character that prevalent tone which marks it as the expression of one personality. "Her characters always hang together, are of a piece, their defects are the defects of their virtues. We are not surprised that a man, so anxious for the good opinion of others as Arthur Donnithorne should selfishly seduce Hetty, because we realise that the controlling force in his character is the desire for immediate enjoyment; so that his wish to sun himself in the pleasant warmth of other people's liking goes along with his inability not to yield to the immediate pleasure of Hetty's embraces. George Eliot can follow the windings of motive through the most torturous labyrinths for firmly grasped in her hand is always the central clue.

Battle in the Mind

George Eliot has an extra-ordinary power of describing mixed characters that extend to mixed states of mind. She emerges triumphant in the moral battlefield. She is capable of penetrating through the core of struggle and elucidate the position of the forces concerned and reveal the trend of their action. She shows how the forces of temptation deploy themselves to attack and how the conscience of man resists or attempts to resist, and how in the conflict in a given circumstances one or the other triumphs. She particularly makes it a point to show the triumph of temptation at first. "No other English novelist has given us so vivid picture of the process of moral defeat, as Donnithorne's gradual yielding to his passion for Hetty. With an inexorable clearness she reveals how temptation insinuates itself into the mind, how it retreats at the first suspicious movement of conscience how it comes back disguised, and how, if once more vanquished, it will sham death only to arise suddenly and sweep its victim away on a single irresistable gust of desire when he is off his guard."

The Moral Chaos

Eliot is equally capable of portraying the moral chaos that takes possession of the mind after the wrong has been done. She exposes the mental battle, the struggling of the spirit striving to make itself at ease at the face of a disturbed conscience. She depicts precisely how an act before it is done looks tempting, shrouded in the softening darkness of the secret heart, and after, exposed in to the harsh day light of other people's judgement takes an ugly turn. Arthur experiences the pricks of consciences and spends sleepless nights after learning how his mistake led innocent Hetty to misery. Eliot with more penetration and insight isolates and detects the various warring elements in Arthur's mind, his horror of being disappointed of his inextinguishable hope that things will come right in the end, his irrationed conviction that with him, at least, things always come right in the end. She mercilessly, and at the same time delicately exposes the human weakness. In exposing Arthur she also exposes the reader.

Arthur Torn between Temptation and Moral Duty

The novelist lays bare the conscious as well as semi-conscious motives of Arthur Donnithrone. His working of the inner mind is exposed for the benefit of the reader to project the struggle of guilt ridden conscience. He had been awake and could rest in bed no longer. Conscious of his status and moral character, the loss of Adam's respect was a shock to his self-contentment which suffered his imagination with the sense that he had sunk in all eyes; as a sudden shock of fear of some unseen danger makes a woman suffer from insomnia. Arthur would have liked to convince himself that he had done no harm, he was not guilty and had no one enlightened him about the situation, he would have went on believing himself.

Conclusion

Eliot's psychological insight into the depth of human soul, the analysis of the causes that regulate human action which earns her a special place among the Victorian novelists. Though she belongs to genre of Victorian novels yet she is different from the rest of the group by virtue of her originality and different handling of subject matter. She leads the list of other modern novelists who have a high conception of their art, who regard the novel as a serious form of art and who are interested in the probing of the human psyche and the subtle analysis of the sub consciences or the unconscious mind.

Q. 7. Consider Arthur as a man of weak moral fibre who yields to temptation.

Or

Through Arthur—Hetty Sorrel love story, the novelist tries to impart a moral lesson depicting the ill consequences of surrendering to temptation. How far would you agree with this view?

Or

The novel *Adam Bede* is a study in moral weakness and its consequences. How far would you agree or disagree with this view? Give reasons for your answer.

Or

"If Arthur had been conventionally wicked Squire's son setting out to seduce the village maiden he could hardly have made a better start. Yet George Eliot enables us to look at this scene—with the additional knowledge that there is no prospect of Arthur's marrying Hetty—and still remains convinced that he means no ill."

Make an analysis of Arthur Donnithorne's character in the light of the above statement.

Or

"His (Arthur Donnithorne's) is the tragedy of a weak man who is unable to line up to his good intentions." Give in your own words an account of Arthur Donnithrone's moral conflict.

Or

How far is Arthur Donnithorne responsible for Hetty's tragedy?

Or

The novel *Adam Bede* traces the movement from weakness to sin and from sin to Nemesis. Comment.

Ans. Drama of Moral Conflict

George Eliot's novels are famous for their moral implications. Her novels are dramas of moral conflict depicting the inner struggle of the soul. "Art for arts sake" did not find expression in her novels, but she upheld the philosophy of art for morality's sake. She believed in the ethical influence of art and that "our deeds determine us, as much as we determine our deeds". If we yield to temptation and sin; suffering and nemesis are sure to follow—that was her philosophy of life. We reap as we sow. Her characters which are real human beings full of life and vigour, suffer because of their violation of some moral codes, because of their inability to resist the temptations of the flesh. In *Adam Bede,* Hetty and Arthur suffer because of this. As creatures of weak moral disposition, Arthur and Hetty yielded to temptation which resulted in sin. Their violation of the moral code led to punishment and intense suffering. Through the Arthur-Hetty affair, the novelist tries to imply the fatal consequences of violation of moral code, how yielding to temptation leads to sin and sin to nemesis.

Hetty : A Real Country Girl

Hetty Sorrel, the central figure of the novel, is neither a temptress who seduces a rich heir in order to blackmail him for marriage nor an innocent virgin who was taken advantage of by a rich young man. Hetty is simply a village girl who lives in a world of dreams. She is sketched as a rustic, a charming but vain girl who has romantic dreams with a handsome and rich lover. She craves for luxury and fineries of life and dreams about marrying a rich and handsome man. She was swept of her feet by the courteous Arthur Donnithorne. She snubs the unassuming hardworking Adam for Arthur and ultimately has to pay a heavy price for her folly. Her suffering makes reader sympathise with the vain, selfish yet intensely human figure. The action of the novel revolves around her story and hence she is considered to be the central character in the novel and she suffers great misfortune. Her suffering gives her special eminence.

Her Cloistered Life

In the very beginning of the novel a happy and contended Hetty lives in her aunt's place. She helps her aunt with the household chores and looks after the daily work in a dairy. Except the occasional reprimands and rebukes from her aunt, she lives a sheltered life otherwise. She was quite unaware of the difficulties and hardships of life as she was hardly ever exposed to the harsh realities of life. Her vanity and frivolousness led her to yield to temptation which came in the form of Arthur Donnithrone.

Her Vulnerability to Temptation

Hetty, a beautiful country girl, full of life and vigour has several admirers. Adam Bede, a carpenter, hard-working and honest, admired and respected for his qualities, is one of them. He is the kind of man whom any woman would be proud to have. Hetty like other woman was quite well aware of the sterling qualities of Adam, but his poverty had put her off. She was too materialistic and too fond of comfort and luxury to give a serious thought to Adam. She knew it too well that Adam would not be able to afford all the luxuries she craves for, he will be unable to provide the splendid life with fine jewelleries and carriages that she often dreams about. Her dreams will remain unfulfilled if she marries Adam. Vain and frivolous, that she is, the admiring glances of Arthur, his flirtation makes her feel her dream turning real. The vain and foolish Hetty is swept of her feet as she feels that her knight in shining armour has come to fulfil her dream. Her imagination takes a galloping turn and she begins to dreams about her marriage with Arthur.

Her World of Fantasy

Commenting on her dream world, Eliot writes, "A new influence had come over Hetty—gay, atmospheric, shaping itself into no self-confessed hopes or prospects but producing a pleasant neurotic effect, making her tread the ground and go about her work in a sort of dream, unconscious of weight or effect and showing her all things through a soft, liquid veil, as if she were living not in this world of bricks and stone, but in a beautiful world, such as the sun lights up for us in the waters."

Like any other girl of seventeen, Hetty was frivolous and vain. The fact that she had several admirers made her even more vain and self-centered. She dreamed about luxuries and fineries—"To sit in a carpeted parlours and always wear white stockings; to have some large, beautiful ear-rings, to have Nottingham lace round the top of her gown and something to make her handkerchief smell nice." The dreaming of such luxuries are quite appropriate to her nature. So such dream of luxuries only add to the realism of her character. She dreams about her marriage with Arthur and her life with him after marriage.

Her Consequent Suffering and Punishment

But destiny had some other plans for Hetty. She was destined to face great pain and suffering as a result of her frivolous nature and her life ended in a great tragedy. Hetty was uneducated, rustic to whom a gentleman with a white hand was dazzling as an Olympian God. She was thus tempted and being a girl of weak moral fibre, she could not resist the temptation and committed the fatal mistake that doomed her life forever. Hetty's world fell apart on the night she received Arthur's farewell letter. She cried her heart out. On learning about her pregnancy she was reluctant to marry Adam and sets out in search of Arthur stepping out of her sheltered life for the first time. Her violation of the social norm, moral code follows swiftly by punishment and suffering "Journey in Hope" and "Journey in Despair"—are the record of her suffering and deep spiritual anguish. She is so desperate that she even contemplates suicide for the fear of shame and disgrace. Though she had visited the church regularly she has no guiding principle to see her through as she had never absorbed a single Christian quality. Worn with her hectic journey to Windsor and back to Stoniton, she gives birth prematurely to a child in the house of a stranger. Her mind was haunted by the thought of shame and guilt. She thought of abandoning her child and return to Hayslope and resume her earlier life of peace and security. The next evening she went out and left her child in the woods. But her conscience did not let her rest in peace, the crying of the child haunted her all night. She returned to the spot where she had hidden the child, but it was too late, the child lay dead there. Convicted with child murder, and faced with the public disgrace of her trial, Hetty "shut her heart against her fellow creatures". She had transformed into a story figure who refused to divulge anything. Dinah, the Methodist preacher through her loving, sympathy and patience could reach out and help her convincing her of God's mercy and removing her fear of perpetual remorse beyond the grave. A sort of spiritual regeneration takes place when Hetty finally opens her heart out to Dinah and makes a confession.

Arthur : His Lack of Self Control

Through Hetty's story the novelist tries to highlight the moral truth that sin or yielding to temptation—is sure to be followed by punishment and suffering. The same truth is illustrated by the character of Arthur Donnithorne. Despite his good intentions he too lacked the self control and yields to temptation that results in the tragedy ruining Hetty's life as well as his. He was well aware of the fact that because of the parity in their social status, he could never marry Hetty, yet it did not stop him from indulging in casual flirtings with her. He was attracted to her beauty and flirted with her. As a man he was mature and superior to Hetty both in years and experience and such he was more responsible than Hetty for the tragedy.

Arthur : The Man behind Hetty's Tragedy

Though Arthur is responsible for Hetty's tragedy, he is not like the conventional villain of a melodrama. The novelist has probed deep inside his mind and soul to make the reader explore the real personality. His tragedy is the tragedy of a weak man who is unable to live up to his good intention. Arthur intends to cultivate a good friendly relations with everybody and never knowingly and willingly harms anybody. Through his thoughts rather by his actions the reader gets a fair idea about his good intentions. He was attracted to Hetty's beauty and flirted with her, but was determined to tell her not to take him seriously. He knew that he could never marry her because of the difference in their social status and tried to avoid her. That he meant no harm can be well guessed by the reader from his thoughts. He fights his impulse to meet Hetty but fails. Despite his good intentions he seduces Hetty. When Adam confronts him, accusing him of seducing innocent Hetty, he denies and laughs it away only as casual flirt not a serious involvement. He even writes a letter to Hetty endirg their affair, but assuring her of his help whenever the need arises.

Critic R.T. Jones comments, "If Arthur had been conventionally wicked Squire's son setting out to seduce the village maiden he could hardly have made a better start. Yet George Eliot enables us to look at this scene — with the additional knowledge that there is no prospect of Arthur's marrying Hetty—and still remains convinced that he means no ill."

The Fatal Error Despite His Best Intention

Arthur tried his best not to allow himself to meet Hetty. Contemplated how he could avoid her : "If he lunched with Gwaine and lingered chatting he should not reach the chase again till nearly five, when Hetty would be safe out of his sight in the House Keeper's room, and when she set out to go home, it would be his lazy time after dinner, so he should keep out of her altogether." He underestimated the strength of his impulse to meet Hetty—'that was the fatal mistake he committed. Aware of his attraction and realisation of the truth that he could never marry a farmer's niece led him to do something to get rid of the foolish temptation. He decided to go over to Mr. Irwine's place and seek his advice. When Arthur reached Mr. Irwine's place he had a second thought regarding the confession he had to make. He decided to wait and talk about it later. He valued other people's opinion about himself greatly and so hesitated to tell him about Hetty. He was determined more than ever to avoid Hetty, he was successful to some extent also. But he could not maintain the consistency of his decision. He danced with Hetty at his brithday party and met her in the woods again. Their secret meeting was discovered by Adam. On being confronted by Adam, Arthur denies anything serious between him and Hetty.

The readers get an idea about Arthur's intentions, his self-deceptions and distortions of truth. All this makes him very real and acceptable to us.

His Punishment

As a result of his moral weakness he also suffers from deep spiritual anguish. He never thought that his casual fling would have a serious and devastating effect on Hetty's life. When he comes to know about Hetty's tragedy, her conviction in child murder and trial, he was shaken. He becomes miserable, wretched and repents for his misdeed at once. He tries his best to save Hetty and is able to secure a pardon from capital punishment but fails to save her from transportation. He is a broken man who falls ill towards the end of the novel. He is remorseful for the pain he inflicted on Hetty, the Poyser family, Adam and himself. His realisation of his guilt makes him more genuine and humane. He confesses to Adam, "I was all wrong from the very first and horrible wrong has come of it. God knows, I'd give my life if I could undo it."

Q. 8. "*Adam Bede* is uneven in the precise sense of having its weight wrongly distributed." Write a note on the technical flaw of the novel in the light of the above statement.

Or

The Dinah Adam marriage is forced, unnatural and lacks credibility. How far would you agree with this view?

Or

Is the ending of *Adam Bede* suitable? Give your own views.

Ans. A Well Constructed Novel

Adam Bede is considered to be one of the finest novels in English literature and also a well constructed one. It has its share of faults and flaws which have been the butt of criticism.

George Eliot is more a philosopher than a novelist. Most of her novels have an undertone of moral and philosophical elements. Her critical and philosophical ability surpasses her artistry in narrating a tale. The author from time to time gives her own comment which holds up the story temporarily and makes it laboured as in chapter XVII titled 'In Which the Story Pauses a Little' Eliot frequently imposes her own opinion on the characters instead of letting them make their own judgement. She labels Hetty a "sinner" who yielded to the temptation of the flesh. Adam and Dinah are presented as near perfect. But for the modern reader Dinah in somewhat lifeless and sanctimonious and Adam too perfect to seem real. Critic Robert Speaight, is of the opinion that "throughout her work George Eliot exercises the perilous prerogative of the creative mind to stand outside her creation, view it in company with the spectator, and say how this or that effect of characterisation strikes her. But in her later novels this tendency is held under increasing control; in *Adam Bede* it is indulged without the least attempt at discipline. The technique seems to us extremely crude, holding up the narrative and frequently spoiling the illusion."

A Melodrama

Adam bede abounds in melodramatic elements. The discovery of Thias Bede's body drowned in the river by Adam and Seth while returning home after the delivery of a coffin is quite melodramatic. The fight that takes place between Adam and Arthur after Adam incidentally comes upon Arthur and his beloved in the woods at night is also melodramatic. The story of seduction of a rustic girl by a rich heir, his ultimate desertion of her after impregnating her, her suffering, child murder, the conviction of the girl are all features of melodrama. The novel is full of such incidents that it can be categorised with heap of melodramas where emotional outburst, unlikely coincidences take place very frequently. It is the novelist's psychological insight, her deep penetration into the mind of the characters that raises it above this level. One of the most unpardonable flaw in the novel is the melodramatic situation of Hetty's pardon. Convicted with the murder of her child Hetty is condemned to death by the law. In the worst tradition of the Victorian novel she was to be executed in public. Arthur on learning about Hetty's dilemma tries his best to secure a reprieve for her. He rushes through the crowd gathered to watch Hetty's execution and is able to save her from being hanged in the nick of time. This incident is quite unacceptable from the otherwise a well constructed novel.

Much Emphasis on the Rural Background

Robert Speaight accuses George Eliot of giving too much time to create the background of the novel. He says that because of laying two much emphasis in building up the background, *Adam Bede* is uneven as its weight has been wrongly distributed. George Eliot was too fond of her native landscape and lingered at describing it. The rural backdrop, the workshop, the dairy, the Hall-Farm, the Chase are described giving minutest detail. While going through the novel the reader live with the characters, share their sorrows and happiness and the placid rhythm of their lives. The readers are so deeply engrossed in the lives of the people, their peaceful chatting and small domestic ambitions that they are forced to sympathise with them during their hours of pain and suffering. But George Eliot being more artistic and with a sheer abundance of creativity in *Adam Bede,* and as a result too much stress is given to the rural background of the novel.

The Use of Biblical Language

The use of Biblical language in conversation by Dinah is also a discredit of the novel. The way Dinah uses Biblical language in personal relation is quite unnatural and unacceptable to the reader. Dinah is too virtuous to be true. The author's treatment of the subject is responsible for the failure to produce the intended effect in the characterisation of Dinah. Dinah has a talent for offering comfort to the distressed soul—a talent that is leased on generous sympathy. The use of Christian doctrine, myth and chreology by her in comforting others enable her to speak with authority without failing humanity. But her methodist language and Christian terminology sound rather inconginous and unnatural when she deals at a personal level. When Seth proposes marriage to her she rejects the offer thus; "I've not turned a deaf ear to your words, Seth, for when I saw as your love was given to me, I thought it might be a leading of providence for me to change my way of life and that we should be fellow helpers; and I spread the matter of the Lord.....And when I opened the *Bible* for direction, I've always lighted on some clear word to tell me where my work lay." The religious language come too easily from Dinah lending a false air of Biblical authority to Dinah. What she could have said in plain simple terms is told in a long winding self deceiving speech making her more obscure. Dinah's conversation sounds too priggish and stilted to be real.

The Inartistic Ending of the Novel

Dinah is not only a preacher but also a priest to whom poor Hetty confesses her sin. Dinah lived a secluded life, she lived in a world of illusion detached from reality. Critics are of the opinion that Dinah observes the human condition with sympathy and compassion but without involvement. She makes a complete withdrawal from life. When Seth proposes marriage to her she rejects him saying that their marriage was not God's will. So her acceptance of Adam and ultimately marrying him comes as a shock to the reader and is often criticised as an artistic anti-climax to the drama of Hetty's fall. The last part of the novel is considered to be a major flaw in the plot construction.

According to Arthur James, Hetty Sorrel is the central figure of the novel around whom the plot develops and hence the story of the novel should have ended with her conviction. The continuation of the story after that point is fatal to the artistic integrity of the novel. The story should have ended with either Hetty's execution or with her reprieve. But the continuation of the story is not logical.

Critics argue that Book VI of *Adam Bede* is a material for another novel. Adam's marriage at some future time was quite possible and quite natural also, but it was a matter for a new story.

David Cecil, though objects to the ending of the novel, justifies it on the basis of George Eliot's concept of structural symmetry and the Victorian concern with poetic justice. The marriage of Adam and Dinah that provides a happy ending to the story is not inevitable but rather unlikely. But for the sake of moral purpose that underlies the story demands that Adam and Dinah, the two virtuous characters in the story should come together as a reward for their virtue. The marriage of the two is the best reward that could be given to the virtuous couple.

Adam Dinah Marriage : A Necessity for Their Regeneration

Critic Joan Bennet justifies the much criticised marriage of Adam Dinah on the ground that it allows the novelist to give a finishing touch to Adam's character, to make him realise about his self pride and follies. The end of the novel also suggests return to normalcy. The bright and contended world of Hayslope was shadowed by the tragedy of Hetty. The Adam Dinah marriage and its celebration symbolises the fact that the agitation has subsided and life resumes its usual course again. This is the justification of the Epilogue which shows Adam, Dinah, their two children and "uncle Seth" living happily in their new home. It suggests that the pretty "preacher-woman" at last has been domesticated and had transformed from the detached, withdrawn, eccentric preacher to a housewife who is totally involved in the fate of common humanity. It is not a fall on her part, but evolution or growth towards the attainment of full humanity. The Dinah Adam marriage after Hetty's conviction is not an anti-climax, but a necessity. It is essential for both Adam and Dinah, because otherwise both of them would have remained incomplete human being. There can be no fulfilment without love and love was necessary for their growth to maturity and fulfilment. This also enables Eliot to suggest the moral implication that common suffering results in sympathy and sympathy is the basis of true love: sorrow is required to make love true and lasting.

Q. 9. "Eliot's stories grow like plants out of a theme or idea in a given social environment." Justify.

Or

Write a note on the plot structure of the novel *Adam Bede*.

Or

Comment on the organic wholeness of the novel *Adam Bede*.

social background. Arthur Donnithorne's flirtation with Hetty, their yielding to temptation and thus violating the established social norms and everything that followed depends on the relation of them to their world, their society. The Poysers, Hetty's uncle's family with whom she lived had their own share of pride and self respect. The vivid picture of their surroundings, their working day, their home life, their Sunday observance and the neighbours, opinion on them, all are responsible in one way or the other for the tragedy and in heightening the bitterness of its effect. The social background alongwith the sheltered life that the Poysers provided for their niece and the code of moral conduct imbibed in her that made it inevitable for Hetty to run away from home. Contemplating how her condition would put her family to shame and disgrace, Hetty escapes from the sheltered life of Hayslope and sets out in search of Arthur. The readers can well imagine their plight, their shame and agony. By their identification with Hayslope the reader can measure their anguish as well as the probability of their contemplated uprooting. On the other hand Arthur's upbringing, his relationship with his grandfather, the Squire, his intention to impress others and draw their love and respect that explain the loss of prestige and the price he pays for his yielding to temptation and his ultimate suffering.

The Integrity of the Characters with the Physical Setting

The story and characters are not only integrated into the social environment but with the physical environment, the background, setting of the novel. They are symbolic of the physical environment. They represent the softness and fertility of Loamshire-Hayslope but at the same time they also possess its hardness and spiritual deadness. Dinah's preach in Hayslope leaves the audience untouched and unmoved except a few. The people of Hayslope do not respond to religion as their easy going life and self indulgence has made them spiritually dead. Adam, the skilful diligent carpenter who draws everyone's respect is self righteous and hard. Hetty, the charming rustic girl full of life and vitality also shows her stubbornness and hardness during her conviction and trial.

Dinah, the Link between Spiritual Barrenness and Physical Barrenness

Dinah, the methodist preacher serves to connect the two world of Loamshire-Hayslope and Stonyshire. She comes from the rocky, hard and barren land of Stonyshire where the people are receptive to religion and in contrast to the physical barrenness, they are spiritually alive. That is why whenever Dinah anticipates the danger that the spiritual deadness of Hayslope might affect her, she retreats to Stonyshire to carry on her vocation. When confronted with Adam's proposal of marriage she escaped to Stonyshire without informing Adam and even missing the Harvest Supper as she sensed spiritual danger. The nature background changes in keeping with the change in the fortune of Hetty. A carefree, rustic, charming and lively Hetty spends her early life in the idyllic physical environment of Hayslope. On discovering her pregnancy, desperate Hetty goes to the baren and rocky Stonyshire where she is convicted and sentenced to death. Seasonal changes are carefully noted and well integrated with the changing fortunes of the principal characters. Adam and Dinah eventually marries but not in the green and golden morning of spring, but on "a rimy morning in departing November", suggesting the attainment of maturity of Dinah and Adam. A tinge of sadness marks the weather as there is joy which accompanies the wedding. The painful memories of Hetty's tragedy colour and subdue their joy in the present.

The Action in Relation to the Social and Physical Environment

Alongwith the thematic organisation of the material there is also a close integration of the novel with the soul and physical environment. The novel consists of heterogenous material which have been organised and patterned through parallelism and contrast forming a symmetrical structure. The novel has six books which divides themselves into three symmetrical parts, each with a central motif of its own. In Book One the villagers of Hayslope assembles on the village green to hear the preaching of Dinah Morris. This shows the influence of Methodism, but at the same time it also hints that the Hayslope village community is not capable of any drastic change in this direction. In Book III the villagers assemble for a feast on the occasion of Arthur Donnithrone's birthday. This can be regarded as a pivotal incident of the Arthur Hetty affair. The harvest supper in Book VI restores back to Hayslope its earlier life. It restores the balance disrupted by the Arthur Hetty affair.

Presentation of Rural Life

Eliot has beautifully presented the rural background to suit the story and action of the novel. She has successfully captured the slow, leisurely pace of rural life as lived in isolated communities like that of Hayslope.

Flames in *Adam Bede*

Despite being considered one of the best novels of its age *Adam Bede* cannot be regarded as a flawless work of literature. It has many a loopholes to come under harsh criticism. Its ending has particularly come under a good deal of criticism. The marriage of Adam and Dinah does not find favour with the critics who consider it as forced, unnatural and in keeping with the contemporary convention that the happy union of the hero and the heroine is a dramatic necessity. Critics argue that Dinah Adam marriage is just a mechanical device used by the author to round up the story, it is not essential to the plot of the novel. The scene of Hetty's pardon is also very dramatic and improbable. Arthur Donnithrone manages to secure a reprieve for the wronged Hetty and rushes through the crowd just in time to save Hetty from being executed in the public. Again while Adam's love for Hetty is convincing, but his final marriage to Dinah, which helps him to emerge as a better human being does not seem inevitable.

In spite of all these flaws, the novelist's skill in construction of the plot cannot but be appreciated. It stands out as one of the most outstanding novel of the Victorian Age.

Q. 10. According to George Cgreeger, in Arthur, Hetty finds, "for a brief time at least, the objectification of her day-dreaming desires, but these in turn are a projection in fantasy of her own ego, sexually translated." Give your own comment.

Or

Hetty's love of Arthur is in reality the exterminations of her day dreams. How far would you agree or disagree with this view?

Ans. Sheltered Life of Hetty

As represented in the novel, the Loamshire-Hayslope world in all its richness, fertility and beauty is a sheltered world, an earthly paradise. In this beautiful and fertile world where nature is generous and abundant, the lively rustic girl Hetty Sorrel lived with her uncle and his family. Till the age of seventeen she led a sheltered life totally free from the cares and bounds of life. Except the occasional rebukes from her sharp tongued aunt she never experienced any hardship in her life in the real sense. As a result of this, she never had the chance to grow up or attain the required maturity of her age. As maturity is closely related to exposure to the world of misery and wretchedness of life, Hetty, because of her sheltered life never knew any pain and suffering and grew up without maturity. Hence despite her attainment of maturity in terms of age she remained a wilful child lacking experience of the real life, yet required to act in a responsible and mature way in an adult world.

Hetty : Immature and Childish in Nature

The sheltered life of home and Hayslope made Hetty a child of nature. She remained childish and immature despite her age unable to reason, to think and to forsee the consequences of her own actions. The same is true of her emotional life which is like the day dreams of a child who does not have any experience or knowledge of hard-reality. Her frivolous nature does not allow her to walk on the firm ground. She eats, sleeps and moves in a world of dreams where everything is beautiful. From the cosiness of her sheltered home she looked at everything through rose tinted glass. Her constant day dreaming does not permit her to act logically and her imagination takes full flight unhampered regardless of the truth and reality of life. When Arthur shows some interest in her, her heart leaps up and her imagination knows no bound. She dreams about her marriage with Arthur and fantasises about the kind of life she would lead, the dresses of rich brocades and the jewels she would wear. She sees herself as a grand lady gorgeous and majestic in the likeness of Mrs. Irwine, riding in a splendid carriage.

Her World of Dreams

In the chapter titled "Hetty's World" the readers are allowed to have a detailed account of her emotional fantasy. She had met Arthur in the Dairy and she constantly thought about him and the admiring glances that he casts upon her. The novelist comments that bright admiring glances from a handsome youngman from a high status was enough to set Hetty's heart ablaze. Hetty was aware of her beauty and also well aware of the number of admirers she had, Adam being the most eligible. She dismissed the idea of marrying Adam as he did not fit in her dreams to be the prince charming. Adam did not live up to her expectation of her man of dream. She knew that Adam, poor as he was with his old parents to keep could not afford to offer her even the simplest luxury that she shared in her uncle's home. And Hetty's dream were full of luxuries : "to sit in a carpeted parlour, and always wear white stockings : to have Nottingham lace round the top of her gown, and something to make her handkerchief smell nice, like Miss Lydia Donnithornes when she drew it out at the church, and not to be obliged to get up early or be scolded by anybody". She even thought that had Adam been rich enough and could have afforded to give her the luxury she craved for she would have loved him well enough to marry him.

The Effect of Arthur's Love on Her

Arthur's admiring glances put Hetty in the seventh heaven. An intoxicated Hetty moved about lost in a world of dream oblivious of the reality around her : "A new influence had come over Hetty—vague, atmospheric, shaping itself into a self confessed hopes or prospects, but producing a pleasant neurotic effect, making her tread the ground and go about her work in a sort of dream, unconscious of weight or effort, and showing her all things through a soft, liquid veil, as if she were living not in this solid world of brick and stone, but in a beautiful world, such as the sun lights up for us in the waters." She being a simple farmer's girl was swept off her feet by the gentlemanly Arthur. Like a strong wine Arthur's admiration goes to her head and takes her to the world of fantasy. In her excitement she conjures up dreams of fantasy. In chapter XV titled "The Two Bed-chambers", Hetty's activity reveals the effect of Arthur's interest in her. She moved about in the world of dreams, her dreams heightened and excited by her recent meeting with Arthur in the woods. She suffers from narcissus complex. She looked at her own reflection in the mirror admiringly. She smiled at her own reflection and let down her dark silken ringlets. She admired her own looks and felt premier than any woman she had ever seen, she imagined that she heard Arthur's soft voice repeating whatever he said in the woods. She imagined Arthur put his arm round her and the delicate rose-scent of his hair was with her still. The novelist comments at this point that "The vainest woman is never thoroughly conscious of her own beauty till she is loved by the man who sets her own passion vibrating in return."

Her Fantasy

She dreams about the day when she would marry Arthur and become a grand lady like Mrs. Irwine. Arthur's manner, his social status, riches everything fascinated her. She imagined about a "ride in her coach, and dress for dinner in a brocaded silk, with feathers in her hair, and her dress sweeping the ground, like Miss Lydia and Lady Dacey, when she saw them going into the dining room one evening, as she peeped through the little round window in the lobby; only she should not be old and ugly like Ms Lydia, or of the same thickness like Lady Dacey, but very pretty with her hair done in a great many different ways, and sometimes in a pink dress, and sometimes in a white on—she didn't know which she liked best; and Marry Burge and everybody would perhaps see her going out in her carriage—or rather, they would hear of it : it was impossible to imagine these things happening at Hayslope in sight of her aunt. At the thought of all this splendour, Hetty got up from her chair, and in doing so caught the little red-framed glass with the edge of her scarf, so that it fall with a bang on the floor; but she was too eagerly occupied with her vision to care about picking it up; and after a momentary start, began to pace with a pigeon-like stateliness backwards and forwards along her room, in her coloured stays and coloured skirt, and the old black lace scarf around her shoulders, and the great glass earrings in her ears." When Dinah, who was in the adjoining room came, Hetty opened the door without speaking as she was vexed and confused. Sensing that Hetty may get into trouble because of the frivolity of her nature Dinah tried to warn her. When Dinah tried to talk some sense into her she pushed her away sobbing : "Don't talk to me so, Dinah. Why do you come to frighten me? I've never done anything to you. Why can't you let me be?"

Hetty lives and moves in an enchanted world. Even her love of Arthur is tinged with the same enchantment because in him she sees the objectification of her day dreams. She knows that only Arthur can fulfil her dreams, her craving for luxury and fineries.

Her emotional life is a continuous stream of fantasy as the novelist suggests with recurring dream and day dream imagery. Hetty is forever taking holiday in dreams of pleasure. Her dreams is shattered when she receives the letter from Arthur where he ends their relationship with her. Her world collapses and she weeps uncontrollably blaming and cursing Arthur. She is dazed and be wildered and her heart rending tragedy begins.

Q. 11. Consider *Adam Bede* as a novel of rural life.

Or

George Eliot gives a picturesque and realistic presentation of country life in her novel *Adam Bede.* Comment.

Or

"Finally George Eliot uses landscape to define, reinforce and foreshadow the events of the plot and moral situation". Write a note on Eliot's presentation of the rural backdrop in *Adam Bede* in the light of the above statement.

Ans. George Eliot's Familiarity with the English Midland

George Eliot was deeply attached to the region in which her youth was passed. Her focus of interest lies in one particular locality i.e. the English Midlands. The English Midlands had a powerful impact on her imagination and in her early literary works, she presented it in detail conjuring up a vivid, and actual picture of a concrete neighbourhood. The Midland setting provide her with the background against which the conflicts and dramas of human life takes place. In the simple provincial situation, life is revealed clearly, wholly and in depth. Even in that regional setting drama of Sophoclean grandeur and intensity takes place. The tragedy of Hetty Sorrel, the charming damsel of Hayslope bears testimony to this.

The Rural World of *Adam Bede*

The story in *Adam Bede* is projected against the backdrop of the countries of Loamsire and Stonyshire (with their villages, Hayslope and Snowfield)

Loamshire

Most of the action in the novel takes place in Loamshire in and around the village of Hayslope. It is presented as a later day Eden which is suggested by the name of the hero Adam Bede. A fertile and sheltered land, "a region of corn and grass", where the arms produce the necessities of life in great abundance is symbolic of paradise. A prosperous village here poverty is rare, the inhabitants consider the exile from that contend and beautiful world of theirs as the worst possible curse that can befall them. The Poysers, Hetty's uncle's family are against going away from there leaving their roots behind.

Stonyshire

In contrast to the fertile, shuttered land of Loamshire, another country Stonyshire is presented keeping in view the change in the theme of the story. Stonyshire is rocky, barren, naked under the sky and "where the trees are few, so that a child might count them, and there's very hard living for the poor in the winter". The people are hard working and earn their bread and butter not by tilling a fertile soil like the Loamshire people but by digging deep beneath the earth's surface in rocky mines or by labouring in the dark mills of cities like Stoniton. In this "dreary bleak place", poverty is the common lot of the people.

Symbolic Significance of the Rural Background

According to George Creeger apparently Loamshire and Stonyshire seem like little more than Victorian variation on the Romantic theme of country vs. city. However Eliot has done more than simply broaden the negative symbol of the city *i.e.* Stoniton to include a surrounding wasteland *i.e.* Stonyshire. She has handled the symbols so skilfully that an inversion of their conventional values nearly takes place. Both Loamshire and Stonyshire are so stringently qualified that it is difficult to distinguish which is a positive and which is a negative symbol. The readers discover that there is an ugly aspect to the green and fertile Loamshire world and despite the barrenness and sterility of Stonyshire it is not a wasteland. Stonyshire is spiritually alive and in reality Loamshire is the spiritual wasteland.

Loamshire is rich and fertile, but it has a core of hardness. Hetty, the central figure is apparently soft and beautiful, but she too has a hardness within her which her aunt can perceive. After her conviction of child murder, during her trial her "stubborn silence" indicates her hardness. Dinah also perceives the hardness and rigidity of the people of Loamshire and tells Mr. Irwine, "But I've noticed, that in these villages where the people lead a quiet life among the green pastures and the still waters tilling the ground and tending the cattle, there's a strange deadness to the world, as different as can be from the great towns....It's wonderful how rich is the harvest of souls up those high walled streets, where you seemed to walk as in a prison-yard and the ear is deafened with the sounds of worldly toil. I think may be, it is because the promise is sweeter when this life is so dark and weary, and the soul gets more hungry when the body is ill at ease". In spite of its physical liveliness, Loamshire people are spiritually dead. The inhabitants of Stonyshire are more responsive to religion and spiritually alert and alive though it is a rocky and hard region where they live.

The Graphic Presentation of Scenes and Sights

The background against which the drama of *Adam Bede* takes place is on the borders of Straffordshire and Derbyshire. The novelist gives a picturesque, graphic, and faithful description of the region in abundance in the novel. The scenes and sights, the beautiful landscapes, the quality of life that goes on within it and its tradition, customs and superstitions have all been rendered so faithfully that the readers feels as if they are a part of that life, actually living there and sharing in the placid rhythm of life disturbed only now and then. The geographical features, the inns, churches, mansions, etc, and everything about the region has been faithfully recorded in the novel.

The Landmarks

In *Adam Bede,* the novelist gives a pen picture of real place and location. The original of the 'Donnithorne Arms' is the 'Bromley Davenport Arms' and it stands at the entrance of the village of Ellastone in Staffordshire.

The'Donnithorne Chase' in the novel is described after the beautiful estate of'Wootton Hall', not so far from the village of Ellaston.

These landmarks play an important role in the novels of Eliot. They appeal again and again in her novels imparting to them a rare continuity and organic unity.

The Graphic Description in the Novel

Eliot uses rich graphic descriptions in the novel to provide a credible setting to the novel. By her realistic description Eliot brings out the individual character of the setting, the place where her characters live and to which they are bound by tradition, love, memory, work and affection. She uses the landscape to define, reinforce and foreshadow the events of the plot and moral situation. The warmth of the sun, the scent of the pine-wood, and elder bushes, the light striking the shavings of wood, all help to create the sense of a calm, ordered existence. Such background highlight, the human action that follows.

Mrs. Poyser, the sharp tongued aunt of Hetty, is the voice of rural tradition and community. Her home, the Hall Farm provides a background that illustrates her character vividly. The Hall Farm is symbolic of orderliness, comfort, love, energy, security and peace of mind. Even Captain Arthur Donnithrone recognises the Hall Farm as symbolic of all these qualities and compliments Mrs. Poyser : "I think yours is the prettiest farm on the estate...."

The novelist lends reality to the presentation of these rural dwellers with the kind of imagery the characters use. The images used by them differ from character to character. Mr. Poyser being a farmer uses the images of unripe grain. The speech of Mrs. Poyser is that of a typical housewife. Their speech is, as it were, generic, the speech of a special category of beings of which each is an individual member.

The Presentation of Midland Life

Critic Anne Morley is of the opinion that Eliot has successfully conveyed to her readers the quality or flavour of life as lived in Hayslope. In *Adam Bede* a true picture of purely rural life is depicted very skilfully by the novelist. Every class that makes up a village community has its representative. The characters not only speaks in the dialect of that locality accurately but are also inflected with distinctness from each other. The field labourers, rude utterances, 'as incapable of an undertone as a cow or a stag', receives a touch of cultivation when it is used by the mechanic, and these two, again are varied in the farm house; while each individual has appropriate peculiarities which give a distinct truth of portraiture. When the readers have a distinct idea of the vocabulary these people use, they are led to a clearer notion of the range of their ideas. The Midland dialect that they speaks faithfully express pathos, commonsense, and humour.

The novel presents a cross-section of the Midland society with people belonging to different occupations and professions. The carpenter, the preacher, the rector, the clergy, the farmer, the dairy maid, the dairy hands, the Squire and his household, the common labourers, wage earners, the vain and frivolous rustic girls all brought to life by Eliot's artistic skill.

Even the customs, traditions, superstitions associated with Midland society has been depicted in the novel. A very common superstition associated with Midland life is that a knock at the door at night is a bad omen which means death in the family. While giving a finishing touch to a coffin, Adam hears a knock on the door and Thias is found dead the very next morning. The celebration of Arthur's 21st birthday gives the novelist a chance to give a detailed account of such celebrations in the rural area and village jealousies in pastoral communities.

The World of Hayslope

In world of Hayslope everything is inter-related. All the incidents have some links and connections. Here the good or ill of one cannot but have repercussions on the rest. Like Arthur's seduction of Hetty led her to pain and suffering and had its effect on Adam, to whom Hetty was betrothed as well as the Poyser's family. The rural community is almost a character in the story. Those who violate the social norms have no place in the Hayslope world and ultimately have to leave it. Hetty Sorrel, who is compared to a plant without roots does not fit in the corporate life of the community. The Poysers stick there despite the threats of the old Squire and misdeeds of the young Squire, as they developed a deep sense of kinship with the community and want to remain as a part of it.

Conclusion

Eliot's intimate relationship with the country life and her power of description have made a masterpiece out of *Adam Bede*. Through her vivid description, she has made rural England come to life in the pages of the novel. The essential features of English rural life—the farms, the lush fields, the brown canal, the rattle of cottage looms, and above all the racy speech of the yeoman and peasant are all to be found in *Adam Bede*.

PART - IV

CHAPTER - 23

SELECT LITERARY CRITICISM

1. Joan Bennet : *Organic Plot*

"there is no part of what we have learnt of the outer circle that does not affect our sense of the inner. The cultured benignity of the Rector, the moral enthusiasm of the Methodists, the simple ignorance of the country-folk, all make their own impact on the central characters and help to determine the events. Although the impression while we read is of a leisurely sequence of naturalistic scenes of comedy or of pathos and of a world richly populated with entertaining characters, when we look back—we find that every individual scene or character is directly or indirectly related to the simple story at the core of the book, of the carpenter's betrothed betrayed by the squire's grandson. In its setting this commonplace story becomes. widely significant. *The simple well-contrived pattern conveys the sense of a social structure enclosing four human beings as completely as the soil encloses the roots of a growing plant and, in so doing, it illustrates one aspect of the author's vision of life."*

2. David Cecil : *Flaws in the Characters*

"Drawing from the inside out, starting with the central principle of the character, she is able to show how it reveals itself in the most apparently inconsistent manifestations, can give to the most varied coloured surface of character that prevalent tone which marks it as the expression of one personality. Her characters always hang together, are of a piece, their defects are the defects of their virtues. We are not surprised that a man so anxious for the good opinion of others as Arthur Donnithorne should selfishly seduce Hetty, because we realise that the controlling force in his character is the desire for immediate enjoyment; so that his wish to sun himself in the pleasant warmth of other people's liking goes along with his inability not to yield to the immediate pleasure of Hetty's embraces. George Eliot can follow the windings of motive through the most tortuous labyrinths, for firmly grasped in her hand is always the central clue."

3. David Cecil : *Universality*

"With rare penetration and insight, George Eliot isolates and detects the various warring elements in Arthur's mind, his genuine compunction, his horror of being disapproved, of his instinctive resentment at disapproval, however justifiable, his inextinguishable hope that things will come right in the end, his irrational conviction that with him, at least, things always must come right. One grows quite uncomfortable as one always must come right. One grows quite uncomfortable as one watches so merciless, so delicate an exposure of human weakness. The truth it embodies is universal. In exposing Arthur Donnithorne, she also exposes her reader."

4. J.W. Cross : *Female Character : Mrs. Poyser*

"His (Robert Evans) second wife was a woman with an unusual amount of natural force; a shrewd practical person, with a dash of the Mrs. Poyser vein in her". Mrs. Evans, like Mrs. Poyser, was a successful dairy women, house-keeper and mother. She was a devoted wife with a sharp tongue which subdued her husband, children and servants. Mrs. Poyser is the wittiest of all George Eliot's characters. She pervades the novel *Adam Bede* and is well known for her sharp tongue, but a kind heart.

5. V.S. Prichett : *Subjectivity*

"George Eliot was punishing herself and Hetty has to suffer for the sins George Eliot had committed, and for which, to her perhaps unconscious dismay, she herself was never punished". Hetty is punished, for her creator in her own life had deliberately broken the rules prescribed by her parentage and education, found herself richer, happier and content, instead of being punished and persecuted. In her remorse she crucifies the pretty, dairy-maid. Hetty Sorel receives what Marian felt to be her due. "As when a child she had driven into her wooden doll's head the nails her wicked aunt should have endured, so now she made her books what her dolls once had been : the sublimation of her vision of retributive justice."

6. David Cecil : *Thematic Unity*

"Her mind was always active; experience set it immediately and instinctively analysing and generalising, to discovering why and how things happened. And when she turned her attention to the world around her it was this analysis that started her creative imagination working. It is inspired, not by what she felt or fancied, but by what she thought; not by a wish to convey her impressions of life but her judgements on it. And it embodied itself not in a picture but in a theme. She did not have a vision of Barechester or Cranford and then invent situations on which to hang her picture of this vision; she had a vision of human society as the expression of certain principles, and she embodied it in a picture of a specific place—Middlemarch. Her novels are built round an idea or theme, and everything not relevant to that idea is rigidly excluded. The end is implicit in the beginning, successive events are logically and usually connected with each other and as the action proceeds, it is seen to be the logical and natural outcome of the character or characters concerned and those characters themselves are the result of their social environment."

7. Jerome Thale : *Art of Characterisation*

George Eliot was interested not so much, "in the disintegration of society, the break-down of structures which seemed so large in mid-Victorian England, as in the delineation of character, particularly the inner man. Instead of concentrating her attention on the external appearance and idiosyncrasies of her characters, she directed her whole attention to the portrayal of the inner man."

8. Lettice Copper : *Some Faults*

"The weakness of the book, besides the oppressive virtue of Adam and Dinah is, as with many Victorian novels, the sacrifice of probability to plot, and the tidiness of the ending. George Eliot was moving towards a new kind of novel in which representation of life was to be more important than the resolution of a plot, but she was still partly bound by the old convention : Hetty's pardon, so dramatically and improbably brought to the place of execution by Arthur Donnithorne is an artificial device to spare the reader. In the relationship between Hetty and Arthur and in all that grows out of it, there is a sense of destiny which is falsified by this resolution. Again while Adam's love for Hetty is utterly convincing and the thing that brings him most to life as a human being, his final marriage to Dinah has none of that inevitability, but seems like a mechanical device to round off the story."

9. Creeger : *Her Retreats*

"Such a psychological state represetns a complete withdrawal from life, and withdrawal (or retreat) is characteristic of Dinah. Whenever, the going gets rough, that is, whenever life begins, paradoxically to seem too pleasant and seductive, Dinah flees back to Stonyshire, barren and sterile under the "overreaching sky". The most notable of these strategic retreats occurs after Adam has told her of his love. Following his declaration, Dinah replies that she could return his love save for the fear that she would 'forget to rejoice and weep with others', even forget the divine presence. Her peace and joy come from having no life of her own. Adam's love only raises the fear that she will forget Jesus, the man of sorrows, and become hard : 'And think how it is with me, Adam : that life I have led is like a land I have trodden in blessedness since my childhood; and if I long for a moment to follow the voice which calls me to another land that I know not, I cannot but fear that my soul might hereafter yearn for that early blessedness which I had forsaken, and where doubt enters there is no perfect love. I must wait for clearer guidance: I must go from you'. Here is clear expression of Dinah's fear of accepting full maturity; for the land which faces her (*i.e.* Loamshire and, of course, Adam) is a strange one, and who knows what life there may hold for her? Better, then, to return to the other land (Stonyshire and the self-contained world of childhood). There is at least no risk to run. If Hetty was incapable of growing up, Dinah is afraid to".

10. Creeger : *Lack of Involvement in Life*

"Implicit in her fear is also, I believe, a kind of unwillingness to become fully involved in life. In this respect she is like her creator, who once said that it was a pity her life could not be managed for her, while she stood by, the passive but interested spectator." Just such a one is Dinah: she observes the human condition, with sympathy and compassion, it is true, but without involvement. Selfless is a word used frequently in describing her but, selfless means not only something different from selfish; it means also lacking in self. To lack this sense of human identity is to become something either less or more than human—a clod, perhaps, or a divinity." Talking of herself to Mr. Irwine, she says : "I'm too much given to sit still and keep by myself : it seem as if I could sit silent all day long with the thought of God overflowing my soul—as the pebbles lie bathed in the Willow brook. For thoughts are so great—aren't they, sir. They seem to lie upon us like a deep flood; and it's my besetment to forget where I am and everything about me, and lose myself in thoughts that I could give no account of, for I could neither make a beginning nor ending of them in words."

11. Dorothy V. Ghent : *The Rhythm of Rural Life*

"The pace of *Adam Bede* is set to Mrs. Poyser's clock, to all that; slow toil and activity that have made daylight and living valuable. Slower, organically, invisibly slow at the months of Hetty's pregnancy;

the Poyser's clock, the clock at *the Chase,* do not keep this time with their eights and nines and half past nines. This other deep, hidden animal time drags the whole pace down to that of poor Hetty's journey in despair, a blind automatism of animal night where the ticking of the human clock cannot be heard."

12. George Creeger : *Enchanted World of Hetty*

"Even her love of Arthur is tinged with the same quality, in him she finds, for a brief time at least, the objectification of her day-dreaming desires, but these in turn are a projection in fantasy of her own ego, sexually translated. What she loves in him is not so much Arthur as her own self—as she wishes it to be."

13. Robert Speaigth : *Creative Mind*

"Throughout her work George Eliot exercises the perilous prerogative of the creative mind to stand outside her creation, view it in company with the spectator, and say how this or that effect of characterisation strikes her. But in her later novels this tendency is held under increasing control; in *Adam Bede* it is indulged without the least attempt at discipline. The technique seems to us extremely crude, holding up the narrative and frequently spoiling illusion.

14. Joan Bennet : *Biblical Concepts*

"If the characterization of Dinah partially fails to produce the effect intended, it is not because she is too virtuous but because of the author's treatment of her subject. It is in part because she intervenes too much, explicitly guiding the reader's response by her own comments, and it is in part the result of Dinah's semi-biblical idiom. Doubtless that idiom is a faithful record of the speech of Aunt Samuel and other Methodists, but it is none the less a self-conscious and irritating mode of speech. When Dinah's conversation is set beside Lisbeth Bede's in a scene in which George Eliot's excellent ear for dialogue probably catches the tune of each with equal fidelity, Lisbeth sounds natural and wins the readers' sympathy, whereas Dinah sounds priggish and stilted. The scene occurs when Dinah visits Mrs. Bede to try and comfort her after the death of her husband.

There is a distasteful over-carefulness about Dinah's idiom. The consciousness of virtue hard to distinguish from self-righteousness, that Dinah's speeches betray, is an obstacle to our sympathy. So also is the case with Dinah's use of Biblical idiom whom she rejects Seth Bede, and also when she puts off Adam before finally accepting him.

15. Creeger : *The Concept of Maturity*

"What George Eliot is presenting through these three characters, with their combination of keenness and mildness, the balance in them of head and heart is, as I have suggested, a concept of maturity—what a fully developed human personality is, or rather ought to be, like. But none of the book's major characters—neither Hetty nor Adam nor Dinah—belongs at first with Mr. Irwine, Bartle Massey, and Mrs. Poyser, though some of them eventually join that company. How difficult the task and how valuable its achievement *Adam Bede* demonstrates."

16. Speaight : *Portrayal of Landscapes*

"*Adam Bede* is uneven in the precise sense of having its weight wrongly distributed. *Too much space is taken up in building up the background.* George Eliot has come home and she is too fond of her native landscape not to linger on it at length. The workshop and the dairy and the *Hall-Farm* are minutely described so that we seem, day by day to believing with the characters and to be sharing the placid rhythm of their lives. This slowness of tempo is seen to have its value when the drama of Hetty's flight and trial takes possession of the book. If we had not known these people in their peaceful gossiping and small domestic ambitions, we should not sympathise with them so deeply in their stress. But the contrast was overdone, not by George Eliot's artistry over reaching itself—she was not yet practised enough for that—by a sheer abundance of creative vigour. The colourist—and she never painted more lusciously than in *Adam Bede*—could not bear to leave her palette.

17. David Cecil : *George Eliot's Originality*

"But George Eliot began with an idea of character or situation, her plot was intended to follow, not a standardised formula, but what she conceived to be the logical development of that idea : and this might entail something quite different from the accepted Victorian notion of a plot. It might entail no marriage, no happy ending, no character answering to the Victorian conception of hero or heroine. Often it did not. In *Silas Marner* the hero is an elderly bachelor; *The Mill on the Floss* ends very badly and has no hero at all. In *Middlemarch* there is no central figure of any kind; the main interest is divided between four separate groups of characters; and none of these, except Dorothea Brooke, approaches the conventional heroic type. Finally, since the action of George Eliot's stories arises logically from the characters, those strokes of fortunes, coincidences, sudden inheritances long lost wills, which are the stock-in-trade of the ordinary Victorian plot, are inevitably omitted. They are the first novels which set out to give a picture of life wholly unmodified by those formulas of a good plot which the novel had taken over from comedy and romance. Her story is conditioned solely by the logical demands of situation or character; it ends sadly or happily, includes heroes or omits them, deals with the married or the unmarried, according as reason and observation lead her to think likely. In fact, the laws conditioning the form of George Eliot's novels are the same laws that condition those of Henry James and Wells and Conard and Arnold Bennett. Hers are the first examples in English of the novel in its mature form; in them it structurally comes of age."

18. David Cecil : *Portraits of the Inner Man*

"Her psychological insight into the springs of human action is best seen in her delineation of her serious characters. She does not begin with the personality that appeared to the outward world, but with the psychological elements underlying that personality. And this meant that her portrait is pre-eminently concerned with these elements. She may clothe them in outward idiosyncrasy, but this idiosyncrasy is never the principal thing about them. We do not remember her serious characters by their appearance or the way they talked, indeed we do not remember these things clearly at all. Her portraits are all primarily portraits of the inner man.

19. Phyllis Bentlay : *Regional Characters*

"Turning to the George Eliot characters we find that many of her important characters are truly regional. They are drawn from humble walks of life and are shown carrying on their day to day activity. They are drawn from the rustics of the Midlands, and their activities are typical of midland life. When we read her novels we meet carpenters, mill-owners, farmers, governors, factory-workers, weavers, maids, gardeners, dairy maids, inn keepers, and schoolmasters. They are drawn from life and so are vital and living. These regional characters are not characters or comic figures introduced for the sake of humour. She treats them with respect, sympathy, and understanding. Her sympathies are with the peasants, who earned their livelihood from the soil, and with regional craftsmen. In *Adam Bede,* in one of her many asides, she expresses her interest in such humble characters "I turn, without shrinking, from cloud-borne angels from prophets, sibyls and heroic warriors, to an old woman bending over her flower pot, or eating her solitary dinner, while the noonday light softened perhaps by a screen of leaves, falls on her."

20. Long : *Development in Characters*

"Her heroes and heroines differ radically from those of Dickens and Thackeray in this respect—that when we meet the men and women of the later novelists, their characters are already formed, and we are reasonably sure what will they do under given circumstances. In George Eliot's novels the characters develop gradually as we come to know them. They go from weakness to strength, or from strength to weakness, according to the works that they do and the thoughts that they cherish. The novelist exhibits the mode by which step by step a character goes down, re-adjusting his principles to suit his practice, till imperceptibly he is transformed, changed or ruined."

21. Hugh Walker : *Memories of The Past*

"It is notorious that in the earlier novels George Eliot drew very freely on the stories of her memory. Scene after scene, character after character in these novels has been identified with some place or person within the range of her early experience. Her mansions and cottages, her lanes and meadows, are those to which she had been accustomed to derive in childhood with her father, or over which she had rambled with her brother. Still more are the characters of her novels, the figures with whom she had been familiar and almost in proportion to the familiarity is the frequency of their appearance. No other group was so often laid under-contribution as her own family. Her father, her mother, her brother, her sister, her aunt and herself, all appear in her pages."

22. David Cecil : *Moralistic Approach*

"Activities were right in so far as they assisted you to be good, they were wrong in so far as they prevented you. And such activities as were neither right nor wrong, were frivolous, unworthy of the attention of a serious person. She believed that the power which rules on high is just and moral. She was sure that, those who live a virtuous life are essentially contented, that those who live a vicious life are essentially discontented. However, well-meaning you might be or however lucky, she was sure that you cannot escape the consequences of your own actions, that your sins find you out, that the slightest slip will be visited on you, if not immediately than later".

23. A.E. Baker : *Psycho-Analysis*

"George Eliot's sphere was the inner man; she exposed the internal clockwork. Her characters are not simply passive, and they do not stand still; they are shown making their own history, continually changing and developing or degenerating as their motives issue into acts, and the acts become part of the circumstances that condition, modify and purify or demoralize the will". "Our deeds determine us, as much as we determine our deeds."

24. George Creeger : *Symbolism*

"At first glance Loamshire and Stonyshire seem like little more than a Victorian variation on the Romantic theme of country vs. city. It soon becomes apparent, however, that George Eliot has done more than simply broaden the negative symbol of the city (Stoniton) to include a surrounding wasteland (Stonyshire); she has handled the symbols in such a fashion that an inversion of their conventional values very nearly takes place. At least both Loamshire and Stonyshire are so stringently qualified that it is impossible to say of one, that it is a positive, of the other a negative symbol. We discover that there is an ugly aspect to the green and fertile Loamshire world: and that despite the barrenness and sterility of Stonyshire it is not altogether a wasteland".

25. Gerald Bullet : *Adam Bede, a Masterpiece*

"George Eliot's intimate knowledge of country life and her matchless powers of description have combined to make *Adam Bede* a masterpiece. She has made rural England come to life in the pages of the novel. England is most English in those Midland shires, and George Eliot knew them, or knew their essential features—the farms, the lush fields, the brown canals, the rattle of cottage looms, and above all the racy speech of the yeoman and peasant—as 'only a child can'. Her descriptions of country people have all the warmth and colour of reality, but and this is important—it is reality with a difference, it is reality at the service of imagination; not usurping imagination's place and function."

SELECT BIBLIOGRAPHY

1. **Dorothy Van Ghent** : *History of English Novel*
2. **Leslie Stephen** : *George Eliot*
3. **George Greeger (ed)** : *George Eliot, 20th Century Views (A Collection of Critical Essays)*
4. **Robert Speaeght** : *George Eliot*
5. **R.T. Jones** : *Adam Bede, A Critical Commentary*
6. **Gerald Bullet** : *George Eliot*
7. **Ian Adam** : *George Eliot*
8. **Joan Bennet** : *George Eliot, Her Mind and Her Art*
9. **Robert Liddel** : *The Novels of George Eliot*
10. **W.J. Harvey** : *The Art of George Eliot*
11. **Gorden S. Haight (ed)** : *A Century of George Eliot Criticism*
12. **Lettice Cooper** : *George Eliot*
13. **Walter Allen** : *George Eliot*
14. **F.R. Leavis** : *The Great Tradition*
15. **Barbara Hardy** : *The Novely of George Eliot*
16. **Lord David Cecil** : *Early Victorian Novelists*
17. **Jerome Thale** : *The Novels of George Eliot*
18. **Elizabeth Drew** : *The English Novel*
19. **Basil Willey** : *Nineteenth Century Studies*
20. **W.K. Cross** : *The Development of the English Novel*
21. **Hugh Walker** : *Literature of the Victorian Era*
22. **Laurence Lerner** : *The Truth Tellers*